"Project Censored is
fear to tread."

—ALAN MACLEOl

MW01138846

"As they've done for nearly a half a century, Project Censored exposes the danger of profit-driven media, honors the brave journalists who keep the ideals of their profession alive, and inspires us all to demand better."

—JULIANNA FORLANO, host of *The Julianna Forlano Show*

"Project Censored has shined the light for more than forty years on those critical stories and investigative reports that government officials, major media companies, and assorted gatekeepers of 'respectable' journalism too often ignore."

—JUAN GONZÁLEZ, co-host of *Democracy Now!* and professor of journalism and media studies at Rutgers University

"*Project Censored's State of the Free Press* sounds the alarm. This series of sobering reports reminds us what critical information the daily news smorgasbord just isn't putting out for us to consume, as the news business rushes headlong into triviality, and flirts with irrelevance."

—RAY SUAREZ, host of *On Shifting Ground* (KQED) and *Going for Broke*

"The state of the free press is miserable despite the great work of Project Censored in holding journalism accountable. They are a finger in the leaky dike of the First Amendment but they can't do it alone. This is the cause the public should most support if democracy is of concern."

—ROBERT SCHEER, Professor of Communication at Annenberg School for Communication and Journalism and publisher of the *ScheerPost*

"*State of the Free Press* is literally the only publication out there that's warning us in plain, well-documented language about what is happening right before our eyes. Read this book. It'll make you angry and it'll spur you to action. Future generations will thank you."

—JOHN KIRIAKOU, CIA torture whistleblower

"Today we mostly shut out news about our darker side, which is why we need Project Censored. Someone has to remind us to look in the mirror."

—MATT TAIBBI, author of *Hate Inc.*

"Now, more than ever, press freedom is at stake. In opposition to the undemocratic censorship of information, I proudly stand with Project Censored."

—SHARYL ATTKISSON, Emmy Award–winning investigative journalist and host of *Full Measure with Sharyl Attkisson*

PROJECT CENSORED'S

STATE OF THE FREE PRESS 2025

The Top Censored Stories and Media Analysis of 2023–24

EDITED BY
Mickey Huff, Shealeigh Voitl,
AND Andy Lee Roth
WITH Project Censored

FOREWORD BY Mnar Adley

ILLUSTRATED BY Anson Stevens-Bollen

THE CENSORED
— PRESS —

SEVEN STORIES

Fair Oaks, CA • New York

A JOINT PRODUCTION OF THE CENSORED PRESS
AND SEVEN STORIES PRESS

The Censored Press   Seven Stories Press
PO Box 1177   140 Watts Street
Fair Oaks, CA 95628   New York, NY 10013
censoredpress.org   sevenstories.com

ISBN 978-1-64421-429-9 (paperback)
ISBN 978-1-64421-430-5 (electronic)
ISSN 1074-5998

College professors and high school and middle school teachers
may order free examination copies of Seven Stories Press titles.
Visit https://www.sevenstories.com/pg/resources-academics
or email academic@sevenstories.com.

9 8 7 6 5 4 3 2 1

Printed in the USA

Book design by Jon Gilbert

Media power is political power.

—BEN BAGDIKIAN

Contents

Foreword

MNAR ADLEY

More than a decade ago, Julian Assange boldly reminded the world that if wars can be started by lies, peace could be started by truth. WikiLeaks shook the world when it published a leaked video showing a US drone operator knowingly shooting into a Baghdad crowd, killing at least a dozen people, including two Reuters journalists—a war crime that only became known to the public years after the US invasion of Iraq had left more than one million civilians dead, and for which no one has been held accountable, except for the publisher who exposed the atrocity.

Until June 2024, Julian Assange had languished in the UK's Belmarsh prison for revealing the empire's crimes, while the architects of the US invasion of Iraq, including Bush, Cheney, and Blair, walked free. Those crimes went unaccounted for because the US establishment press worked in lockstep to beat the drums of war, pushing the lies of weapons of mass destruction. Anyone who spoke out against the war or challenged the media's official narrative was accused of supporting the enemy and targeted with McCarthyite smears. Back then, however, Project Censored was on the case, highlighting the voices of independent journalists and news outlets that provided a radically different understanding of those leaders and the motives for their actions.

Today, in 2024, a genocide in Gaza is unfolding before our eyes. We have witnessed dismembered children, helpless fathers carrying their dead children's body parts in plastic bags, mothers calling for their dead babies to awaken, and wives embracing the bodies of their murdered husbands, giving them one last kiss goodbye.

The period since the October 7, 2023, attack has felt even more sinister than the efforts to demonize Hussein and his regime in the build-up to the 2003 invasion of Iraq. We have heard on repeat horrifying allegations of Palestinians beheading Israeli babies, mass rape of Israeli women whose breasts were severed and scattered on the streets of an Israeli kibbutz, and of their children baked in ovens. As Robin Andersen addresses in Chapter 4 of this book, these were lies presented to the public on the front pages of the *New York Times*, *Washington Post*, and *Wall Street Journal*, and broadcast daily on cable television stations such as CNN. US corporate media published stories fed to them by the Israeli government and its proxies without independent verification or investigation. Again, Project Censored has highlighted independent reporting that challenges the accuracy and legitimacy of these accounts.

Meanwhile, local reporters risked their lives to reveal the reality of events on the ground in war-torn Gaza. For their efforts to report the truth, these courageous individuals have been directly targeted by a regime desperate to cloak its genocidal actions from the world's scrutiny by committing violence against journalists. See Chapter 2 of this volume for an update on Project Censored's previous coverage of the repression of Palestinian media.

In zones of conflict around the world, wearing a flak

jacket marked "Press" is supposed to provide a measure of protection for reporters. But right now in Palestine, the designation functions like a target, as Israel has turned Gaza into what Reporters Without Borders has called a "cemetery for journalists." Nevertheless, journalists, including Motaz Azaiza, Hind Khoudary, Younis Tirawi, and Wael Al-Dahdouh, have used their social media platforms to show the world what they have witnessed.

October 7 marked a new era in how people around the globe consume news. In the months following the attack, we became witnesses of another sort, experiencing how corporate media outlets, such as the *New York Times* and CNN, use atrocity propaganda in blatant ways to manufacture consent and, specifically, to justify Israel's slaughter of Palestinians.

Manufacturing consent is often a top-down process. The management of the *New York Times*, for example, sent its reporters a memo instructing them not to use words such as "genocide," "slaughter," or "ethnic cleansing" when discussing Israel's military actions. In fact, *Times* staff are restricted from using the terms "refugee camp," "occupied territory," and even "Palestine," robbing them of the very language necessary to report accurately on the situation if they wish to do so.

Meanwhile, CNN exercises similar control over its reporters. Upper management issued a series of messages to all staff in October 2023, instructing them to submit all Gaza-related content to its Jerusalem bureau, which is strongly pro-Israel, before publishing. CNN also directed its staff to always use the moniker "Hamas-controlled" when discussing the Gaza Health Ministry and its casualty figures, to make sure that every story framed Hamas as responsible for the violence, but not to quote Hamas officials because their statements were "not newsworthy" and amounted to no more than "inflammatory rhetoric and propaganda."

This framing was used to dehumanize the entire Palestinian population as barbaric, inhumane, and deserving of assault. Israel has dropped more than seventy thousand tons of munitions on what it had already transformed into the world's largest concentration camp, leaving tens of thousands of civilians dead.

Perhaps it is not surprising that US media have shown so little interest in the victims of imperial violence. After all, these news outlets are giant corporations with deep ties to the US government. In 1983, when journalism scholar Ben Bagdikian first published *The Media Monopoly*, he warned that barely fifty large companies controlled nearly all of what Americans saw, read, and heard. Today, that number has dropped to five controlling corporations. The picture is similar online, with Silicon Valley juggernauts such as Alphabet, Meta, and X controlling the market. Project Censored refers to these outlets as "corporate" rather than "mainstream" media because they reflect corporate interests and world views.

As Bagdikian noted and Project Censored has long documented, the consolidation of media is a serious threat to democracy. By and large, these corporations sing from the same hymn sheet, providing only the illusion of choice and debate while constantly banging the drums for war. As esteemed media critic Noam Chomsky famously observed, "Any dictator would admire the uniformity and obedience of the US media."

This is why independent media organizations and

critical media literacy groups are essential. For example, *MintPress News*, the independent journalism outlet that I founded and direct, has been at the forefront of penetrating the fog of war, deconstructing corporate media frames that center militarism and exclude settler colonialism while presenting a different understanding of conflict in the Middle East.

Likewise, Project Censored has been a pioneer in promoting independent news outlets like *MintPress News* and developing critical media literacy tools for students and the public. Founded in 1976, nearly fifty years later, it abides as one of the nation's leaders in championing a better-informed, more democratic United States. Generations of scholars, critics, students, and journalists have relied on Project Censored to shine a light where the darkness of censorship otherwise prevails, to highlight the best work by truly independent journalists, and to promote civic engagement based on critical media literacy. It was an honor to be asked to pen this foreword; now, I encourage you to read *State of the Free Press 2025* and use the knowledge you glean from it to inform your own political action.

MNAR ADLEY is an award-winning journalist, editor, and the founder and director of *MintPress News*. She is also president of the non-profit media organization *Behind the Headlines* and the host of the video series it produces.

Notes

1. "Israel is Eradicating Journalism in Gaza, with Ten Reporters Killed in Three Days, 48 Since Start of War," Reporters Without Borders,

November 22, 2023; see also, "Journalist Casualties in the Israel-Gaza War," Committee to Protect Journalists, June 10, 2024.

2. Jeremy Scahill and Ryan Grim, "Leaked NYT Gaza Memo Tells Journalists to Avoid Words 'Genocide,' 'Ethnic Cleansing,' and 'Occupied Territory,' *The Intercept*, April 15, 2024.

3. Chris McGreal, "CNN Staff Say Network's Pro-Israel Slant Amounts to 'Journalistic Malpractice'," *The Guardian*, February 4, 2024.

Reporting the Truth to Resist Injustice

ANDY LEE ROTH and MICKEY HUFF

US PRESS FREEDOMS: FROM "SATISFACTORY" TO "PROBLEMATIC"

A 2024 Pew Research Center poll found that a remarkable 73 percent of adult Americans believe a free press is either extremely or very important to the well-being of society—though only a third of those polled believe that US media are completely free to report news.[1] Indeed, half of those surveyed believe that US news organizations are influenced a great deal by corporate/financial interests (51 percent) or government/political interests (49 percent). Citing reports by the Associated Press and the *Columbia Journalism Review*, the Pew Research Center noted that "recent high-profile incidents such as a police raid on a Kansas newsroom and a government seizure of a Florida journalist's materials have raised questions about press freedom in the U.S."[2]

Pew reported its findings in anticipation of World Press Freedom Day and before Reporters Without Borders (RSF) published the 2024 edition of its annual World Press Freedom Index. The United States ranked fifty-fifth among 180 nations for press freedoms in 2024, according to RSF, which defines press freedom as "the ability of journalists as individuals and collectives to select, produce, and disseminate news in the public interest independent of political, economic, legal, and social interference and in the absence of threats to their physical and mental safety."[3] RSF found press freedom is "problematic" in the United States, which earned a score of 66.59 out of a 100, a decline of nearly five points, compared to 2023 when the United States ranked forty-fifth in the world based on "satisfactory" levels of press freedom.[4] Noting that the United States was "once considered a model for freedom of expression," RSF reported that in 2024, "major structural barriers to press freedom persist," including, for instance, highly concentrated media ownership that appears "to prioritize profits over public interest journalism," declines in both local news and public trust in media, and the enactment of state and local laws that limit journalists' access to public spaces.

From a global perspective, RSF noted "a worrying decline" in respect for media autonomy, increased pressure from state or other political actors, and "a clear lack of political will on the part of the international community to enforce the principles of protection of journalists." Nowhere has the latter been more evident than in Israeli-occupied Palestine, including Gaza especially, where RSF reported a "record number of violations against journalists and the media" since October 2023, including the killing of more than a hundred Palestinian journalists by Israel Defense Forces.[5]

REPORTING FROM GAZA AS A BLOODIED KLAXON

In May 2024, the Committee to Protect Journalists (CPJ) reported that the sustained intensity of violence in Gaza, including specifically a surprise Israeli attack on the Al-Shifa hospital in northern Gaza, which killed hundreds of Palestinians, had produced "a morass of contradictory information."[6]

The CPJ's report linked the "trail of confusion" about the attack on Al-Shifa hospital to pervasive threats against journalists working in Gaza and the wider repercussions of ongoing violence there: "An unprecedented number of deaths ... displacement, and censorship are all making it exponentially harder to confirm information about the conflict's devastating impact on Gaza's media community—and, by extension, about the broader impact of the war." The loss of local sources, precarious living conditions, communications breakdowns, deteriorating due process, and fear of retribution combined, the CPJ explained, to make reporting from Gaza a harrowing challenge.

Early in the conflict, the Israel Defense Forces had informed Reuters and *Agence France-Presse* (*AFP*) that it could not guarantee the safety of their journalists operating in Gaza, ominously urging the news agencies "to take all necessary measures for their safety."[7] In November 2023, Access Now, a nonprofit that documents global internet censorship, published an extensive report on how Israel was cutting vital internet access in Gaza.[8] Amidst "a devastating near-complete communications blackout," people in Gaza were "left without the ability to stay informed, keep connected with loved ones, access life-saving information, or document the human rights violations and atrocities occurring on the ground," Access Now reported.[9]

More recently, in May 2024, the Israeli cabinet voted to ban Al Jazeera from operating in Israel. The global satellite news network had been providing 24/7 live coverage of Israel's assault on Gaza. As *Common Dreams* reported, the order was believed to be "the first of its kind targeting a foreign media outlet operating in Israel."[10] Al Jazeera reported that it would "pursue available legal channels to protect its journalists from Israel's 'slanderous' shutdown."[11] Also in May 2024, Israel targeted the Associated Press, invoking a new law that empowers the government to shut down foreign media outlets' operations if they are deemed threats to national security. Israeli authorities seized from a home in the southern Israeli city of Sdero cameras and equipment that AP staff had been using to provide live video coverage of northern Gaza.[12] As this volume went to press, Reporters Without Borders had just filed a third complaint with the International Criminal Court about Israeli war crimes against journalists in Gaza.[13]

Critics—including the Palestinian Journalists' Syndicate (PJS)—have decried Western news outlets for failing to meet "basic journalistic standards" in covering the Israeli assault on Palestinians since October 7.[14] "Shorn of any pretense of objectivity or truth, some Western media organizations have parroted Israeli government talking points, failed to challenge or even *attempt* to verify blatant misinformation and propaganda, and adopted dehumanizing and violent language about the Palestinian people," the PJS stated.[15] In doing so, these news outlets have been "facilitating genocide" amid Israel's "wholesale ethnic cleansing" of Gaza, according to a statement issued by the PJS in October 2023 and reported by *Truthout*.[16]

In contrast to their corporate counterparts—not to mention the Biden White House, which has continued to reject claims that Israel's mass killing of Palestinians in Gaza constitutes genocide—from early in the conflict, independent news outlets gave voice to experts who characterized Israel's assault on Gaza as genocide.[17]

News media omissions often function as tacit permission for abuses of power.[18] As we noted in December 2023, US corporate media have treated "Gaza's inhabitants as nonpersons, and daily life in Gaza as non-news" for decades. This "shameful legacy of narrow, pro-Israel coverage indirectly laid the groundwork for the atrocious human suffering taking place there now."[19]

VIOLENCE ABROAD ENGENDERS ATTACKS ON PRESS FREEDOMS AT HOME

The pressures of Israel's asymmetric war on Gaza have also impacted journalists working in the United States. Early in the conflict, news workers at CNN, *The Hill,* and the Associated Press were fired for crossing red lines by advocating for a free Palestine or characterizing Israel as an apartheid state, Alan MacLeod reported in late October 2023.[20]

Since October 7, 2023, the U.S. Press Freedom Tracker has used the tag "Israel-Gaza war" to note the wave of press freedom violations involving journalists covering domestic reactions across the United States, including demonstrations on college campuses, public streets, and city halls, from California and Washington to Texas, Illinois, and New York.[21] Between October 7, 2023, and May 2024, the Tracker documented thirty-eight arrests of journalists, thirty-seven assaults on them, eleven instances of equipment damage, and three chilling statements, all connected to journalists' work covering local reactions to the

Israel-Gaza war. These figures do not include journalists temporarily detained by police but not formally charged, a "catch-and-release" tactic that "takes journalists away from the news until the story is over."[22]

Threats against journalists are "the most basic and blunt form of press censorship," effectively silencing the public's source of news.[23] But journalism in the United States has also been subject to legislative attacks that threaten press freedoms and the public's right to know.

LEGISLATIVE ATTACKS ON MEDIA FREEDOM

In April 2024, Congress passed what is known as the TikTok "divestment-or-ban" bill, which President Biden quickly signed into law. In the Senate, the legislation passed as a rider on a measure to provide $95 billion in mostly military aid to Ukraine, Israel, and Taiwan, the international news agency Reuters reported.[24] The military aid warrants concern in its own right, but the added censorship of the popular social media platform is deeply problematic. As Omar Zahzah observed in a June 2024 article for *Electronic Intifada*, "It is no surprise that a bill furthering US funding for imperialism and genocide should also fortify US imperialism on the digital front."[25]

Senator Ron Wyden (D-OR) warned that the legislation "provides broad authority that could be abused by a future administration to violate Americans' First Amendment rights."[26] Senator Ed Markey (D-MA) went further, warning, "We should be very clear about the likely outcome of this law. It's really just a TikTok ban ... Censorship is not who we are as a people. We should not downplay or deny this trade-off."[27]

TikTok was ostensibly targeted because it is owned by ByteDance, a Chinese company. Even though other popular social media platforms also share user data for profit, violate users' rights to privacy, contribute to the spread of misinformation and disinformation, and foster internet addiction, Congress and the White House singled out TikTok as the real threat. Their reasoning was that TikTok alone operated under Chinese influence and could share US users' data with the Chinese government.[28]

Not long after Biden enacted the ban, which would force ByteDance to divest and allow a US company to assume control of the platform by early 2025, Secretary of State Antony Blinken and Senator Mitt Romney (R-UT) publicly admitted that the *real* reason TikTok had been targeted was its potential influence on the American public regarding Israel's relentless bombardment of Palestinian civilians.[29]

As protests spread across US colleges and universities in the spring of 2024, Romney questioned why Israel's messaging on Gaza had been so "awful," noting that "typically the Israelis are good at PR. What's happened here?"[30] Blinken quickly replied that those who opposed Biden's support for Israel were being manipulated by social media, and TikTok in particular. Blinken went on to say that those pushing for a ceasefire were "on an intravenous feed of information with new impulses, inputs every millisecond," and "the way this has played out on social media has dominated the narrative." Ryan Grim of *The Intercept* called the exchange an "incredible historical document" that revealed how high-ranking US officials seek to control narratives and restrict information, especially around Israel and Gaza.

Congressional zeal to throttle freedom of information did not stop at TikTok. Echoing the xenophobia that fueled anti-terrorism legislation after 9/11, in April 2024, the House of Representatives took aim at nonprofits, passing—by a vote of 382–11—legislation that would authorize the secretary of the treasury to unilaterally remove the tax-exempt status of any 501(c)3 nonprofit determined to be a "terrorist supporting organization."[31]

The legislation prompted the Charity & Security Network, a resource and advocacy center for nonprofit organizations that work in conflict zones, to warn policymakers to beware of "the parade of horribles that could cascade from this broad legislation that uses the targeting of charities as a vehicle for larger political motives."[32]

Although numerous anti-terrorism laws already restrict nonprofits—like other organizations—from providing funding to foreign terrorist organizations, making the proposed legislation "redundant and unnecessary," according to the Charity & Security Network, the Senate quickly introduced a companion measure, S. 4136, after the House voted its approval.[33]

Seth Stern, director of advocacy at the Freedom of the Press Foundation, explained that the legislation could provide new, more robust tools for government officials to target nonprofit news organizations.[34] Noting that elected officials have already called for terrorism investigations of the *New York Times*, Reuters, CNN, and the Associated Press, Stern warned against "passing overbroad and unnecessary new laws" that provide government officials with "brand new ways to harass and silence journalists who don't toe the line."

The legislative attack on nonprofits, like the TikTok ban, is rooted in the United States's support of Israel.

AIPAC, the American Israel Public Affairs Committee, and other pro-Israel lobbying groups significantly backed seven of the eight representatives who sponsored or cosponsored the House's version of the bill; and, overall, 355 of the House's 435 members have received lobbying funds from pro-Israel groups during the 2024 election cycle, suggesting that bipartisan support for the legislation "may reflect the influence of lobbying money as much as the House's desire to restrict financial support for terrorism."[35]

A PULITZER FOR THE *NEW YORK TIMES* DESPITE TROUBLING QUESTIONS

In 2024, the Pulitzer Prize Board awarded the *New York Times* a Pulitzer for international reporting, citing the newspaper's "wide-ranging and revelatory coverage of Hamas' lethal attack in southern Israel on October 7, Israel's intelligence failures and the Israeli military's sweeping, deadly response in Gaza."[36] Established in 1917 and administered by Columbia University in New York, the Pulitzer Prize is widely recognized as the most prestigious award for newspaper journalism in the United States.

The Pulitzer announcement cited seven examples of the *Times*'s "winning work," published between October 13 and December 30, 2023. Conspicuously missing from the Pulitzer's record of the *New York Times*'s reporting on Gaza was the newspaper's front-page report from December 31, 2023, "'Screams Without Words': Sexual Violence on Oct. 7."[37] In this article, the *Times* reported the results of a two-month investigation that "uncovered painful new details" based on "video footage, photographs,

GPS data from mobile phones and interviews with more than 150 people," which allegedly documented Hamas attacks against Israeli women as "part of a broader pattern of gender-based violence on Oct. 7." In more direct language, the article alleged mass rape of Israeli women by Hamas.

The report by the *Times* immediately came under intense scrutiny, first on social media and then via independent news outlets, as Robin Andersen examines in detail in the News Abuse chapter of this volume. For example, Max Blumenthal and Aaron Maté of *The Grayzone* submitted an open letter to the *Times*, posing serious questions about the credibility of the article's key sources and its "sensationalism, wild leaps of logic," and lack of "concrete evidence to support its sweeping conclusion."[38] Subsequent investigative reporting by Jeremy Scahill, Ryan Grim, and Daniel Boguslaw of *The Intercept* exposed that one of the article's authors, a freelancer named Anat Schwartz, was a former Israeli intelligence officer who "had no prior reporting experience."[39] Its exposé also documented internal criticism of the mass rape story. *The Intercept* quoted a *Times* reporter who also worked as an editor: "A lot of focus will understandably, rightfully, be directed at Schwartz but this is most clearly poor editorial decision making."

Galvanized by the deep concerns raised about the integrity of the *New York Times*'s mass rape story and the editorial judgment that led to its publication, some two hundred professors of journalism and scholars of news media at colleges and universities across the United States sent an open letter to the publisher of the *New York Times* on April 29, 2024, recommending that the newspaper "immediately commission a group of journalism experts to conduct a thorough and full independent review of the reporting, editing and publishing processes for this story."[40] Noting that the impact of the newspaper's report was "impossible to fathom," in part because it "fueled the fire at a pivotal moment" when there was an opportunity to contain the situation before it devolved into what the International Court of Justice has since deemed "the 'plausible' realm of genocide," the authors of the open letter urged the *New York Times* to "waste no time in extending an invitation for an independent review."

All these concerns regarding the *Times*'s December 31, 2023, report of mass rape on October 7 by Hamas were public knowledge in early May 2024, when the Pulitzer Prize Board awarded the *New York Times* its prize for international reporting. It remains to be seen whether the newspaper's leadership will heed the well-founded recommendations by many of the country's leading journalism professors and scholars. In the meantime, it is cold comfort that the Pulitzer Prize Board did *not* cite the *Times*'s "Screams Without Words" report among the newspaper's "winning work." But the announcement of the award specifically lauded the *Times*'s "wide-ranging and revelatory coverage of Hamas' lethal attack in southern Israel on October 7," the very topic of the now-discredited report. How could the Pulitzer jury not consider the unanswered questions and deep doubts raised by the *Times*'s problematic story and the newspaper's subsequent lack of transparency about the editorial decisions that led to its publication?

The Pulitzer honoring the *New York Times* for its reporting on Gaza reveals a great deal about the state of the free press in the United States. Under the dark shadow cast by the *Times*'s handling of its alleged mass rape story, the luster of the Pulitzer Prize for international reporting is dimmed, if not degraded. Missing from the glossy presentation of the Pulitzers are nearly all of the journalists, many now deceased, who have risked their lives, and often those of their families, in order to provide the global public with fact-based reports from conflict zones such as Gaza.

"REFUSE TO SEE INJUSTICE AS NORMAL": INDEPENDENT JOURNALISTS SPEAK OUT

Not all the news coming out of Columbia University this past year was bleak. By contrast, longtime Israeli journalist Amira Hass, a *Haaretz* correspondent for the Occupied Palestinian Territories, received the 2024 Columbia Journalism Award for her reporting.[41] Hass has spent three decades in Gaza and the West Bank reporting on the plight of Palestinians. In May 2024, she addressed the graduating class of Columbia's journalism school. She exhorted the graduates, who belong to the next generation of journalists, to "refuse to accept Hell as normal" and explained her own experience: "The journalism that I chose to practice is based on the refusal to see injustice as normal, the refusal to normalize it to a point that we do not see it."[42]

The Park Center for Independent Media honored another staunch independent voice reporting from Palestine, awarding a prestigious Izzy Award for "outstanding achievement in independent media" to Mohammed El-Kurd, the first Palestine correspondent to work for *The Nation* in its 160-year history.[43] The Izzy announcement specifically cited two of El-Kurd's reports, "Western Journalists Have Palestinian Blood on Their Hands" and "The Right to Speak for Ourselves."[44] In the latter article, based on a lecture he delivered at Princeton in honor of the late Edward Said, El-Kurd explained why he steadfastly refuses what he called "the politics of appeal."

He described how this news frame, developed by "well-meaning journalists and cultural workers," aimed to humanize oppressed Palestinians but ultimately produced "a false, flattening dichotomy between terrorists and victims." The politics of appeal, he explained, requires of Palestinians and other human targets of oppression "a perfect victimhood" as an "ethnocentric requirement for sympathy and solidarity." Many people engage in the politics of appeal "in good faith," El-Kurd acknowledged, but he refuses it. "I don't want to appeal to anyone," El-Kurd stated, especially if doing so means denying the human feelings of rage and disdain that are necessary to be brave and resist.

Amira Hass and Mohammed El-Kurd remind us of the elementary differences between conventional journalistic objectivity and viewpoint transparency. Historically, journalists have sought to achieve objectivity through *balance*—presenting "both sides" of a story—and *depersonalization*—refraining from inserting their own evaluations or experiences into the story.[45] By contrast, as Cassandra Kunert of *Weave News* notes in Chapter 5 of this volume, journalism committed to viewpoint transparency involves a disclosure of intent.[46] Hass and El-Kurd, for example, each disclose journalistic intent in the form of refusals: Hass's refusal to "see injustice as normal" and El-Kurd's rejection of the victimizing "politics of appeal."

These disclosures of intent break from the ideal of objectivity—an *impossible* ideal—to fulfill one of the cardinal demands of journalism, which is the commitment to being accountable and transparent.[47] By doing so, viewpoint transparency may also fulfill two additional demands of ethical journalism: the commitment to seeking and reporting truth while also minimizing harm. These ethical guidelines are the compass for the journalism and media criticism presented in *State of the Free Press 2025*.

INSIDE *STATE OF THE FREE PRESS 2025*

Chapter 1 presents Project Censored's twenty-five most important but under-reported stories of 2023–2024. The stories and topics covered here by independent news outlets are "catalysts for change," as noted in the chapter's introduction. Some of these stories detail injustices so egregious that a well-informed public might be spurred to organize and demand change if the story were more widely known—as exemplified by reporting from *The Appeal* about the number of people serving long prison sentences despite having been acquitted in trial (story #9). Additional stories from this year's list document grassroots efforts that could serve as models for change in similarly impacted communities, as illustrated by this year's #12 story about Indigenous activists in Panama shutting down a notorious multinational copper mine in order to defend their community's freshwater sources and forest ecosystems. Each of the featured stories has been "censored" in the broad sense established by Project Censored founder Carl Jensen, who defined censorship as "the suppression of information, whether purposeful or not, by any method—including bias, omission, underreporting or self-censorship—that prevents the public from fully knowing what is happening in its society."[48] Compiled by Nicole Mendez-Villarrubia, Cam Lippincott, Amy Grim Buxbaum, Steve Macek, and Andy Lee Roth, this year's Top 25 story list represents the collective effort of 206 students from nine colleges and university campuses who identified, vetted, and summarized Validated Independent News stories through the Project's Campus Affiliates Program.

In Chapter 2, Nicole Mendez-Villarrubia, Grace Harty, Olivia Rosenberg, and Steve Macek revisit five Top 25 stories from previous Project Censored yearbooks to update subsequent developments in those stories and reassess whether they remain blockaded by corporate news outlets. This year's Déjà Vu News chapter reviews reporting on the repression of Palestinian media, from *State of the Free Press 2023*; Canary Mission's efforts to blacklist pro-Palestinian activists, from *State of the Free Press 2022*; the global wave of violence against women, also from the 2022 yearbook; fascists in the Ukraine training White supremacists from the United States, from *Censored 2020*; and the causes and consequences of a backlog in unprocessed rape kits, from *Censored 2016*.

Barbie mania takes over Junk Food News in Chapter 3 as Reagan Haynie, Sierra Kaul, Gavin Kelley, Jennifer Lyons, Marcelle Swinburne, and Mickey Huff deliver another overstuffed junk news menu, focused on how women, even despite fame and fortune, cannot seem to catch a break in our patriarchal and misogynistic culture. In a year that saw *Barbie* (2023) "snubbed" at the Academy Awards, Taylor Swift, who doubles as International Superstar Barbie, was accused of taking over the NFL while being a psyop for Joe Biden's campaign *and* destroying the environment. Who says women can't do it all? This year's chapter shines a light on one of our popular culture's dark fixations, summarized in an apt line from *Barbie*, "Everyone hates women. Men hate women and women hate women. It's the one thing we can agree on." There's something else we all can agree on—the patriarchy has got to go. As the Junk Food News chapter suggests, nodding to Taylor, it's time to *shake it off!*

In Chapter 4, media scholar Robin Andersen analyzes News Abuse in corporate coverage of Israel's attack on Gaza, showing how this reporting obscures or distorts some of the most important facts about the crisis. The chapter analyzes how Western news outlets have produced what Andersen characterizes as atrocity propaganda. It also documents Israeli government efforts to censor news coming out of Gaza and how US establishment media have followed suit, repeatedly promoting false or debunked stories while downplaying the slaughter of civilians. Andersen's chapter reminds us why an ethical, independent press is so desperately needed to break through the fog of war.

Chapter 5, Media Democracy in Action, highlights individuals and organizations who champion the rights to freedom of expression and information and foster grassroots civic engagement. In her introduction, Mischa Geracoulis reminds readers that, in a year of high-stakes elections taking place around the world, "political pressures are testing the limits" of press freedom. The chapter's contributors highlight important counters to those pressures. Kirby Thomas West, an attorney specializing in constitutional rights, describes how the Freedom of Information Act empowers independent journalists and public interest attorneys to inform the public and spur civic engagement. Sarah Leah Whitson, executive director of Democracy for the Arab World Now, addresses the impact of Israel's war in Gaza on First Amendment rights in the United States. Dorothy Kidd, professor of media studies at the University of San Francisco, describes transforming her classroom into a "media-active *dojo*," where students develop critical media literacy skills to challenge dominant media structures and organize for social change. Cassandra Kunert of *Weave News* describes citizen journalists whose reporting aims to explain "how complex global structures and relationships function in their own lives." Finally, Jeje Mohamed, co-founder of Aegis Safety Alliance, describes the development of safety and security trainings for journalists that help them "navigate the inherent risks and occupational hazards associated with their work" while also considering each journalist's own unique identity and experience.

Media scholar Bill Yousman concludes *State of the Free Press 2025* with "Eleven Theses on Disinformation." Outcries over "fake news" after the 2016 election led to a moral panic focused on the media's role in promoting disinformation. In eleven pithy, carefully documented theses—such as "The social impact of disinformation is real," his sixth thesis—Yousman addresses the concerns of disinformation skeptics, argues for taking disinformation seriously, and advocates for change in our media practices informed by the values of plurality and critical opposition. In what amounts to a fitting finale for *State of the Free Press 2025*, Yousman concludes that efforts to challenge concentrated media power must ultimately be "collective and political, not individual."

This year, careful readers may notice a subtle change in how we format the names of news organizations. In accordance with the *Chicago Manual of Style*, Project Censored has historically used italicization for print publications but not for digital-only news outlets. Beginning with this volume, we have revised our house style to use italics for online news outlets. While the previous style carried with it an implication of elitism—legacy media publications deserved italics, but newer online outlets did not—as Project Censored has long documented, some of the most valuable independent journalism is found online. This change in our house style reflects that reality.

MEDIA POWER IS POLITICAL POWER

Although the 2024 Press Freedom Index clearly demonstrates the deep challenges that US journalism now faces, journalists have been a central force for social justice and political change in the United States in other perilous times, as exemplified by the muckraking journalists of the Progressive Era.[49] The contributions to this volume suggest the potential influence of today's independent journalism. Media scholar Ben Bagdikian, author of the seminal study *The Media Monopoly*, regularly reminded people that media power *is* political power.[50] This is particularly the case when we see independent journalism covering key stories the corporate news media either ignore, spin, or botch.

That noted, the United States could have the best journalism in the world, but that reporting will have little societal impact so long as political leaders ignore the realities reported by journalists, especially those who raise critical questions about established policies and institutions. This reality highlights the need for public engagement—not just to support public interest journalism but also to pressure elected officials to implement laws and policies informed by it.

Educating people to use critical media literacy tools to determine for themselves whether specific news stories or outlets are worthy of their trust and support is one way to mobilize that necessary public engagement. The kind of critical media literacy (CML) curriculum promoted by Project Censored and its allies helps people develop the skills necessary to determine for themselves which media outlets produce ethical journalism that serves public interests.[51] In the past year, we have seen renewed efforts to elevate critical media literacy education through legislation at the state level.[52] Although state-level mandates are a welcome development, the need for CML education is so great that we should not leave the efforts to state legislators alone, especially when some have shown themselves vulnerable to the lure of corporate-sponsored versions of media literacy.[53]

Project Censored's own efforts—including the *Decoding Democracy* video series, which draws connections between CML, independent media, and civic engagement, and our recent book for young people, *The Media and Me*—are examples of the kind of educational materials that ought to be taught across the curriculum, from an early age, to nurture a more media savvy and literate society.[54] As these resources emphasize, the challenge, moving forward in uncertain political times, is to determine how best to convert the burgeoning power of the independent press into meaningful political power in service of true democracy and civic engagement.

One hopeful example of what this might look like is the Protect Reporters from Exploitative State Spying (PRESS) Act, which has broad, bipartisan support. If enacted, the PRESS Act would protect journalists from being coerced into revealing their sources to government officials. The legislation would safeguard *anyone* engaging in journalism, not just those employed by establishment outlets, which would be a significant win for independent and nonprofit newsrooms that are often marginalized or excluded by authorities.[55] As Seth Stern of the Freedom of the Press Foundation and Clayton Weimers of Reporters Without Borders USA noted, "It's the strongest 'shield' bill to protect journalists and their sources ever introduced in Congress."[56] This shield law is one example of how policy can be made to support journalism in the public interest.

Despite the challenges to the Fourth Estate presented in *State of the Free Press 2025*, from various forms of censorship to direct attacks on journalists themselves, it is vital to recognize and recall the many positive developments and creative solutions in the works.

As we complete this book, news broke that Julian Assange, the persecuted WikiLeaks publisher, will be freed from confinement after striking a surprising plea deal with the US Department of Justice. His freedom is to be celebrated—even if the terms of the deal could still have a chilling effect on public interest journalism.[57] Those concerns noted, collective action on behalf of Assange clearly made a difference. But for the sustained, multi-year, global campaign to free him, Assange would probably still be languishing in prison today.[58]

Collective efforts on behalf of media reform, and especially journalistic integrity, are difficult; the stakes are high, but the payoffs are well worth the effort. From the classroom to the public square, with critical media literacy and a truly independent press, we the people can better connect media power to political power to create a more just and well-informed society. We make the first steps in this direction when, following the leads of independent journalists Amira Hass and Mohammed El-Kurd, we refuse to accept injustices as normal, and vow to bravely report the truth.

Andy Lee Roth, Winthrop, Washington
Mickey Huff, Fair Oaks, California, and Ithaca, New York
June 2024

Notes

1. Kirsten Eddy, "Most Americans Say a Free Press Is Highly Important to Society," Pew Research Center, April 23, 2024.
2. Eddy, "Most Americans Say." See also John Hanna, "Kansas Lawmakers Want a Report on Last Year's Police Raid of a Newspaper," Associated Press, January 24, 2024; and Mathew Ingram, "Indictment of Florida Journalist Raises Troubling Questions," *Columbia Journalism Review*, February 29, 2024.
3. "2024 World Press Freedom Index–Journalism under Political Pressure," Reporters Without Borders, 2024. For analysis of RSF's 2024 Press Freedom Index, see Mischa Geracoulis, "Reporters Without Borders Finds Significant 'Barriers to Press Freedom' in the United States," Project Censored, June 13, 2024.
4. The Index assigns a score for each country—from 0 to 100, with 100 representing "the highest possible level of press freedom"—based on a quantitative assessment of abuses against media and journalists and a qualitative analysis based on responses from press freedom specialists in each country. For comparison, Canada ranked fourteenth with a score of 81.7 ("satisfactory") and Norway ranked first, with a score of 91.89 ("good"). See "Methodology Used for Compiling the World Press

Freedom Index 2024," Reporters Without Borders, undated [accessed May 28, 2024].

5.   "2024 World Press Freedom Index."
6.   CPJ Staff, "Why Impact of Israel-Gaza War Has Become Harder to Document," Committee to Protect Journalists, May 6, 2024.
7.   "Israeli Military Says It Can't Guarantee Journalists' Safety in Gaza," Reuters, October 27, 2023.
8.   Marwa Fatafta et al., "Palestine Unplugged: How Israel Disrupts Gaza's Internet," Access Now, November 10, 2023, updated November 28, 2023.
9.   Fatafta et al., "Palestine Unplugged." Internet shutdowns often serve as cover for atrocities; see Hugo Sousa and Andy Lee Roth, "2016: A Record Year for Global Internet Shutdowns," in *Censored 2018: Press Freedoms in a 'Post-Truth' World*, eds. Andy Lee Roth and Mickey Huff with Project Censored (New York: Seven Stories Press, 2017), 64–67, also archived on the Project Censored website.
10. Brett Wilkins, "Israel Bans Al Jazeera in 'Assault on Freedom of the Press'," *Common Dreams*, May 5, 2024.
11. Al Jazeera Staff, "Israel Bans Al Jazeera: What Does It Mean and What Happens Next?" Al Jazeera, May 6, 2024.
12. Brett Wilkins, "AP and Free Press Defenders Blast Israeli Shutdown of Gaza Live Feed," *Common Dreams*, May 21, 2024.
13. "RSF Files Third Complaint with ICC about Israeli War Crimes against Journalists in Gaza," Reporters Without Borders, May 27, 2024. Israel has fallen to the rank of 101st on the 2024 World Press Freedom Index referenced earlier.
14. Sharon Zhang, "Palestinian Journalists' Union Says Western Media Is 'Facilitating Genocide'," *Truthout*, November 2, 2023.
15. Palestinian Journalists' Syndicate, "Some of the Global Media's Unethical Coverage Is Facilitating Genocide in Gaza," The Real News Network, November 7, 2023; see also Zhang, "Palestinian Journalists' Union Says."
16. Zhang, "Palestinian Journalists' Union Says." See also Mohammed El-Kurd, "Western Journalists Have Palestinian Blood on Their Hands," *The Nation*, October 20, 2023.
17. See, for example, Lara Witt and Tina Vásquez, "US Media Is Evading Its Responsibility to Acknowledge the Gaza Genocide," *Prism*, October 26, 2023. On the Biden administration's denials, see, e.g., Trevor Hunnicutt and Jeff Mason, "White House Sees No Genocide in Gaza, Condemns Aid Convoy Attacks," Reuters, May 13, 2024.
18. Andy Lee Roth and Liam O'Connell, "Omission Is the Same as Permission," *Index on Censorship* 50, no. 4 (January 2022).
19. Andy Lee Roth and Mickey Huff, "How Corporate Media Helped Lay the Groundwork for Israel's Genocide in Gaza," *Truthout*, December 2, 2023.
20. Alan MacLeod, "Propaganda Blitz: How Mainstream Media Is Pushing Fake Palestine Stories," *MintPress News*, October 13, 2023. Also see Roth and Huff, "How Corporate Media."
21. Kirstin McCudden, "Israel-Gaza War: Journalists Covering Local Reaction," U.S. Press Freedom Tracker, April 30, 2024. The U.S. Press Freedom Tracker is a nonpartisan news database—produced by a coalition of press freedom organizations and managed by the Freedom of the Press

Foundation—that provides information on the number of press freedom violations in the United States, including arrests, assaults, and seizures of equipment.

22. Seth Stern, "Settlement Hasn't Stopped NYPD's Press Abuses at Protests," Freedom of the Press Foundation, May 22, 2024.

23. Andy Lee Roth, "The Deadly Business of Reporting Truth," Project Censored, August 17, 2022, updated December 19, 2023.

24. David Shepardson, "US Senate Passes TikTok Divestment-or-Ban Bill, Biden Set to Make it Law," Reuters, April 24, 2024.

25. Omar Zahzah, "US TikTok Ban Sign of Imperial Anxiety," *Electronic Intifada*, June 6, 2024.

26. Shepardson, "US Senate Passes TikTok Divestment-or-Ban Bill."

27. Shepardson, "US Senate Passes TikTok Divestment-or-Ban Bill."

28. Mickey Huff and Nolan Higdon, "The Press Freedom Clock is Tik-Toking," Project Censored, May 2, 2024.

29. Julia Conley, "Romney Admits Push to Ban TikTok is Aimed at Censoring News Out of Gaza," *Common Dreams*, May 6, 2024.

30. Conley, "Romney Admits."

31. Andy Lee Roth, "Pro-Israel Legislators Have Concocted a Dangerous Ruse to Shut down Nonprofits," *Truthout*, May 3, 2024. Despite "fundamental concerns," the legislation had received "nearly no news coverage to date," Roth reported.

32. "Charity & Security Network Opposes Legislation That Targets Charities," Charity & Security Network, April 25, 2024.

33. Roth, "Pro-Israel Legislators Have Concocted a Dangerous Ruse."

34. Seth Stern, "Criticizing Israel? Nonprofit Media Could Lose Tax-Exempt Status without Due Process," *The Intercept*, May 10, 2024.

35. Roth, "Pro-Israel Legislators Have Concocted a Dangerous Ruse." See also the subsequent report by Sheera Frenkel, "Israel Secretly Targets U.S. Lawmakers with Influence Campaign on Gaza War," *New York Times*, June 5, 2024, updated June 6, 2024.

36. "The 2024 Pulitzer Prize Winner in International Reporting," The Pulitzer Prizes, 2024.

37. Jeffrey Gettleman, Anat Schwartz, and Adam Sella, "'Screams Without Words': Sexual Violence on Oct. 7," *New York Times*, December 31, 2023. The online version of the article was published December 28, 2023, and updated on March 25, 2024.

38. Max Blumenthal and Aaron Maté, "Screams without Proof: Questions for NYT about Shoddy 'Hamas Mass Rape' Report," *The Grayzone*, January 10, 2024.

39. Jeremy Scahill, Ryan Grim, and Daniel Boguslaw, "'Between the Hammer and the Anvil': The Story behind the *New York Times* October 7 Exposé," *The Intercept*, February 28, 2024. See also, Robin Andersen, "Investigating the *New York Times* 'Investigation' of Hamas Mass Rape," *CounterPunch*, February 11, 2024.

40. "A Call from the Journalism Academy for an External Review at the *New York Times*," *Literary Hub*, April 30, 2024.

41. "Columbia Journalism Award," Columbia Journalism School, undated [accessed May 31, 2024].

42. "'Refuse to Accept Hell as Normal': Amira Hass Delivers Graduation Speech as Students Keep up Protests," *Democracy Now!*, May 16, 2024. See also, Amy Goodman, interview with Amira Hass, "'Resist the Normalization of Evil': Israeli Reporter Amira Hass on Palestine and the Role of Journalism," *Democracy Now!*, May 17, 2024.

43. "Izzy Award for Independent Media to Be Shared by In These Times, Mohammed El-Kurd, Lynzy Billing, and Trina Reynolds-Tyler and Sarah Conway," *IC News* (Ithaca College), April 2, 2024.

44. Mohammed El-Kurd, "Western Journalists," and "The Right to Speak for Ourselves," *The Nation*, November 27, 2023.

45. See Robert M. Entman, *Democracy without Citizens: Media and the Decay of American Politics* (New York: Oxford University Press, 1990), 30.

46. Also see Jay Rosen, "The 'Here's Where We're Coming From' Statement in Journalism," *PressThink*, November 8, 2021.

47. "SPJ Code of Ethics," Society of Professional Journalists, September 6, 2014.

48. Carl Jensen, "Project Censored: Raking Muck, Raising Hell," in *Censored: The News That Didn't Make the News—and Why*, ed. Carl Jensen (Chapel Hill, North Carolina: Shelburne Press, 1993), 1–14, 7.

49. See Carl Jensen, *Stories That Changed America: Muckrakers of the Twentieth Century* (New York: Seven Stories Press, 2000), and Andy Lee Roth and Mickey Huff, "What If Journalism Disappeared?" in *State of the Free Press 2024*, eds. Andy Lee Roth and Mickey Huff, 6–7.

50. Ben H. Bagdikian, *The Media Monopoly* (Boston: Beacon Press, 1983).

51. Kate Horgan, Reagan Haynie, and Shealeigh Voitl, "Navigating the Digital Democracy," *The Progressive*, May 29, 2024; and "SPJ Code of Ethics."

52. See, for example, Michael Leedom, "Building Media Literacy into School Curriculums Worldwide," *News Decoder*, February 29, 2024; and Sharon Johnson, "Media Literacy Becomes a State Issue," *The Progressive*, June 3, 2024.

53. See, for example, Nolan Higdon and Mickey Huff, "Mandatory Media Literacy Education Could Be Coming to California Schools Soon," Project Censored, July 18, 2023, updated February 19, 2024.

54. See "Decoding Democracy: Exploring Critical Media Literacy Education, Independent Journalism, and Civic Engagement," Project Censored, May 3, 2024; Project Censored and the Media Revolution Collective, *The Media and Me: A Guide to Critical Media Literacy for Young People* (Fair Oaks: The Censored Press; New York: Triangle Square, 2022), which is supplemented by a resource guide for educators available, at no charge, via the "Classroom" page on the Project Censored website.

55. "Sen. Durbin Should Advance the PRESS Act before Time Runs Out," Freedom of the Press Foundation, May 30, 2024; Seth Stern, "Frequently Asked Questions about the PRESS Act," Freedom of the Press Foundation, January 25, 2024.

56. Clayton Weimers and Seth Stern, "Why Political Rivals Can and Should Come Together for Press Freedom," *The Hill*, February 1, 2024; see also Geracoulis, "Reporters Without Borders Finds Significant 'Barriers to Press Freedom.'"

57. As Trevor Timm, director of the Freedom of the Press Foundation, and others have noted, the charge the DOJ forced Assange to plea to for his

freedom—conspiracy to violate the Espionage Act, based on his having obtained secret documents and communicated them to persons not entitled to receive them, including the public—is a "crime" that journalists at establishment news outlets across the country commit nearly every day. See Trevor Timm, "At Last, Julian Assange Is Free. But It May Have Come at a High Price for Press Freedom," *The Guardian*, June 25, 2024; and "WikiLeaks Publisher Julian Assange Finally Freed," Reporters Without Borders, June 25, 2024.

58.   Kevin Gosztola, "The End of the Biggest Press Freedom Case of the Century," *The Dissenter*, June 25, 2024.

CHAPTER 1

The Top *Censored* Stories and Media Analysis of 2023–2024

Compiled and edited by
NICOLE MENDEZ-VILLARRUBIA, CAM LIPPINCOTT,
AMY GRIM BUXBAUM, STEVE MACEK,
and ANDY LEE ROTH

INTRODUCTION: EXPOSING GAPS IN CORPORATE CONTROL OVER NEWS

ANDY LEE ROTH

*The power to keep an occurrence out of the
news is power over the news.*
—GAYE TUCHMAN, *Making News*[1]

News today is so abundant, so pervasive, and so easily accessible that it might seem improbable, if not impossible, that any genuinely important events or issues could remain unreported or not widely known. Confronted with an overwhelming torrent of media, it's no wonder that few Americans think the problem with news is that we do not have *enough* of it.[2]

Instead, from the launch of the twenty-four-hour news cycle in the late 1980s to the proliferation of news-focused websites and social media spurred by the development of the internet, we seem to be inundated with more and more news. In 2001, Project Censored's founder Carl Jensen characterized this development as "news inflation," noting "there seems to be more [news] than ever before—but it isn't worth as much as it used to be."[3]

This abundance of news, now available at our fingertips thanks to mobile devices, promotes the delusion that nothing of genuine significance can ultimately escape our attention.[4] With news media increasingly tailored to particular groups and communities, every possible interest and perspective appears to be fulfilled by one outlet or another.

Yet, as Jensen observed, the fundamental problem is not the quantity of news but the quality of it. Stipulating that news ought to be "nutritious" for society, informing members of the public about threats to its economic, political, and physical health, Jensen quipped, "We need more steak and less sizzle from the press."[5]

The nation's most prominent outlets seek to convince us that their reporting is comprehensive, impartial, and definitive: "All the News That's Fit to Print," as the *New York Times* first asserted on its front page in 1897. Nevertheless, since 1976—for nearly fifty years now—college students and faculty working with Project Censored have identified, vetted, and promoted public awareness of trustworthy stories produced by independent news outlets on significant topics that have gone unnoticed or under-reported by the establishment press. This ongoing, critical investigation of "missing" news stories exposes gaps in corporate news coverage that raise basic questions about just how comprehensive, impartial, or definitive a view of the world they provide.

This year's Top 25 chapter represents the collective effort of 206 students from nine college and university campuses across the United States, who have developed and engaged their critical media literacy skills by identifying, vetting, and summarizing important but under-reported independent news stories and helping to bring them to wider public attention. They are the forty-ninth cohort of students who have worked with their faculty mentors and Project Censored to expose and publicize what Jensen called "The News That Didn't Make the News—and Why."

The specific stories gathered and summarized here each stand on their own as vital dispatches on issues that deserve more extensive news coverage and broader public engagement than they have received thus far. For example, this year's featured stories cover censorship by the world's most popular social media platforms of information about abortion services (story #5), school hospital programs supporting students' mental health and education (story #23), and a report that more than six thousand US workers died on the job in 2022, according to records maintained by the federal Bureau of Labor Statistics—an astounding rate of one workplace death every ninety-six minutes (this year's #1 story). These are certainly newsworthy issues, but for one reason or another, the corporate news media have not covered them. Without the independent news coverage highlighted here, the public would know little to nothing about these concerns.

But readers can only appreciate the full significance of the Project's annual listing of important but underreported stories by stepping back to perceive deeper, less obvious *patterns of omission* in corporate news coverage. Thus examined, the Project's annual story lists provide an evidence-based rejoinder to anyone who would doubt that US establishment news outlets produce a *filtered* version of who and what counts as "newsworthy." Every year, a number of genuinely important events or issues are blocked or marginalized by the establishment press, as Project Censored systematically documents.[6]

When corporate news media consistently omit or underplay the types of stories highlighted in this chapter and previous years' top story lists, that news judgment distorts the public's comprehension of the world and, by extension, undermines one of the fundamental conditions for democracy, a well-informed and engaged electorate.

As sociologist Gaye Tuchman noted in her pioneering study of how news shapes our understanding of what we want to know, need to know, and should know, conventional news frames both "produce and limit meaning."[7] These limits, Tuchman argued, typically work to block inquiry and transform dissent.[8]

How do they do this? By providing what Tuchman, drawing on the work of feminist sociologist Dorothy Smith, referred to as "methods of not knowing" that normalize and ultimately reproduce the existing social order.[9] For example, Tuchman presented an extended analysis of how "successful" news coverage of the women's movement in the 1960s and 1970s eventually "limited its ability to carry forth radical issues."[10]

What Tuchman demonstrated regarding news coverage of social movements that challenge the status quo also holds true for news more generally. Even when news outlets seek to fulfill their role as watchdogs, alerting the public to abuses of power, news based on official sources and conventional narratives tends nonetheless to legitimize established institutions. Consequently, "News gives the feeling that there is novelty without change," as another sociologist, E. Barbara Phillips, noted in 1976.[11] That enduring pattern may explain why so many Americans today remain not only disinterested in news but also convinced that political gridlock is inevitable, corporate dominance is inescapable, and substantive reform is a pipe dream.

By contrast, the stories reported by independent news outlets and highlighted by Project Censored serve as potential catalysts for change. They break the typical patterns of news coverage that Tuchman criticized. Some of these stories detail abuses of power so egregious that an informed public might well be outraged and spurred to organize and demand change; additional stories document innovative solutions that could serve as models for change in similarly impacted communities or as inspiration for grassroots campaigns to tackle other seemingly unsolvable problems. Perhaps that is why these stories appear in this volume—as important but *under-reported* news stories—rather than on the front pages of the nation's most prestigious newspapers or the headlines of its most popular cable and television news programs.

Tuchman was right that much of what passes for news promotes "not knowing" in service of the status quo. However, an independent press committed to ethical journalism provides the public with meaningful alternatives. The intrepid journalists and news outlets whose work is celebrated here demonstrate the power of independent journalism to inform the public about issues and perspectives that challenge the status quo. The following stories promote critical inquiry, a plurality of perspectives, and informed dissent in the face of systemic injustices and deep-rooted inequalities.

Can independent journalism effectively contest the corporate media's power to legitimize the status quo? The answer hinges not only on the dogged commitment of independent journalists and news outlets to continue reporting stories that raise fundamental questions about systemic injustices and inequalities but also on whether we, the public, harness that power to envision and enact new, more just, equitable, and inclusive futures.

NOTE ON RESEARCH AND EVALUATION
OF *CENSORED* NEWS STORIES

How do we at Project Censored identify and evaluate independent news stories, and how do we know that the Top 25 stories we bring forward each year are not only relevant and significant but also trustworthy? The answer is that every candidate news story undergoes rigorous review, which takes place in multiple stages during each annual cycle. Although adapted to take advantage of both the Project's expanding affiliates program and current technologies, the vetting process is quite similar to the one Project Censored founder Carl Jensen established more than forty years ago.

Candidate stories are initially identified by Project Censored professors and students or are nominated by members of the general public, who bring them to the Project's attention.[12] Together, faculty and students evaluate each candidate story in terms of its importance, timeliness, quality of sources, and inadequate corporate news coverage. If it fails on any one of these criteria, the story is deemed inappropriate and is excluded from further consideration.

Once Project Censored receives the candidate story, we undertake a second round of judgment, using the same criteria and updating the review to include any subsequent competing corporate coverage. We post stories that pass this round of review on the Project's website as Validated Independent News stories (VINs).[13]

In early spring, we present all VINs in the current cycle to the faculty and students at all of our affiliate campuses and to our panel of expert judges, who cast votes to winnow the candidate stories from more than one hundred to twenty-five.

Once the Top 25 list has been determined, Project Censored student interns begin another intensive review of each story using Nexis Uni and ProQuest databases. Additional faculty and students contribute to this final stage of review.

The Top 25 finalists are then sent to our panel of judges, whose votes rank them in numerical order. At the same time, these experts—including media studies professors, professional journalists and editors, and a former commissioner of the Federal Communications Commission—offer their insights on the stories' strengths and weaknesses.[14]

Thus, by the time a story appears on the pages of the *State of the Free Press* yearbook, it has undergone at least five distinct rounds of review and evaluation.

Although the stories that Project Censored brings forward may be socially and politically controversial—and sometimes even psychologically challenging—we are confident that each is the result of serious journalistic effort and deserves greater public attention.

Thousands Killed and Injured on the Job, with Significant Racial Disparities in Deaths and Injuries

Tyler Walicek, "1 US Worker Dies on the Job Every 96 Minutes, Latest Data Shows," *Truthout*, February 17, 2024.

"87% of Service Workers in the US South Were Injured on the Job Last Year," *Peoples Dispatch*, April 5, 2023.

Student Researchers: Adrien Louis (City College of San Francisco) and Olivia Rosenberg (North Central College)

Faculty Evaluators: Jennifer Levinson and Sentura Tubbs (City College of San Francisco) and Steve Macek (North Central College)

Working in the United States is becoming more dangerous, and Black and Latiné workers in particular are at heightened risk of being killed or injured on the job, according to recent studies reported on by *Truthout* and *Peoples Dispatch*.

According to a February 2024 report for *Truthout* by Tyler Walicek, the Bureau of Labor Statistics (BLS)'s Census of Fatal Occupational Injuries (CFOI) found a "5.7 percent increase in workplace deaths in the U.S. during the relevant 2021-2022 census period."[16] In 2022,

"Nearly 6,000 U.S. workers died on the job," Walicek wrote, and "a startling total of 2.8 million were injured or sickened." On average, a US worker was killed at work every ninety-six minutes in 2022, *Truthout* reported. All told, deaths due to injuries sustained in the workplace have reached the highest level since 2007.

The BLS data also reveal "marked racial disparities" in fatal occupational injuries, with the average rates of workplace deaths for Black workers (4.2 per hundred thousand full-time workers) and Latiné workers (4.6 per hundred thousand) "distinctly higher" than the average rate of 3.7 workplace deaths per hundred thousand full-time workers.

Immigrant employees are especially vulnerable. *Truthout* quoted Tracey Cekada, chair of the Department of Safety Sciences at Indiana University of Pennsylvania (IUP), "Fatalities among foreign-born Hispanic or Latiné workers need to be addressed, as we are seeing a growing number of Spanish-speaking employees enter the workforce. These communication barriers put workers at risk."

The rate at which service workers, particularly people of color who work in the service sector, sustain non-fatal injuries on the job is also alarmingly high, according to an April 5, 2023, report by *Peoples Dispatch* which summarized findings from the Strategic Organizing Center (SOC). The SOC's March 2023 survey sampled workers from eleven Southern states in an area known as the "Black Belt," which refers to states with "historically large Black populations," including North Carolina, South Carolina, Alabama, Tennessee, Georgia, Virginia, Louisiana, Florida, Texas, Mississippi, and Arkansas. Of the 347 service workers polled, 87 percent were injured on the job in 2022. The survey also noted that service industry workers in the South are predominantly Black.

Most of those injured on the job were hurt by carrying or lifting items, being struck by falling items, getting cut by a sharp tool, or from heat-related illness due to broken air conditioners.

Around half of the respondents reported noticing unsafe conditions in their workplace, and just under half reported facing harassment or violence. The Strategic Organizing Center reported that 70 percent of workers surveyed did not report harassment or violent behavior for fear of retaliation by their employers.

Compared to other developed countries, the United States consistently underperforms in providing workers with on-the-job safety. In his *Truthout* article, Tyler Walicek argued that this is a direct consequence of "the diminution of worker power and regulatory oversight" in the United States. A 2021 assessment by Arinite Health and Safety, a consulting firm, found that US workplace fatality rates exceeded those in the UK, Canada, Australia, and much of Europe, Walicek reported.[17]

Workers are increasingly organizing to fight back against hazardous working conditions.

Members of the Union of Southern Service Workers (USSW) filed a civil rights complaint against South Carolina's Occupational Safety and Health Administration (SC OSHA) for failing to protect Black workers from hazardous working conditions, as the *Post and Courier* of Charleston, South Carolina, reported.[18] In its federal complaint, the USSW wrote that "from 2018 to 2022, SC OSHA conducted no programmed inspections in the food/beverage and general merchandise industries, and only one such inspection in the food services and ware-housing industries."[19]

On April 4, 2023, the USSW went on a one-day strike in Georgia, North Carolina, and South Carolina to expose unsafe working conditions in the service industry.

Surprisingly, there has been almost no coverage of the BLS findings by corporate news media. The BLS released its Census of Fatal Occupational Injuries report in December 2023, and yet, as of May 2024, no major US daily newspaper had covered the report. In December 2023, FOX 9, the Minneapolis-St. Paul Fox News affiliate, ran a story focused on the census findings for Minnesota, which found that eighty-one state residents were fatally injured on the job in 2022.[20] But this local coverage focused on Minnesota and did not address the national trends detailed in the full BLS report. On April 12, 2024, WBAY, the local ABC affiliate in Green Bay, Wisconsin, ran a package that reviewed the BLS data on workplace fatalities as part of its coverage of "Work Zone Safety Awareness Week."[21]

Corporate coverage of the conflict between the USSW and SC OSHA has also been scant. Independent, not-for-profit news outlets, such as *DC Report*, have consistently paid more attention to the issue.[22] In December 2023, the Associated Press and *Bloomberg Law* both reported on another development related to workplace safety: the Service Employees International Union petitioning the federal government to investigate South Carolina's failure to protect its service workers, but the articles did not address the issue of racial disparities in workplace safety.[23]

The corporate media's refusal to cover the harsh realities of workplace deaths and injuries—and the obvious racial disparities in who is hurt and killed on the job—makes the task of organizing to address occupational safety at a national level that much more difficult.

A "Vicious Circle" of Climate Debt Traps World's Most Vulnerable Nations

Natalia Alayza, Valerie Laxton, and Carolyn Neunuebel, "Developing Countries Won't Beat the Climate Crisis without Tackling Rising Debt," World Resources Institute, September 22, 2023.

Katie Surma, "How Developing Nations Battered by Climate Change Are Crushed by Debt from International Lenders," *Inside Climate News*, March 6, 2024.

Student Researcher: Tyler Sarro (Saint Michael's College)

Faculty Evaluator: Rob Williams (Saint Michael's College)

Low-income countries are disproportionately impacted by poverty and climate-related disasters.[24] Many of the developing nations most vulnerable to climate change are also "operating on increasingly tight budgets and at risk of defaulting on loans," Natalia Alayza, Valerie Laxton, and Carolyn Neunuebel reported for the World Resources Institute in September 2023. They described the pattern—which has been worsened by the pandemic and a global recession—as a "climate debt trap" for the affected countries.

Confronted by a combination of natural disasters intensified by climate change—such as flooding and drought—and compounding debt, these nations' governments face challenges in funding basic social programs, leading to public distrust, further impoverishment, and reduced credit ratings that make future loans even more costly.

Global standards for climate resilience require immense national budgets. Developing countries borrow from international creditors, and as debt piles up, governments are unable to pay for essential needs, including public health programs, food security, and climate protections.

"High-interest rates, short repayment periods, and . . . the coexistence of multiple crises (like a pandemic paired with natural disasters) can all make it difficult for governments to meet their debt servicing obligations," according to the World Resources Institute's report. It quoted the Minister of State for Finance in Belize, Christopher Coye, "How do we pursue climate action? We are fiscally constrained." Similarly, the finance minister of Barbados, Ryan Staughn, called for a debt crisis solution that "allows countries to be able to continue to respond to the climate crisis without getting ourselves into trouble."

Debt distress in developing nations is a growing problem.[25] The World Resources Institute reported that the number of developing countries for which debt liabilities exceeded 60 percent of the nation's gross domestic product nearly tripled (from twenty-two nations to fifty-nine) between 2011 and 2022. Around the world, approximately 41 percent of people live in countries that spend more on interest payments than on development, a situation that undermines public trust in those nations' governments and in the belief that "international cooperation works to everyone's benefit," Alayza, Laxton, and Neunuebel noted.

The World Resources Institute reported that among the world's fifty most climate-vulnerable nations, twenty-three countries are either in debt distress—being unable to repay the principal and interest owed to creditors—or at risk of it.

A 2018 study, commissioned by the UN Environment Programme and produced by the Imperial College Business School and SOAS University of London, determined that "climate vulnerability" had already raised "the average cost of debt in a sample of developing countries by . . . USD 40 billion in additional interest payments" during the previous ten years.[26] This report examined five nations to show how climate risks manifest as actual impacts on the environment, resulting in economic expenditures that require the government to seek loans from development banks, other nations, or private investors, often leading to debt distress or debt defaults that, in turn, make it more difficult and costly to secure future loans.

One of this report's key messages was the need for investments that "enhance the resilience of climate vulnerable countries" in order to help them deal not only "with the consequences of climate risks, but also bring down their cost of borrowing."

In March 2024, Katie Surma reported for *Inside Climate News* that the climate crisis is "driving some climate-vulnerable nations deeper into debt, locking them into unsustainable cycles of economic crisis and hampering their governments' ability to provide basic services." Surma's report focused on a United Nations study of the Bahamas, where five major hurricanes since 2012 have forced the island nation of four hundred thousand citizens to take on "billions of dollars in debt for reconstruction." As Surma reported, the UN study's author, Attiya Waris—a UN Independent Expert on foreign debt, other international financial obligations, and human rights—characterized the Bahamas as representative of other climate-vulnerable nations. Waris called on the international community to offer below-market-rate loans, cancel debts related to climate-induced disasters, and make contributions to the Loss and Damage Fund, which began operation in November 2023 following its creation at COP27, the 2022 United Nations Climate Change Conference.

The climate debt trap described by the World Resources Institute has received limited news coverage. *The Guardian* deserves credit for running an important story on how nations in the global south are "forced to invest in fossil fuel projects to repay debts," describing lending policies that critics have characterized as a "new form of colonialism."[27] Otherwise, independent news coverage has been limited to outlets that specialize in climate news.[28] Among corporate news outlets, *Bloomberg* reported in May 2023 on a looming "debt crisis" for nations "most vulnerable to climate change," but its analysis catered to the financial interests of international investors.[29] A December 2023 report by the *New York Times* detailed how debt defaults threaten a "lost decade" for poor countries. But this report focused primarily on defaults to the United States and China, with less focus on how poorer countries will combat deficits, especially as climate change escalates.[30]

A prescient report published by *Dissent* in 2013, Andrew Ross's "Climate Debt Denial," provides a stark reminder that the climate debt trap now highlighted by the World

Resources Institute and others was predictable more than a decade ago.[31]

Saltwater Intrusion Threatens US Freshwater Supplies

Delaney Nolan, "Saltwater Threat to Louisiana Drinking Water to Grow across US, Experts Warn," *The Guardian*, October 10, 2023.

Holly Michael, "What Is Saltwater Intrusion? A Hydrogeologist Explains the Shifting Balance between Fresh and Salt Water at the Coast," *The Conversation*, October 11, 2023.

Student Researcher: Brianna Hickey (Frostburg State University)

Faculty Evaluator: Andy Duncan (Frostburg State University)

In fall 2023, saltwater traveling from the Gulf of Mexico up the Mississippi River infiltrated the freshwater systems of the delta region, contaminating drinking and agricultural water supplies as well as inland ecosystems. This crisis prompted a scramble to supply potable water to the region and motivated local and federal officials to issue emergency declarations.

While the danger at that time was specific to the region, a pair of articles published in October 2023 by Delaney Nolan for *The Guardian* and Holly Michael for *The Conversation* highlighted the escalating threat of saltwater intrusion across the United States and beyond.

Earth Island Journal republished the *Guardian*'s report, and *Sierra*, the Sierra Club magazine, similarly underscored the "nationally looming threat" highlighted by the Gulf region's latest water crisis.[32]

In coastal areas of the United States and across the globe, sea levels are rising dramatically because of climate change. As Nolan explained in the *Guardian*, "Deep below our feet, along every coast, runs the salt line: the zone where fresh inland water meets salty seawater. That line naturally shifts back and forth all the time, and weather events like floods and storms can push it further out. But rising seas are gradually drawing the salt line in." Severe drought, such as that experienced in the Gulf Coast and Midwest regions in 2023, drew the salt line even further inland.

Although coastal Louisiana has been one of the first US regions "to reach crisis levels since it is experiencing some of the most rapid sea-level rise on Earth," along with record high ocean surface temperatures and the loss of coastal wetlands, the problem is not confined to the Gulf region. "As seas rise as a result of the climate crisis, and weather events grow more extreme, the threat of saltwater reaching other major US cities grows," according to experts interviewed by the *Guardian*. Communities along the eastern seaboard, including those in New York, New Jersey, Rhode Island, and South Carolina, as well as major cities such as Philadelphia and Los Angeles, are threatened by saltwater intrusion of freshwater aquifers, Nolan reported. Jeeban Panthi, a coastal hydrologist at Kansas State University, told the *Guardian*, "The problem is everywhere."

In *The Conversation*, Holly Michael, a hydrogeologist

at the University of Delaware, wrote that "fresh water is essential for drinking, irrigation and healthy ecosystems. When seawater moves inland, the salt it contains can wreak havoc on farmlands, ecosystems, lives and livelihoods." Michael reported that "seawater intrusion into groundwater is happening all over the world, but perhaps the most threatened places are communities on low-lying islands," such as the Marshall Islands, which is "predicted to be uninhabitable by the end of the century."

Saltwater intrusion has many negative consequences, according to Michael's reporting: "Drinking water that contains even 2% seawater can increase blood pressure and stress kidneys. If saltwater gets into supply lines, it can corrode pipes and produce toxic disinfection by-products in water treatment plants. Seawater intrusion reduces the life span of roads, bridges and other infrastructure." As stated in *Sierra*, "Experts warn it's bound to get worse if cities don't prepare."

Major corporate news outlets, including *Time*, CNN, and CBS News, did cover saltwater intrusion in fall 2023 but focused almost exclusively on the threat to coastal Louisiana that garnered a federal emergency declaration in late September.[33] A number of news outlets, including FOX Weather and *Axios*, hastened to report that the threat in Louisiana was only temporary rather than a long-term problem.[34] Instead, corporate media typically treat saltwater intrusion as a localized issue affecting specific coastal regions such as New Orleans, the Delmarva Peninsula, and the Gulf Coast of Florida.[35] Aside from a brief article in *Forbes* acknowledging the growing problem for coastal regions in the US and around the world, corporate media have largely resisted portraying saltwater intrusion as a more widespread and escalating consequence of climate change.[36]

Natural Gas Industry Hid Health and Climate Risks of Gas Stoves

Rebecca Leber, "The Forgotten Gas Stove Wars," *Vox*, February 5, 2023.

Rebecca Leber, "The Gas Stove Wars Are Far from Over," *Vox*, March 21, 2023.

Jeff Brady, "How Gas Utilities Used Tobacco Tactics to Avoid Gas Stove Regulations," NPR, October 17, 2023.

Rebecca John, "Burning Questions: A History of the Gas Industry's Campaign to Manufacture Controversy over the Health Risks of Gas Stove Emissions," Climate Investigations Center, October 17, 2023.

Student Researcher: Grace Harty (North Central College)

Faculty Evaluator: Steve Macek (North Central College)

The natural gas industry adapted the tobacco industry's tactics to promote the use of gas stoves, reported environmental journalist Rebecca Leber for *Vox* in 2023. In a series of articles, Leber documented how the gas utility industry used strategies previously employed by the tobacco industry to avoid regulation and undermine scientific evidence establishing the harmful health and climate effects of gas stoves.[37] On October 17, 2023, NPR and the watchdog group Climate Investigations Center (CIC) also published wide-ranging investigations detailing the industry's multi-decade disinformation campaign.

As the public controversy surrounding gas stoves erupted as a culture war issue in 2023, these independent investigations meticulously documented longstanding efforts by the natural gas industry to hide health risks by diluting the scientific evidence with industry-backed studies and to promote gas stovetop cooking through public relations campaigns modeled on those previously employed by Big Tobacco.[38]

"The basic scientific understanding of why gas stoves are a problem for health and the climate is on solid footing," Leber reported in *Vox* in March 2023, "It's also common sense. When you have a fire in the house, you need somewhere for all that smoke to go. Combust natural gas, and it's not just smoke you need to worry about. There are dozens of other pollutants, including the greenhouse gas methane, that also fill the air."

Although the science is complicated, the gas industry itself privately acknowledged in 2020 that "gas cooking does generate indoor air emissions of contaminants, including carbon monoxide, oxides of nitrogen, trace amounts of materials, such as formaldehyde and so forth." In a recording obtained by *Vox*, Ted Williams, a senior executive for the American Gas Association (AGA), a powerful industry lobbying group, admitted that "it's not an issue that's going to be easy to paper over, because it does—these products do have emissions."

Documents obtained by NPR and CIC show exactly how the AGA tried to paper over its pollution problem by:

convincing consumers and regulators that cooking with gas is as risk-free as cooking with electricity. As the scientific evidence grew over time about the health effects from gas stoves, the industry used a playbook echoing the one that tobacco companies employed for decades to fend off regulation. The gas utility industry relied on some of the same strategies, researchers and public relations firms.[39]

This approach was part of a marketing campaign called "Operation Attack," which included prominent product placements ranging from *Julia Child & Company* and other popular programs in the 1970s to enlisting celebrity chefs and social media influencers today, according to Leber.[40]

The gas stove was the centerpiece of the campaign because it "plays an outsized role in the gas utility business," Jeff Brady explained for NPR, "It doesn't use much natural gas, but house builders and real estate agents say many buyers demand a gas stove. That requires gas utility service to a home, which makes it more likely customers will also use appliances that consume more gas, such as a furnace, water heater and clothes dryer. That's why some in the industry consider the stove a 'gateway appliance.'"

Although *Vox*, CIC, and NPR offered the most substantive accounts of industry influence, a smattering of local and independent outlets, such as *Grist*, have published related coverage.[41] Alex Baumhardt at the *Oregon Capitol Chronicle* reported on an initiative "to investigate the state's largest natural gas utility for spreading misinformation about the health and climate risks of gas-burning stoves."[42] Fittingly, advocacy groups, including the Sierra Club and the Union of Concerned Scientists, have also called out the industry for "gaslighting."[43]

By covering gas stoves as a culture war controversy, corporate media have ignored the outsize role of the natural gas industry in influencing science, regulation, and consumer choice.[44] Instead, corporate coverage has focused on individual actions, like cooktop comparisons and how to improve kitchen ventilation, or on governmental actions, such as local moves to phase out gas hookups for new buildings and opposition to regulatory efforts to improve the efficiency of home appliances, including the "Hands Off Our Home Appliances Act" which passed the US House in May 2024.[45]

One notable exception is a November 2023 *Los Angeles Times* editorial by Jonathan Levy, an environmental health scientist at Boston University. Despite years of scientific evidence linking gas stoves to health concerns, Levy wrote, "The gas industry's campaign was largely successful. Industry-funded studies muddied the waters and helped to stall further federal investigations or regulations addressing gas stove safety."[46] Levy concluded, "Regulators, politicians and consumers need accurate information about the risks of gas stoves and other products in homes. There is room for vigorous debate that considers a range of evidence, but the public has a right to know where that evidence comes from." As this case shows, the work of independent outlets like *Vox*, NPR, and CIC helps to make that possible.

Abortion Services Censored on Social Platforms Globally

Susan Buttenwieser, "Abortion Information Facing Online Censorship Globally," Women's Media Center, November 2, 2023.

Vittoria Elliott, "TikTok Keeps Removing Abortion Pill Content," *Wired*, June 24, 2023.

Weronika Strzyżyńska, "Meta and Google Accused of Restricting Reproductive Health Information," *The Guardian*, March 27, 2024.

Jennifer Neda John, "How Meta Created a Wild West for Abortion Misinformation," *Slate*, July 31, 2023.

Student Researcher: Olivia Rosenberg (North Central College)

Faculty Evaluator: Steve Macek (North Central College)

In the aftermath of the US Supreme Court's 2022 ruling in *Dobbs v. Jackson Women's Health Organization*, online abortion services are facing global censorship on social media platforms. Instagram, Facebook, TikTok, and Google have all allegedly restricted digital access to reproductive health organizations, according to a November 2023 report by the Women's Media Center (WMC).

Women's rights advocacy groups are calling the Supreme Court's overturning of *Roe v. Wade* the catalyst for the suppression of reproductive health information on social media. Hashtags for #mifepristone and #misoprostol, two drugs used in medical abortions, were hidden on Instagram after the *Dobbs* decision, the WMC reported. Other posts discussing medical abortions were removed from social platforms, including Instagram, TikTok, and Facebook. According to a June 2023 *Wired* article by Vittoria Elliott, "Advocates worry that in order to avoid regulation and sidestep possible legal issues, TikTok may be over-moderating, blocking access to any relevant information, and that this began before 2022." TikTok has denied censoring abortion content.

In 2022, US Senators Elizabeth Warren (D-MA) and Amy Klobuchar (D-MN) wrote to Meta and questioned what measures the company was taking to stop abortion censorship on their platforms, *Ars Technica* reported.[47] They cited instances when Facebook and Instagram "removed 'posts providing accurate information about how to legally access abortion services' within minutes and placed sensitivity screens over a post promoting an abortion documentary," along with "censorship of health care workers," which included the temporary account suspension of a reproductive rights organization.

US state legislatures are currently considering banning access to telehealth abortion care. Furthermore, CNN reported that "at the end of 2023, nine states where abortion remained legal still had restricted telehealth abortions in some way."[48]

Tech giants are censoring reproductive health information beyond the United States. A March 2024 *Guardian* article by Weronika Strzyżyńska reported that Meta and Google are accused of obstructing such information across Africa, Latin America, and Asia. In Argentina, where abortion remains legal, Google blocked ads regarding reproductive health. Several national governments are also restricting online abortion information, according to WMC's findings. For instance, Women On Web

(WOW), a website that provides abortion information and services internationally, is facing blockages in South Korea, Turkey, and Spain. The international legal organization Women's Link Worldwide took the issue to the Supreme Court of Spain, where the court ordered partial reinstatement of WOW's website.

Advocates also cite widespread misinformation as a threat to those seeking reproductive healthcare information. Crisis pregnancy centers (CPC), facilities that masquerade as reproductive healthcare clinics but do not provide abortion services, have spent $10 million on Google ads within the last two years. After many CPC ads were flagged as disinformation, Google "claimed to have removed particular ads for fake clinics that violated its policies, but they did not take action on the systemic issues with fake clinic ads," WMC reported. The Center for Countering Digital Hate posted a report in 2023 detailing Google's promotion of Google Search ads for fake abortion clinics.[49] A December 2023 *Rolling Stone* article described how "Democrats on the House Oversight Committee...demand[ed] that Musk's and Zuckerberg's platforms take 'immediate action to combat the spread of abortion misinformation,' and request[ed] that the companies deliver briefings to Congress on the matter by December 14."[50]

Women's rights organizations and reproductive health advocates have been forced to squander scarce resources fighting this sort of disinformation online. In October 2023, Reproaction, a national abortion advocacy organization, produced a report with data highlighting a "clear and immediate uptick" in the suppression of reproductive justice content and the spread of disinformation online six months after the *Dobbs* decision, with content suppression especially problematic on Facebook, Google, and TikTok.[51]

"It goes to show that our rights are at risk and how the fight for abortion access is moving online," Venny Ala-Siurua, executive director of WOW, told WMC, "The internet has become the main source of information around abortion, and access to high-quality and accurate information is critical for people to access abortion care."

According to a July 2023 report by Jennifer Neda John for *Slate*, "Advocates have struggled to disseminate accurate information about abortion under Meta's policies. We Testify, an organization that uses storytelling to shift perceptions of abortion . . . tried to run an ad with information from the World Health Organization explaining how to undergo a self-managed abortion [and the] submission was denied."

As of June 2024, corporate coverage of abortion censorship has been limited, but CNN did mention the topic in a June 2022 article.[52] There appeared to be more corporate media focus on abortion disinformation rather than censorship. Independent reporting from *Jezebel*, and Reproaction via Medium, have done more to draw attention to this issue.[53]

Global Forest Protection Goals at Risk

Olivia Rosane, "'The World Is Failing Forests': Report Finds Leaders Way off Track from Halting Deforestation by 2030," *Common Dreams*, October 24, 2023.

Mary Gagen, "Forests Are Vital to Protect the Climate, Yet the World Is Falling Far behind Its Targets," *The Conversation*, November 1, 2023.

Student Researcher: Sophie Cramer (Frostburg State University)

Faculty Evaluator: Andy Duncan (Frostburg State University)

According to an independent assessment, a much-publicized United Nations goal to end deforestation by 2030 is unlikely to be achieved, as Olivia Rosane reported for *Common Dreams* in October 2023.

The problem is money and where it's directed, according to the latest Forest Declaration Assessment, released in October 2023.[54] "We are investing in activities that are harmful for forests at far higher rates than we are investing in activities that are beneficial for forests," said Erin Matson, senior consultant at Climate Focus and coordinator of the report.

The Forest Declaration Assessment determined that protecting and restoring the world's forests requires a commitment of $460 billion per year in "green" financing; but, every year between 2013–2018, national governments provided at least $378 billion and up to $635 billion in "gray" financing that has "clear" harmful impacts on forests.[55] During that time, governments invested just $2.2 billion to protect, conserve, and restore forests, or "less than 1 percent of gray flows," according to the report, which concluded that governments "must align fiscal and financial policies with forest goals."[56]

The latest Forest Declaration Assessment, the work of "a strong and diverse group of research organizations, think tanks, NGOs, and advocacy groups spanning the globe," is sure to fuel complaints that UN climate summits generate more headlines than substance. The goal to end deforestation by 2030 was set in 2021 in Glasgow, Scotland, at the twenty-sixth United Nations Climate Change Conference, or COP26.

Even so, not all countries are failing their forests. More than fifty countries still have the potential to halt deforestation by 2030, and they have laid the groundwork for everyone else to follow, according to the assessment.

Alongside the Forest Declaration Assessment, the World Wildlife Fund (WWF) issued its first Forest Pathways Report.[57] As the report's lead author, Mary Gagen, noted in an article published by *The Conversation*, "Global forest loss in 2022 was 6.6 million hectares, an area about the size of Ireland. That's 21% more than the amount that would keep us on track to meet the target of zero deforestation by 2030, agreed in Glasgow." At 33 percent over the necessary target, loss of tropical rainforests was "even more pronounced," Gagen reported.

In her article for *The Conversation*, Gagen emphasized four key recommendations made by the WWF to protect forests: (1) accelerating the recognition of Indigenous land and resource rights; (2) mobilizing public and private financial institutions to support sustainable forest economies; (3) reforming global trade so supply chains do not rely on commodities tied to deforestation; and (4) shifting the economy to value nature.

In contrast to the celebrity-studded, TV-friendly highlights from the 2021 UN summit in Glasgow, these major reports on deforestation and how to combat it have received scant attention from corporate media. Corporate news outlets appear to have ignored the Forest Declaration Assessment and the Forest Pathways Report, except for a November 2023 article published by the *Washington Post*, which reported, "Forest loss and methane emissions are climbing, despite pledges at the U.N. climate talks in Scotland in 2021."[58] Although the *Post*'s coverage came after the release of the Forest Declaration Assessment and the Forest Pathways Report, it made no direct reference to either of them. International outlets, including Germany's *DW* and France 24, a state-owned television network, did produce substantive reports based on the Forest Declaration Assessment.[59]

Military Personnel Target Gen Z Recruits with Lurid Social Media Tactics

Alan MacLeod, "From Simp to Soldier: How the Military is Using E-girls to Recruit Gen Z into Service," *MintPress News*, June 1, 2023.

Student Researcher: Ashton Sidford (Diablo Valley College)

Faculty Evaluator: Mickey Huff (Diablo Valley College)

The US military is taking the old adage "sex sells" to another level by using sexually suggestive social media posts on TikTok and Instagram—known as thirst traps—in an effort to recruit members of Generation Z in response to military recruitment numbers falling below goals in recent years.[60] The main subject of Alan MacLeod's *MintPress News* investigation is Army Psychological Operations Specialist Hailey Lujan, who has amassed more than nine hundred thousand TikTok followers and three hundred thousand followers on Instagram, based on her videos which feature "sexually suggestive content alongside subtle (and sometimes not-so-subtle) calls to join up."

This drastic change from soldiers bringing pull-up bars for recruitment sessions during high school lunch periods to using female sexuality online to lure teenage boys into an institution with a horrendous record of sexual assault against female soldiers adds new questions about what exactly the military seeks to accomplish with these videos. Lujan's videos seemingly violate the code of conduct of the image-conscious US military, and it is unclear what role the military has in producing Lujan's content. Nonetheless, Lujan appears to remain an active member of the army. According to MacLeod, "Multiple videos suggest Lujan is connected with the 101st Airborne Division. Location data shows she is based at Fort Campbell, a large military installation on the Tennessee-Kentucky border that houses the storied division."

The self-aware nature of these accounts sticks out. Lujan frequently references the allegations that she is a federal agent and a psyop (a psychological operation), captioning her videos with comments such as, "My handlers made me post this" or "Not endorsed by the DoD

[Department of Defense] :') :3," MacLeod reported. Videos often include Lujan flaunting heavy weapons, modeling high-end clothes she supposedly bought with her signing bonus, and one of her in Donald Trump Jr.'s penthouse. None of these videos explain the actual responsibilities of military life. "Lujan's content appears to be a part of a weird new strategy of military outreach, shocking academics and military experts alike," MacLeod reported. Lujan is not the only online military influencer, but her overt use of her sensuality and her constant encouragement of her followers to enlist make her noteworthy.

"I can't believe she's getting away with posting some of this stuff," said journalist and veteran Rosa del Luca in an interview with *MintPress News*, "Everyone learns in boot camp that when you are in uniform, you cannot act unprofessionally, or you get in deep trouble." MacLeod reached out to the Department of Defense for clarification but received no response.

Additionally, the Army has been sponsoring various popular content creators—such as YouTube stars Ben Azelart (27 million subscribers) and Michelle Khare (4.5 million)—to "join" for a day. These videos portray military training as nothing but fun obstacle courses similar to those featured on some television game shows. Unlike Lujan's videos, these "join for a day" videos make clear that the US Army has total control of production, with the obvious goal of rebranding the military's image for a generation that sees military service in increasingly negative light.[61] The branches of the US military are no stranger to partnerships with entertainment giants that traditionally engage viewers from all walks of life—as in armed forces' partnerships with the National Football League.[62] But this new attempt to appeal to niche youth audiences has not been scrutinized, which is especially troubling because studies show the young targets of these videos often have trouble distinguishing between sponsored and un-sponsored content.[63]

"It is now well-established (if not well-known) that the Department of Defense also fields a giant clandestine army of at least 60,000 people whose job it is to influence public opinion, the majority doing so from their keyboards," MacLeod reported, noting that, in doing so, "this troll army was likely breaking both domestic and international law."

Using social media for military recruiting is not a new strategy, and the military's venture in e-sports has received previous corporate coverage, notably when Rep. Alexandria Ocasio-Cortez sought to bar the use of funds for recruiting efforts on live-streaming websites, such as Twitch, and in e-sports.[64] However, this new psychosexual recruiting method has not received the same level of pushback from the media or politicians.

As of May 2024, there has been no new coverage on this specific instance from either corporate or independent news outlets, though the pop culture magazine *Dazed* has reported on Lujan's Israeli counterparts in the Israel Defense Forces (IDF).[65] As *Dazed* reported, these influencers post popular trends, such as "get ready with me" videos, on the IDF's official social media accounts. This appears to be the only other coverage of using Gen Z's cultural references as a military recruitment strategy.

New Federal Rule Limits Transcript Withholding by Colleges and Universities

Sarah Butrymowicz and Meredith Kolodner, "Holding Transcripts Hostage May Get a Lot Harder, Thanks to New Federal Rules," *The Hechinger Report*, December 1, 2023.

Katherine Knott, "U.S. Bans Most Withholding of Transcripts," *Inside Higher Education*, October 25, 2023.

Student Researchers: Caroline Brussard, Dempsey Campbell, Samantha Druckenmiller, Grace Ferguson, and Ashley Santos (University Of Massachusetts Amherst)

Faculty Evaluators: Allison Butler and Jeewon Chon (University Of Massachusetts Amherst)

A new federal regulation will make it more difficult for colleges and universities to withhold students' transcripts to force them to repay loan debts, Sarah Butrymowicz and Meredith Kolodner reported for *The Hechinger Report* in December 2023. Transcript withholding is a strategy colleges use to recover outstanding debt despite questions about the practice's fairness and effectiveness. Butrymowicz and Kolodner's report focused on the case of Florina Caprita, a student who was unable to transfer credits earned in a paralegal training program after Ashworth College, a for-profit school, withheld her transcript. As Katherine Knott reported for *Inside Higher Education*, more than six million students have "stranded credits" due to the controversial practice.[66]

At present, Department of Education (DOE) regulations prevent schools from withholding transcripts for students receiving federal aid, but these protections do not apply to institutions that accept no federal student aid, including many for-profit colleges, such as Ashworth.[67] Another agency, the Consumer Financial Protection Bureau, is also investigating transcript withholding, which the Bureau has deemed abusive because the practice is "designed to gain leverage over borrowers and coerce them into making payments."

Many states have banned transcript withholding by public universities. In 2022, for example, Colorado required state schools to provide records of students' transcript requests. The difficulty lies in differences between state legislation and state and federal regulations. Currently, no single law or regulation bans transcript withholding across all colleges and universities.

A new DOE rule regulating transcript withholding will take effect in July 2024. As Katherine Knott reported for *Inside Higher Education*, the rule will "prevent a college or university from withholding a student's transcript for terms in which a student received federal financial aid and paid off the balance for the term." Knott reported that the new policy is part of a set of regulations intended to enhance the DOE's oversight of institutions by providing additional tools to hold all colleges accountable.

Knott's article quoted the Under Secretary of Education, James Kvaal, "This change will ensure that students receive credit for the education that they have completed and help them with transfer and finding a job."

The new rule also aims to protect students impacted by sudden college closures. "Too many students have been abandoned by shady colleges that close their doors and leave borrowers with unaffordable debt and little hope of completing their educational journeys and embarking on rewarding careers," Education Secretary Miguel Cardona said in a statement. From 2013 to 2022, the Department of Education sought more than $1.6 billion in liabilities from closed institutions but was only able to collect $344 million, according to a DOE news release cited by Knott.

As of May 2024, there has been only limited corporate news coverage of the new federal rules intended to regulate transcript withholding. In October 2023, the *Washington Post* published a substantive report, which emphasized the new rule's protections for students from sudden college closures but only briefly noted colleges' use of transcript withholding as a way to force students to repay debts.[68] In January 2023, *U.S. News & World Report* published an article on students with stranded credits that provided some background on state and federal bans against transcript withholding.[69] In September 2022, the *New York Times* published an article, produced in partnership with the *Hechinger Report*, on transcript withholding.[70] Notably, this article was written by Meredith Kolodner, a contributor to the *Hechinger Report*'s ongoing series, "Hidden Debt Trap," on student loan debt.[71]

Controversial Acquitted-Conduct Sentencing Challenged by US Commission

Stewart Bishop, "Sentencing Commission Limits Acquitted Conduct Sentencing," *Law360*, April 17, 2024.

C.J. Ciaramella, "U.S. Sentencing Commission Restricts Federal Judges' Ability to Use Acquitted Conduct at Sentencing," *Reason*, April 18, 2024.

Meg O'Connor, "New Hearing for Man Sentenced to Life in Prison despite Not Guilty Verdict," *The Appeal*, February 2, 2024.

Meg O'Connor, "A Jury Found Them Not Guilty Of Killing A Cop. A Judge Sentenced Them to Life Anyway," *The Appeal*, November 21, 2023.

Student Researcher: R'riana Crawford-King (City College of San Francisco)

Faculty Evaluator: Jennifer Levinson (City College of San Francisco)

Under a legal practice known as acquitted-conduct sentencing, judges presiding over federal cases can determine defendants' sentences based on charges that juries previously acquitted them of. However, in April 2024, the United States Sentencing Commission (USSC) voted to "exclude conduct for which a person was acquitted in federal court from being used in calculating a sentence range under the federal guidelines."[72] The Sentencing Commission's amendment will significantly limit federal judges' use of acquitted-conduct sentencing, as the legal news service *Law360* and *Reason* magazine reported. The practice, which has been condemned by "a wide range of civil liberties groups, lawmakers, and jurists," has "raised defendants' scores under the federal sentencing guidelines, leading to significantly longer prison sentences," C.J. Cia-ramella reported for *Reason*.

The Commission voted unanimously "to prohibit judges from using acquitted conduct to increase the sentences of defendants who receive mixed verdicts at trial," Stewart Bishop reported for *Law360*, but was "divided" on whether its proposal ought to apply retroactively.

"Not guilty means not guilty . . . By enshrining this basic fact within the federal sentencing guidelines, the Commission is taking an important step to protect the credibility of our courts and criminal justice system," chair of the USSC, US District Judge Carlton W. Reeves, said in a press release.[73] Congress established the Sentencing Commission in 1984 as a bipartisan, independent government agency whose mission is to "reduce sentencing disparities and promote transparency and proportionality in sentencing."[74]

"The acquitted conduct amendment comes with a rather large caveat," *Law360* acknowledged. It still allows federal judges to consider acquitted conduct that "establishes, in whole or in part, the instant offense of conviction," including either an admission of guilt by the defendant during a guilty plea or the finding by a judge or jury of guilt beyond a reasonable doubt.[75]

Acquitted-conduct sentencing, which the Supreme Court affirmed in a 1997 ruling, *United States v. Watts*, is premised on the idea that judges can use lower standards of proof—a preponderance of evidence—when sentencing than used by juries when deciding guilt, which requires proof beyond a reasonable doubt. In effect, even after jurors acquitted defendants of charges, judges could determine their sentences based on those same charges.

However, in June 2023, when the Supreme Court declined to rule on a case involving acquitted-conduct sentencing, *McClinton v. United States*, several Supreme Court Justices—including Sonia Sotomayor, Brett Kavanaugh, Neil Gorsuch, and Amy Coney Barrett—suggested that the USSC ought to resolve the question of how acquitted conduct is considered under federal sentencing guidelines. The USSC's April 2024 amendment will take effect in November 2024 unless Congress acts to disapprove the changes before then.

Acquitted-conduct sentencing partly explains why two Black men from Virginia, Terence Richardson and Ferrone Claiborne, have been serving life sentences for the murder of police officer Allen Gibson in 1998 despite being found not guilty by a federal jury in 2001. Meg O'Connor's reporting for *The Appeal* highlights the egregious injustices that result when federal judges enhance defendants' sentences based on acquitted conduct.

No physical evidence linked Richardson or Claiborne to the murder of the police officer. However, their attorney warned that, as poor Black men accused of murdering a White police officer, they risked the death penalty if found guilty. Horrified, Richardson pled guilty to involuntary manslaughter and was sentenced to five years in state prison. After the family of Gibson, the dead police officer, pushed for harsher sentences, resulting in further public outcry, federal prosecutors brought additional charges against Richardson and Claiborne, accusing them of selling crack cocaine and murdering Gibson in a drug deal gone wrong. In 2001, both men were found guilty of selling crack cocaine but not guilty of Gibson's murder. However, based on acquitted-conduct sentencing, District Judge Robert E. Payne sentenced both Richardson and Claiborne to life in prison.

After years of rejected appeals, in February 2024, the Virginia Supreme Court approved an evidentiary hearing for Richardson in May.[76] In that hearing, the judge permitted new evidence to be introduced, opening the possibility that Richardson might be released from prison.[77]

Corporate news outlets have barely covered acquitted-conduct sentencing and the US Sentencing Commission's amendment to restrict the practice. *Bloomberg Law* covered the proposed amendments.[78] But, as of June 2024, neither the *New York Times* nor the *Washington Post* appear to have covered this news from April 2024. Likewise, Richardson's and Claiborne's cases have received nearly no national coverage by corporate outlets, with one exception being a March 2023 BET report, which addressed coerced confessions but not acquitted-conduct sentencing.[79] The case has been covered by local news outlets, among which ABC 8 News, serving the Richmond, Virginia, region, deserves recognition for providing extensive reporting on the case since January 2017.[80] In addition to recent independent reporting by *The Appeal*, in May 2022, *The Atlantic* published a detailed profile of Richardson's attorney, Jarrett Adams, and how police hid exonerating evidence from Richardson's and Claiborne's original attorneys.[81]

Generative AI Apps Raise Serious Security Concerns

Priya Singh, "After ChatGPT, US Congress Bans Use of Microsoft's AI Tool Copilot for Staff Members," *Business Today*, April 1, 2024.

Paolo Passeri, "The Risk of Accidental Data Exposure by Generative AI Is Growing," *Infosecurity Magazine*, August 16, 2023.

Tiernan Ray, "ChatGPT Can Leak Training Data, Violate Privacy, Says Google's Deepmind," *ZDNet*, December 4, 2023.

Eileen Yu, "Employees Input Sensitive Data into Generative AI Tools despite the Risks," *ZDNet*, February 22, 2024.

Student Researcher: Makenzie Haughey (Saint Michael's College)

Faculty Evaluator: Rob Williams (Saint Michael's College)

Generative artificial intelligence (AI) apps, such as OpenAI's ChatGPT and Microsoft's Copilot, can be used to accomplish a range of tasks, from coding programs and analyzing massive collections of data to generating completely unique texts, images, and videos. Use of such apps is increasingly popular with businesses, government agencies, and other organizations. Yet, reliance on AI apps entails serious risks of exposing sensitive data and potentially exposing organizations to opportunistic attacks from bad actors, Paolo Passeri reported for *Infosecurity Magazine* in August 2023. According to an April 2024 *Business Today* article by Priya Singh, this is the main reason why the US Congress and tech firms such as Apple and Samsung have "restricted their employees from using generative AI tools like ChatGPT."

The number of people accessing AI apps at work is

exploding and, according to Passeri, increased by 22.5 percent in May and June 2023 alone. In an article for the business tech news website *ZDNet*, Eileen Yu cited a survey by Veritas Technologies of some 11,500 employees worldwide, including respondents from the United States, China, France, Germany, and the United Kingdom, that found "57 percent of employees used public generative AI tools in the office at least once weekly, with 22.3 percent using the technology daily."

Despite these apps' growing popularity, "the risk of accidentally sharing sensitive information or intellectual property" when using them "is a significant issue," Passeri reported. The Veritas Technologies survey discussed by Yu revealed that 31 percent of employees polled admitted entering sensitive information such as addresses and banking details for customers, confidential HR data, and proprietary company information into publicly accessible AI programs (and another 5 percent were unsure if they had done so).

Not only do users sometimes inadvertently share sensitive data with AI apps, but the apps themselves have been known to accidentally expose their users' personal data due to security design flaws. As an example, Passeri mentioned a March 2023 ChatGPT data breach that caused the app to be temporarily taken offline, which ChatGPT's parent company, OpenAI, attributed to a bug in an open-source library. Passeri wrote that the breach "exposed some customers' payment-related information and allowed titles from some active users' chat history to be viewed."

Tiernan Ray noted in a December 2023 article for *ZDNet* that ChatGPT "could also be manipulated to reproduce individuals' names, phone numbers, and addresses, which is a violation of privacy with potentially serious consequences." Ray's article described how researchers from Google DeepMind, an AI research lab, have discovered a simple "way to break the alignment of OpenAI's ChatGPT." "Alignment" is the term AI researchers use for safeguards established in AI programs to keep them from "emitting objectionable output."

By asking the program to repeat a word, such as "poem," over and over, the researchers could force ChatGPT to produce "whole passages of literature that contained its training data, even though that kind of leakage is not supposed to happen with aligned programs." The researchers, Ray reported, "call this phenomenon 'extractable memorization', which is an attack that forces a program to divulge the things it has stored in memory."

As Anuj Mudaliar of Spiceworks, a professional network for the information technology industry, wrote in February 2024, "Leading artificial intelligence companies such as OpenAI, Google, and Anthropic must focus on vigilant security postures and specific measures to prevent such risks."[82]

Alarm about the risks associated with AI tools such as ChatGPT has led a growing number of organizations to place stringent restrictions on their workplace use. In *Business Today*, Singh explained that the new policy adopted by the US Congress only permits lawmakers and staff to access ChatGPT Plus, a paid version of the app with enhanced privacy features, and forbids them from using other AI apps or pasting blocks of text that have not already been made public into the program. In May 2024, the National Archives and Records Administration completely prohibited employees from using ChatGPT at work and blocked all access to the app on agency computers, "citing 'unacceptable risk' to the agency's data."[83]

Corporate media have given a lot of breathless coverage to the existential threat to humanity allegedly posed by AI. In the past two years, the *New York Times, Wall Street Journal, Washington Post,* and *Time* have each published multiple articles, news analyses, and op-eds mulling over apocalyptic scenarios in which AI takes over nuclear weapons, stock markets, elections, or the power grid and brings about the collapse of the economy, the end of democracy, or even the extinction of the human species.[84] Yet these outlets have been far less attentive to AI apps' documented data security risks and vulnerability to hackers, issues that have been given exhaustive coverage by smaller, tech-focused news outlets. Etay Maor, in an April 2024 opinion piece for *Forbes,* claimed that "much of the perceived risk associated with GenAI is excessive fear-mongering" and that better security controls over AI app users could address concerns that have led organizations to ban their use.[85] Otherwise, the corporate news media have mentioned these issues only in passing, if at all.

One-Third of Children Globally Face Water Scarcity Due to Climate Change

"'Staggering' 347 Million Children Facing Water Scarcity in South Asia: UN," Al Jazeera, November 13, 2023.

Student Researcher: Ian Wroblewski (Frostburg State University)

Faculty Evaluator: Andy Duncan (Frostburg State University)

Nearly one-third of all children on the planet face water scarcity, including a "staggering" 347 million in South Asia alone, according to reports from Al Jazeera and several additional international news sites in November 2023. This news was based on a report from the United Nations Children's Fund (UNICEF), "The Climate-Changed Child," which detailed "the myriad ways in which children bear the brunt of the impacts of the climate crisis."[86] UNICEF's November 2023 report, which supplemented its groundbreaking 2021 Children's Climate Risk Index, spotlighted water issues specifically.[87]

According to UNICEF's analysis, almost one billion children worldwide are exposed to high or extremely high water stress (where demand outstrips surface water supply); 739 million children are exposed to high or extremely high water scarcity; 436 million children live in areas with high or extremely high water vulnerability; and 470 million face high or extremely high drought risk.

"Every region of the world, including high-income

countries, faces challenges related to water," according to UNICEF, but "the largest number of youngsters are exposed in the Middle East and North Africa and South Asia regions—meaning they live in places with limited water resources and high levels of seasonal and interannual variability, ground water decline or drought risk."[88] Al Jazeera reported that "more children in South Asia are struggling due to severe water scarcity made worse by the effects of climate change than anywhere else worldwide." That hardest-hit region includes eight nations—Afghanistan, Bangladesh, Bhutan, India, Nepal, Maldives, Pakistan, and Sri Lanka— and is home to a quarter of the world's children.

"Safe water is a basic human right," said Sanjay Wijese-kera, UNICEF South Asia chief, quoted in Al Jazeera, "yet millions of children in South Asia don't have enough to drink in a region plagued by floods, droughts and other extreme weather events, triggered increasingly by climate change." The lack of water threatens drinking, cooking, and cleaning, as well as agriculture and economic growth.

UNICEF's report was released just ahead of the 2023 United Nations Climate Change Conference, where the agency called for change on multiple fronts, including youth empowerment and education and across-the-board emissions reductions.[89] UNICEF's Executive Director, Catherine Russell, stated in the report, "The global failure to confront the climate crisis—the greatest threat of this generation—has created a child rights crisis. It is jeopardizing every child's fundamental right to health and well-being."

In addition to Al Jazeera, several international publications, including the *Vatican News*, *The News International*, *The New Arab*, and the *Morung Express*, covered the UNICEF report—but as of May 2024, no corporate media outlet in the United States bothered to break this astonishing news.[90]

Indigenous Activists in Panama Shut Down Notorious Copper Mine

Christopher Pollon, "What Happens When a Country Says 'No' to Mining?" *National Observer*, January 8, 2024.

Maxwell Radwin, "Panama Copper Mine to Close after Supreme Court Rules Concession Unconstitutional," *Mongabay*, November 28, 2023

Michael Fox, "Panama Celebrates Court Order to Cancel Mine Even as Business Is Hit," Al Jazeera, November 30, 2023.

Owen Schalk, "Ottawa Silent As Panama Rises up against Canadian Copper Mine," *Canadian Dimension*, November 5, 2023.

Student Researcher: Isabel Cramer (Frostburg State University)

Faculty Evaluator: Andy Duncan (Frostburg State University)

In November 2023, following years of protest by Indigenous activists, Panama's Supreme Court struck down Canadian company First Quantum Minerals's twenty-year concession to operate a controversial thirteen-thousand-hectare open-pit copper mine, Cobre Panamá, 120 kilometers west of Panama City. After the ruling, Panamanian President Laurentino Cortizo announced the mine would be closed.

As Maxwell Radwin reported for environmental news

site *Mongabay*, in 2022, the Cobre Panamá mine produced 1 percent of the world's total copper production, generated 5 percent of Panama's GDP, and employed 2 percent of the country's workforce. The mine is infamous for threatening forest ecosystems and ruining local drinking water.

Like other metals behemoths, First Quantum profits from colonialist mining in some of the world's poorest nations. In 2022 alone, it generated nearly $10 billion in revenue.

The mine's devastating environmental impact has been the focus of ongoing protests since 2011, when the Panamanian government sought to limit the Indigenous Ngäbe-Buglé people's right to self-government so that foreign companies could mine on their land. In response, *Canadian Dimension* reported, "Panamanians rose up, demanding the annulment of mining and hydroelectric concessions on Indigenous territory." Protesters blocked the mine entrance in an action that turned violent amid a heavy-handed government crackdown. The Panamanian government eventually caved, promising that mining would not take place on Ngäbe-Buglé lands after all.

Nevertheless, in October 2023, Panama's parliament renewed First Quantum's concession to operate Cobre Panamá. The mass demonstrations that followed, which Al Jazeera called Panama's "largest protest movement in decades," left the nation "in a state of siege," emptying hotel rooms, grocery shelves, and gas pumps. According to *Canadian Dimensions,* demonstrators demanded "a greater share of profits from foreign mining activity, the protection of Indigenous rights, and stronger environmental regulations." Protests blocked access roads and shipping routes used by the mining company. Several hundred people were arrested, and two people died during the protests.

In a bid to placate protestors, Panama's National Assembly on November 3, 2023, passed an indefinite moratorium on new mining concessions but preserved First Quantum's existing contract.[91] Then, on November 28, the nation's nine-member Supreme Court declared the concession unconstitutional.[92]

In January 2024, First Quantum announced that it planned to take Panama to Investor-State Dispute Settlement (ISDS) arbitration—a process for settling disputes between corporations and sovereign nations—for violating a free trade agreement with Canada. As Christopher Pollon explained in an article for *The National Observer*, ISDS arbitration has increasingly been used by "extractive companies in oil and gas and mining" to combat environmental regulations in Latin America and Africa and often results in awards of billions of dollars for foreign investors.[93]

In May 2024, Panama held a presidential election in which the fate of First Quantum's giant copper mine was a top issue.[94] The winner, José Raúl Mulino, said he would speak with the company about a temporary reopening of the mine only if all arbitration proceedings are suspended.[95]

Environmental news sites, such as *Mongabay*, and Canadian-owned media outlets Reuters and the *Financial Post* gave the protest movement, the mine's shutdown, and First Quantum's ensuing demand for ISDS arbitration copious coverage.[96] However, the years of Indigenous rights struggles and the massive outcry against the mine made scarcely a blip in the US corporate media. *The*

Washington Post ran a single story on the historic wave of protests.[97] And the *New York Times* made passing mention of the mine's closure in its coverage of the recent Panamanian elections.[98]

Homeland Security, ICE Using Cell-Site Simulators for Illegal Tracking

Matthew Guariglia, "Report: ICE and the Secret Service Conducted Illegal Surveillance of Cell Phones," *Deeplinks Blog* (Electronic Frontier Foundation), March 2, 2023.

Student Researcher: Blake Licata (Saint Michael's College)

Faculty Evaluator: Rob Williams (Saint Michael's College)

The Secret Service, Homeland Security Investigations (HSI), and Immigration and Customs Enforcement (ICE) are illegally tracking Americans using cell-site simulators, Matthew Guariglia reported for the Electronic Frontier Foundation in March 2023. The devices, often referred to as "stingrays," mimic cell phone towers, tricking cell phones in the vicinity to connect to the device rather than a tower and then collecting data from those phones.

As Dell Cameron detailed in a June 2023 article for *Wired*, stingrays can single out individual phones in geographically specific locations, and some current versions allow "operators to eavesdrop on calls, or ... force devices to execute unauthenticated commands that disable encryption or downgrade the connection to a lower and less secure network."[99]

Guariglia's EFF article drew on the findings of a redacted report, titled "Secret Service and ICE Did Not Always Adhere to Statute and Policies Governing Use of Cell-Site Simulators," produced by Homeland Security's Office of Inspector General (OIG) in February 2023.[100] According to the report, HSI and ICE used overly broad warrants to collect financial information on those believed to be sending money across international borders.

The OIG report explained that, in cases of "exigent" circumstances, agencies are not legally required to obtain a search warrant before deploying a cell-site simulator. However, even in such cases, a court order is required under the Pen Register Statute for investigations using the technology. Only in genuine emergencies, or "exceptional" circumstances, may stingrays be used without at least a court order. In a review of cases from 2021 and 2022, Homeland Security's inspector general found that "in exigent circumstances, the Secret Service and ICE HSI did not always obtain pen register court orders pursuant to the Pen Register Statute."[101]

Moreover, the report found instances in which ICE or HSI did not document supervisory approval for the use of cell-site simulators and in which data was not deleted at the conclusion of a mission, as required by cell-site simulator policy.[102]

"The fact that government agencies are using these devices without the utmost consideration for the privacy and rights of individuals around them is alarming but not surprising," Guariglia wrote, noting that government agencies such as HSI and ICE have "a dubious and troubling relationship with overbroad collection of private data on individuals."[103]

To date, no major US daily newspapers, news sites, or TV news programs have covered the OIG's February 2023 report on federal agencies' failures to follow policies governing the use of cell-site simulators. Tech news sites and sites devoted to cybersecurity issues, such as *The Register* and *Commsrisk*, covered the OIG's finding that the Secret Service and ICE have repeatedly broken the law with their improper cell phone surveillance.[104]

Companies' Net-Zero Promises Have Near Zero Credibility

Taylor Connelly, "Why Are Companies Reneging on Emissions Reductions?" *E–The Environmental Magazine,* February 22, 2024.

Joseph Winters, "Net-Zero Targets Are More Popular than Ever, but Less than 5% Are Credible," *Grist,* June 12, 2023.

Joseph Winters, "Inside Climate Activists' Uneasy Relationship with 'Net-Zero'," *Grist,* April 11, 2023.

Student Researcher: Sophia DiSpirito (Frostburg State University)

Faculty Evaluator: Andy Duncan (Frostburg State University)

Despite heralding their intent to implement "net-zero" policies to limit carbon emissions, most of the world's biggest companies are spectacularly failing to live up to those commitments. "Hundreds of companies across the world are backtracking on commitments toward green policies, despite growing concerns that the planet is reaching a crisis point," reported Taylor Connelly in *E–The Environmental Magazine* on February 22, 2024.

Connelly's article highlighted the work of Net Zero Tracker, which was also featured prominently in a pair of 2023 articles by Joseph Winters in *Grist*. Run by a consortium of four environmental watchdog groups, Net Zero Tracker is a comprehensive open-source database that provides an independent review of the quality and quantity of net zero targets across countries, regions, cities, and companies.[105]

In November 2023, Net Zero Tracker marked a major milestone, analyzing the thousandth company in its mission to document the veracity of net zero pledges made by the world's top two thousand publicly traded companies.[106] While more companies than ever are making such commitments, few have plans in place that will come anywhere close to fulfilling those pledges. As reported in *E–The Environmental Magazine*:

> Less than 4 percent of the 1,000 companies were doing the bare minimum to be considered in line with the goals of the 2015 Paris [A]greement. The rest of the companies were not even meeting the so-called "starting line criteria" laid out by the United Nations. The "starting line" calls for companies to track their carbon footprint across

supply chains, cut emissions, create a plan for using carbon offsets, and have annual reports on meeting climate targets.

What's more, some companies have actively "stepped back from efforts to limit climate-damaging emissions," wrote Connelly, citing recent moves by several investment firms, including JPMorgan Chase, State Street, and BlackRock, to curtail their involvement in climate agreements, following similar moves by Amazon, BP, Shell, and major insurance firms like AIG.

Corporate media, including the *Los Angeles Times* and Reuters, noted when major companies walked back their climate commitments due to political or investor pressure, often treating it primarily as a business story.[107] A few outlets explained that holding large corporations accountable for their net-zero promises is exceedingly difficult because of supply chain complexity and a lack of regulatory oversight.[108] Among the establishment press, the *Washington Post* stands out for its detailed coverage revealing "the shortcomings of voluntary corporate action."[109]

Bottled Water Consumption Exacerbates Socioeconomic Inequalities

Daniel Jaffee, "The Real Cost of Bottled Water," *CounterPunch*, November 30, 2023.

Student Researcher: Olivia Rosenberg (North Central College)

Faculty Evaluator: Steve Macek (North Central College)

Bottled water is the top-selling beverage in the United States, and annual global sales are in the hundreds of billions of dollars.[110] Much of that market consists of people from low-income communities. "This commodity is vastly more expensive than the tap water it often replaces for consumers," reported Portland State University sociologist Daniel Jaffee in a November 2023 report for *CounterPunch*. Citing a 2019 *Consumer Reports* analysis, Jaffee concluded, "Poorest families spend the most."[111]

"It has long been argued that bottled water is a discretionary good, consumed most by higher-income households," but Jaffee cited research that "tap water consumption was higher at higher incomes, whereas the consumption of bottled water was higher at lower incomes."

Furthermore, "Bottled water use and its impact on household income map onto—and exacerbate—existing social inequalities along lines of race, ethnicity, and class," Jaffee wrote. Most of the water consumed by Black and Hispanic households, immigrants, and those with less than a high school education is bottled. *Consumer Reports* found that Black households spent an average of $19 a month on bottled water, Hispanic households spent $18, and White households spent $9.[112]

Jaffee cited research by Asher Rosinger, Director of the Water, Health and Nutrition Lab at Pennsylvania State University, which determined (in Jaffee's words) that "higher-income adults drink bottled water for convenience, whereas lower-income adults may drink bottled water because of tap water access issues" due to a deteriorating water infrastructure that disproportionately affects marginalized communities. For this reason, Jaffee noted, bottled water companies have been known to target their advertising in Black and Hispanic communities.

Jaffee summarized that the groups who "can least afford to pay for a constant supply of bottled water are precisely those who tend to trust their tap water the least, who are targeted by the industry's advertising, and who spend the highest percentage of household income to buy packaged water."

Moreover, "Bottled water might actually slow the progress of providing universal access to safe drinking water" across the globe, Carla Delgado reported in *Popular Science* in March 2023.[113] Delgado's report quoted Sara Hughes, a water policy expert at the University of Michigan, who explained, "In many places, bottled water is an important source of safe drinking water absent adequate public water supply systems … but the bottled water industry actively encourages distrust of tap water, which does erode public support and investment in public drinking water systems even where the water is available and safe to drink."[114]

Corporate news media do cover the nation's crumbling water infrastructure—particularly when there are local crises, such as in Flint, Michigan—which likely leads to even greater demand for bottled water.[115] But the disproportionate economic impact of reliance on bottled water by marginalized communities has been given scant attention by the establishment press.

Activists Rally outside Insurance Giants, Denouncing Fossil Fuel Investments

Keerti Gopal, "'Insure Our Future:' A Global Movement Says the Insurance Industry Could Be the Key to Ending Fossil Fuels," *Inside Climate News*, March 8, 2024.

Olivia Rosane, "Activists to Insurance Giants: 'End Your Support for Oil and Gas Now'," *Common Dreams*, February 28, 2024.

Student Researcher: Christopher Walker (Diablo Valley College)

Faculty Evaluator: Nolan Higdon and Mickey Huff (Diablo Valley College)

Environmental activists rallied globally from February 26 to March 3, 2024, to protest insurance companies' support of the fossil fuel industry, according to reports by *Common Dreams* and *Inside Climate News*. The movement was organized by Insure Our Future, a coalition whose mission is to promote a healthy transition to clean energy and hold insurance companies that still support fossil fuel projects accountable.

One of the biggest protests took place in New York City at the headquarters of three key companies: Chubb, Tokio Marine, and AIG. According to *Common Dreams*,

"The protest came days after a report from Insure Our Future, Rainforest Action Network, and Public Citizen revealed that at least 35 insurers are underwriting controversial liquefied natural gas (LNG) export infrastructure along the U.S. Gulf Coast." Activists noted that LNG sites have negatively impacted the health of their communities and also pose threats to tribal lands.

The Colorado Times Recorder reported on protests coordinated by Insure Our Future in cities in Colorado, while *Connecticut Public Radio* and *Between the Lines* reported on protests targeting Travelers and The Hartford insurance companies because of their rankings on the Insure Our Future scorecard.[116]

Both Insure Our Future and the Center for International Environmental Law (CIEL) were interviewed for a *KPFA* segment discussing California's climate and insurance crisis.[117] According to a Consumer Watchdog report, "Insure Our Future reported that 12 California insurance companies that have announced coverage restrictions in the state made an estimated $3.6 billion by insuring fossil fuel infrastructure."[118]

As of June 2024, coverage of this issue was limited to a *Wall Street Journal* article discussing how insurance companies were facing pressure from regulators, legislators, and activists.[119] Although the climate change crisis has dominated media circuits and made headlines, corporate media have failed to cover organized efforts to hold the insurance industry accountable for its role or to address the long-term effects of fossil fuel insurance policies on the public. *Inside Climate News*'s article briefly mentions the Biden administration pausing liquefied natural gas export terminals, which did get some coverage from the

Washington Post last year, when environmentalists called on the administration to block exports, noting that the project could be "a 'megabomb' for the climate."[120]

Palestinians in Gaza Suffering from Chronic Illnesses Cannot Access Medical Care

Firas Ramlawi, "Fatima's Story, an Update from Gaza," American Friends Service Committee, December 20, 2023.

Weronika Strzyżyńska and Kaamil Ahmed, "Patients with Chronic Illnesses in Gaza Failing to Get Treatment, Doctors Warn," *The Guardian,* February 17, 2024.

Student Researcher: Kay Woon Lau (City College of San Francisco)

Faculty Evaluator: Jen Levinson (City College of San Francisco)

Palestinians in Gaza suffering from chronic illness are unable to get necessary medical care due to Israel's ongoing bombardment of the occupied territory. While the war has been a focal point of global news coverage since October 7, few reports have addressed the lack of medicine and treatment for chronically ill patients, whom a February 2024 report by the *Guardian* characterized as "the hidden casualties of war." The conflict is jeopardizing "the health of thousands of people with chronic illnesses such as kidney disease, diabetes and asthma," Weronika Strzyżyńska and Kaamil Ahmed reported for the *Guardian.*

Noting that only fourteen of thirty-six hospitals in Gaza were able to provide any medical services, the *Guardian's* report quoted Guillemette Thomas of Doctors Without Borders, who explained that the remaining hospitals were "overwhelmed with injured people" and "not able to deal with chronic illness at all."

"We don't know how many people are dying because they can't access healthcare," Thomas stated.

One of the few organizations to provide detailed reporting on the issue has been the American Friends Service Committee (AFSC). In December 2023, Firas Ramlawi, an AFSC staffer providing humanitarian aid in Gaza, reported the story of Fatima Shahin, a Palestinian woman in her sixties who suffers from kidney failure. Before the war, Shahin underwent dialysis treatment three days a week at Al-Shifa Hospital. When Israeli forces began bombing her residential area, she initially took refuge in a nearby UNRWA school but eventually chose to leave the school after learning that Israeli forces were also targeting shelters. She was evacuated to Al-Shifa Hospital, "hoping to feel safe and, at the same time, undergoing dialysis to stay alive," Ramlawi reported.

Shahin was trapped in Al-Shifa for fourteen days while Israeli forces bombed the hospital. She survived and was eventually able to evacuate with her family to Abu Yousef Al-Najjar Hospital in Rafah. After two days, Ramlawi reported, "The hospital apologized to all kidney patients and asked them to leave because they were trying to cover only injury cases."

As Strzyżyńska and Ahmed reported for the *Guardian*, aid trucks have brought medicine, including insulin, to Gaza; however, distribution is a problem. Thomas, the

Palestine coordinator for Doctors Without Borders, explained, "We have some insulin coming in aid trucks, but patients can't get to the places where it is stocked because of the airstrikes. People are bombed on their way to the hospital." Interim UN humanitarian coordinator Jamie McGoldrick said in a briefing that insulin pens for diabetic children "seem to be prohibited by the Israelis," an accusation that Israel has denied. People with diabetes in Gaza have also struggled to monitor their blood sugar levels and obtain meals that correspond with their medical needs. One woman with asthma told the *Guardian* that, without her medication or even cough syrup, she has resorted to taking morphine to relieve her chest pain.

The lack of medicine is aggravated by a lack of adequate food and clean water. The UN estimated that 70 percent of Palestinians have been forced to drink contaminated water, 50 percent are experiencing food insecurity, and 25 percent of the population is starving.[121] Livestock in Gaza are also starving due to a lack of food, compounding food insecurity.

This issue is not new, according to Abdelkader Hammad, a surgeon at the Royal Liverpool University Hospital. In an interview with the *Guardian*, he explained that around half of kidney dialysis patients in Gaza died during the 2008 Gaza war: "That was why we decided to move on to kidney transplants. We thought that a person with a transplant was more likely to survive a war than someone on dialysis."

Corporate news coverage of medical needs in Gaza has focused on Palestinians suffering from injuries due to Israeli bombings and artillery fire.[122] Although such coverage is essential, it fails to address how overcrowding of besieged hospitals has affected patients suffering from kidney disease, cancer, or other chronic diseases.

Constitutional Loophole Propels Xenophobic Border Policies in Texas

Erum Salam, "Texas's Use of 'Invasion' Clause against Immigrants Is Racist and Dangerous, Rights Groups Say," *The Guardian*, May 29, 2023.

"Texas Rep. Greg Casar Condemns Gov. Greg Abbott's 'Dangerous Stunts' at the Border," *Democracy Now!*, August 30, 2023.

Kate Huddleston, "White Supremacist Conspiracy Theory is Fueling Extreme Border Policy in Texas," *Just Security*, October 24, 2023.

John Knefel, "How the Border-Cop-to-Pundit Pipeline Fuels Anti-immigrant Coverage," Media Matters for America, October 24, 2023.

"US: Texas Border Policies Threaten Deadly Outcomes," Human Rights Watch, February 1, 2024.

Student Researcher: Olivia Jang (Loyola Marymount University)

Faculty Evaluator: Kyra Pearson (Loyola Marymount University)

The federal government has controlled US immigration policy since the 1800s. However, in 2023, Texas Republicans, led by far-right Governor Greg Abbott, proposed legislation—SB 4—that invokes the Invasion Clauses of the United States and Texas constitutions to challenge the federal government's sovereignty over the Texas-Mexico border. The clause authorizes the Texas governor to deploy a "militia to execute the laws of the State, to suppress insurrections, and to repel invasions," according to Erum Salam of *The Guardian*. This legislation describes migration as an "invasion," appealing to White supremacist fears rather than facts.

Standard immigration procedure requires states to release undocumented migrants into federal custody. The new legislation allows Texas to arrest, jail, and deport migrants who are in the country illegally and, according to Kate Huddleston of *Just Security*, provides "no due process before such summary expulsion." This legislation unconstitutionally places Texas state law above US federal law.

Governor Abbott first implemented the border programs in November 2022, with Operation Lone Star being its showpiece. According to Human Rights Watch, despite no evidence that Operation Lone Star has reduced migration, "The program has led to injuries and deaths, consistently violated the rights of migrants and US citizens, and suppressed freedoms of association and expression of groups providing basic aid in Texas."

Furthermore, dangerous vehicle chases by Texas troopers or local law enforcement in Operation Lone Star counties have led to crashes that killed at least 74 people and injured another 189 between March 2021 and July 2023, "a rate of nearly 3 deaths and 7 injuries per month" since Operation Lone Star had been in existence, according to a separate Human Rights Watch report published in November 2023.[123]

Migrant rights groups have opposed Texas border policies, noting that Abbott's comparison of migrants to a foreign public enemy only fans conservative fears with racist language. Roberto Lopez, senior advocacy manager for the Texas Civil Rights Project's "Beyond the Border" program, told the *Guardian*, "Calling immigrants an invasion is extremely dangerous." Noting "many shootings" and a "rise in hate crimes" against migrants, Lopez explained, "This is all connected to this rhetoric of associating people who are trying to seek safety with being like a literal attack on the United States."

On March 20, 2024, the US Supreme Court authorized Texas to continue enforcing SB 4, but hours later, a 5th Circuit Court of Appeals found the law unconstitutional.[124] As of June 2024, the Texas law continues to be litigated.

According to John Knefel of Media Matters for America, conservative outlets such as Fox News and NewsMax have skewed coverage of the issue by employing former Border Patrol and ICE officers to report on immigration, often presenting them as "experts" based on their law enforcement experience. "Their claimed expertise, supposedly gleaned from firsthand experience, allows them to mask xenophobia as hard-won knowledge about public safety," Knefel wrote. On air, these pundits frequently call for US military intervention in Mexican territory, an idea that has become a mainstream conservative position.[125]

Rightwing media have also fixated on false claims of migrants being fentanyl mules. However, an August 2023 NPR analysis of US Customs and Border Protection data found that 90 percent of fentanyl crossing the US-Mexico border between October 2022 and June 2023 was seized at legal points of entry. "Nearly all of that is smuggled by people who are legally authorized to cross the border, and more than half by U.S. citizens," NPR reported, adding that "virtually none is seized from migrants seeking asylum."[126]

The Texas border policies have received partial corporate media coverage. These reports typically fail to address either the policies' violent consequences or their invocation of the Invasion Clause. Corporate coverage treated the issue as a political battle rather than a humanitarian issue with lives on the line. For example, an October 2023 CNN report focused on the legal battles between the Texas state government and the Biden administration but did not describe the ramifications of the disputed policies for asylum seekers.[127]

Unregulated PFAS Harming Native American Communities

Frances Madeson, "PFAS Contamination and the Scourge of Cancer in Odawa Nation," The Real News Network, May 9, 2023.

Zoya Teirstein, "What One School's Fight to Eliminate PFAS Says about Indian Country's 'Forever Chemical' Problem," *Grist*, August 14, 2023.

Student Researcher: Riley Cummins (Diablo Valley College)

Faculty Evaluator: Mickey Huff (Diablo Valley College)

Native Americans have been disproportionately affected by the presence of PFAS—often referred to as "forever chemicals"—in their water sources, according to 2023 reports by The Real News Network and *Grist*. PFAS chemicals are widely used in consumer and industrial products, ranging from food wrappers to firefighting foam, because of their water- and oil-resistant properties. Exposure to them has been linked to increased cancer risk, among other illnesses.

The Real News Network reported high rates of cancer among members of the Odawa Nation, in line with scientific findings on PFAS exposure, the effects of which are "devastating Indigenous and rural communities." Local news media such as *The Maine Monitor*, *Minnesota Reformer*, *Wisconsin Watch*, and WRAL News have highlighted this issue in their areas.[128]

In December 2022, *E&E News* reported on a study that found "water systems used by Indigenous communities do not get the same level of EPA testing for 'forever chemicals' as the general public," despite evidence that tribal public water systems have higher rates of contaminants.[129] Military bases, airports, industrial plants, and landfills are significant contributors to PFAS pollution and are commonly located in non-White and low-income areas, as reported by *The Verge* and *NC Newsline*.[130]

The PFAS problem extends beyond drinking water. A December 2023 article for *Scientific American* cited an Environmental Working Group study that found "eating a single serving of freshwater fish can be the equivalent of drinking water contaminated with high levels of PFAS for a month."[131] This particularly impacts Indigenous groups who rely on subsistence fishing.

The Fond Du Lac Band of Lake Superior Chippewa filed a lawsuit against 3M and twenty-three other companies for contaminating their water and fish with PFAS, according to a July 2023 report by Minnesota Public Radio.[132] The Red Cliff Band of Lake Superior Chippewa and the Kalispel Tribe in Washington filed similar suits in 2022 and 2020, respectively. A $10.3 billion proposed settlement by 3M "would resolve current and future drinking water claims" but would not include tribal water systems.

On June 28, 2023, the EPA announced $278 million of funding for water infrastructure in Indigenous communities, including PFAS management, according to the *Engineering News-Record*.[133] A May 2024 article for *Wisconsin Watch* mentioned an EPA proposal to incorporate treaty rights, such as fishing and wild rice gathering, within the Clean Water Act's standards.

The negative health consequences from PFAS pollution have received some corporate news coverage, but the disproportionate impact on Native American communities has gone under-reported. Local news outlets and publications focused specifically on environmental and Indigenous issues have provided the most coverage. As of May 2024, larger corporate news coverage has been limited to a 2022 *Washington Post Magazine* article.[134]

Kids Online Safety Act (KOSA) Poses Serious First Amendment Concerns

Jason Kelley, Aaron Mackey, and Joe Mullin, "Don't Fall for the Latest Changes to the Dangerous Kids Online Safety Act," *Deeplinks Blog* (Electronic Frontier Foundation), February 15, 2024.

Molly Buckley, "The U.S. House Version of KOSA: Still a Censorship Bill," *Deeplinks Blog* (Electronic Frontier Foundation), May 3, 2024.

Student Researcher: Vincenzo Champion (City College of San Francisco)

Faculty Evaluator: Jennifer Levinson (City College of San Francisco)

Growing concerns about social media use allegedly causing mental health problems in young people have spurred a bipartisan push in Congress for the Kids Online Safety Act (KOSA), an ill-considered piece of internet censorship legislation.

First introduced in the US Senate in 2022, KOSA (S. 1409) has gone through multiple revisions and gained the support of more than sixty-two senators despite criticism from digital rights advocates, child safety organizations, and civil rights groups.[135] The most recent version of the bill would impose a "duty of care" on platforms requiring them to mitigate possible harms to minors, such as cyberbullying, eating disorders, substance abuse, and sexual exploitation.[136] It mandates that underage social media users be permitted to opt out of algorithmic recommendations and turn off potentially addictive features of platforms while also providing parents with tools to protect their children. The latest version of KOSA assigns responsibility for enforcing the bill's "duty of care" provision to the Federal Trade Commission.

A companion House bill introduced in May, H.R. 7891, parallels the Senate bill in most respects but would impose the strictest "duty of care" obligations only on "high impact" social media, messaging, and video game platforms with more than $2.5 billion in annual revenue or more than 150 million monthly users.[137]

In a February 15, 2024, article for the Electronic Frontier Foundation (EFF), Jason Kelley, Aaron Mackey, and Joe Mullin argued that updates to S. 1409 weren't enough to fix its core First Amendment issues. The authors claimed the bill would endanger LGTBQ youth, young people seeking mental health information, and many other at-risk communities. When KOSA was first introduced, it was opposed by advocacy groups such as GLAAD and the Human Rights Campaign for similar reasons. EFF contends that "KOSA remains a dangerous bill that would allow the government to decide what types of information can be shared and read online by everyone."

Kelley, Mackey, and Mullin noted that because there is no case law defining "reasonable care," KOSA would put platforms in a compromising position for hosting otherwise legal content on their websites, such as information about support groups for vulnerable and marginalized youth and suicide prevention resources. Moreover, they argued that KOSA mandates that platforms "restrict access to content based on age," forcing them to adopt some sort of age verification system.

In her analysis of H.R. 7891 for EFF, Molly Buckley noted that, though the House bill would limit liability for the least popular platforms, it "still incentivizes large and mid-size platforms ... to implement age verification systems that will threaten the right to anonymity and create serious privacy and security risks for all users."

Corporate outlets, such as the *Washington Post* and *New York Times*, have covered successive iterations of KOSA but have not examined thoroughly the implications of provisions such as its "duty of care," which EFF has called a "duty of censorship."[138] Independent, technology-oriented news sites, such as *Techdirt*, have investigated those implications in greater detail and centered young people's voices in their coverage.[139]

California's Groundbreaking Investment in Education for Incarcerated Youth

Jeremy Loudenback and Sara Tiano, "California Invests in Education for Incarcerated Youth," *The Imprint*, July 7, 2023.

Betty Márquez Rosales, "California's Most Vulnerable Students May Be Seeing Increased Funding Soon," *EdSource*, June 27, 2023.

Student Researchers: Raeghan Brousseau, Amara Padula, Tara Shea, and Natasha Tykulsky (University of Massachusetts Amherst)

Faculty Evaluators: Allison Butler and Jeewon Chon (University of Massachusetts Amherst)

Genuine education reform is based on the premise that every young person deserves access to high-quality education. Although federal law guarantees the right to education to all, incarcerated youth are often disregarded.[140] However, efforts to build robust education programs for young people in California juvenile detention facilities have received a boost, according to 2023 reports by *The Imprint* and *EdSource*.

An education budget trailer to the California state budget for 2023–24 included funding for higher education programs for incarcerated youth and greater oversight of educational institutions in juvenile detention facilities, Jeremy Loudenback and Sara Tiano reported for *The Imprint* in July 2023. Katie Bliss, the California higher education coordinator at the Youth Law Center, described the state's investment of $80 million for education programs serving incarcerated youth as "nationally historic."

The state committed funding to support education for incarcerated youth amidst uncertainty about the direction of its troubled juvenile justice system. In June 2023, California closed the last of its eleven Division of Juvenile Justice facilities, which will be replaced by what the *Los Angeles Times* described as "an array of programs devised by probation departments in California's 58 counties."[141] As Betty Márquez Rosales reported for *EdSource*, the 2023–24 budget consequently allocated funds to county offices of education to support juvenile court schools and alternative education schools.

The budget includes a number of accountability measures for court and community schools, including assurances from community colleges, California State University, and the University of California, that juveniles with high school diplomas or a California high school equivalency have access to public postsecondary academic and career technical education courses, independent evaluation of county court and community schools, and annual reporting of data regarding justice-involved youth.

Research supports the value of providing education to incarcerated individuals. For example, a 2019 analysis by the Vera Institute of Justice concluded that postsecondary education in prison increases employment and earnings for formerly incarcerated people and reduces recidivism rates, which the Vera study estimated could reduce taxpayer spending on reincarceration by more than $365 million per year.[142]

Funding for public education in California is often deemed newsworthy by corporate and independent news outlets.[143] Nevertheless, investments in education specifically for the state's incarcerated youth have received little to no coverage by establishment news outlets. Coverage from independent outlets such as *The Imprint* and *EdSource* are rare but welcome exceptions to this pattern of limited news coverage.

FBI's Annual Crime Report Misunderstood and Misrepresented by Media

Ethan Corey, "FBI Crime Data for 2022 Is Out. Here's What You Need to Know," *The Appeal*, October 16, 2023.

Weihua Li and Jasmyne Ricard, "4 Reasons We Should Worry about Missing Crime Data," *The Marshall Project*, July 17, 2023.

Student Researcher: Quinlan Stacy (Frostburg State University)

Faculty Evaluator: Andy Duncan (Frostburg State University)

In an October 2023 article, *The Appeal* highlighted the FBI's latest annual report on crime in the United States for 2022. Although crime rates are on a steady decline, messaging from corporate media conveys the opposite, with alarmist headlines announcing "the most dangerous cities in America" and conflating crime rates with single policies or politicians, author Ethan Corey reported. Such attention-grabbing articles don't tell the whole story— and neither do the statistics themselves, according to *The Marshall Project*.

The FBI's Uniform Crime Reporting (UCR) Program obtains data from law enforcement agencies through the newer, more comprehensive National Incident-Based Reporting System (NIBRS) and the older Summary Reporting System (SRS).[144]

An October 2023 *Stateline* article reported that the transition to NIBRS presented challenges for many law enforcement agencies, leading to incomplete and not entirely comparable statistics for 2021 and 2022 crime reports.[145] According to *The Marshall Project*, "Experts predict that the national crime data is likely to be incomplete for years to come, and will leave more room to politicize crime statistics without concrete evidence." But data was incomplete even before 2021, as submitting it to the UCR was not mandatory.

The Appeal explained how the FBI has failed to prioritize sexual assault, organized crime, and white-collar crime within the UCR. Moreover, police departments have previously been found to skew their data to make their cities seem safer or to gain more funding. However, that doesn't make the FBI's statistics useless—they still highlight crime trends across longer periods and can cast light on racially disparate policing and the use of force. "Crime data can be a valuable tool in this context, but only to the extent that it's accurate and the public is aware of its shortcomings," Corey wrote.

As of June 2024, comprehensive coverage of FBI crime statistics and holistic interpretation of them has been scarce. NBC News and *USA Today* did note that Americans' perceptions of crime aren't in line with FBI statistics.[146] Independent sources such as the *Guardian* and local news media reported in greater depth.[147]

Hospital School Programs Support Students' Mental Health and Education

Rebecca Redelmeier, "As More Young People Receive Psychiatric Care, Some Hospitals Have Opened Their Own Schools," *The Hechinger Report*, August 31, 2023.

Student Researchers: Adehl Bavar, Ruby Bochiccio-Sipos, Osei Dixon, Ryan Hunt, and Rianna Jakson (University of Massachusetts Amherst)

Faculty Evaluators: Allison Butler and Jeewon Chon (University of Massachusetts Amherst)

In-hospital schools are developing groundbreaking means to address the mental health crisis among young people, Rebecca Redelmeier reported in August 2023 for *The Hechinger Report*. Amidst a surge of in-patient mental health hospitalizations, original programs such as the University of North Carolina's Hospital School are providing transformative educational support for students, contributing to what Redelmeier described as "a marked difference in their recovery," both mentally and academically.

As part of the local school district, the UNC Hospital School operates year-round. Teachers "serve as a bridge between the hospital and the student's regular school," Redelmeier reported, meeting daily with students and their treatment teams. Principal Marny Ruben explained that a major aim of the program is to provide a sense of normalcy to students whose lives have been upended by a mental health crisis. Regardless of the school district they attend, children admitted to UNC's hospitals have access to its school program. Offering educational opportunities to hospitalized students has been shown to improve their response to treatment.

Although past research indicates that young people are at high risk of attempting suicide after being discharged from hospitalization for mental health issues, more recent studies show that young people's feelings about their school community, including whether they feel cared for by teachers and peers, help curb that risk, Redelmeier reported.[148] In-hospital schools foster school connectedness and promote communication between hospital staff and school staff, reducing the likelihood of fragmented care that potentially makes young people more vulnerable to added risks.

Redelmeier's report focused on UNC's Hospital School, but other hospitals also provide school programs, including the Children's Hospital of Philadelphia, Stanford's Lucile Packard Children's Hospital School Program, and the New York City Department of Education's Hospital Schools Program. In the absence of shared standards for the support students receive in hospital schools, one organization, the Hospital Educator and Academic Liaison Association, or HEAL, has begun tracking hospital school programs across the country to ensure consistently high-quality academic programming.

The establishment press, including the *Washington Post* and the *New York Times*, have reported frequently on the student mental health crisis, though this reporting has tended to focus on the national shortage of mental healthcare providers and counselors, especially since the onset of the COVID-19 pandemic, or questions about the efficacy of large-scale interventions.[149] This coverage has failed to address how in-hospital school programs build connectedness and contribute to effective psychiatric care for patients who are students. One exception to this pattern of omission was a substantive report by NPR in June 2021 about a successful partnership between several school districts in Long Island, New York, and Cohen Children's Medical Center, which provides a "mental health safety net" for children experiencing mental health crises and their families.[150]

Forced Labor Traps Adopted Children in Paraguay

Jazmin Bazán, "Criadazgo: La Explotación Infantil Atrapada Entre Las Paredes Del Silencio," *El Surti*, January 30, 2024.

Student Researchers: Eva Creighton, Mathias Lundgren, and Andrew McCleery (College of St. Benedict and St. John's University)

Faculty Evaluator: Bruce Campbell (College of St. Benedict and St. John's University)

In January 2024, the Paraguayan news outlet *El Surtidor* published an article by Jazmin Bazán about the practice of *criadazgo*, forced domestic labor involving adopted children who receive neither wages nor an adequate standard of living. Paraguay's Instituto Nacional de Estadisticas estimates that about forty-seven thousand children, ages 5-17 (approximately 2.5 percent of Paraguay's total population), are subject to *criadazgo*, working without adequate time to rest, appropriate pay, or opportunities to leave.

Many of these adopted children are girls or young women, some are sexually abused, and most of them keep silent about their situations.

As Bazán noted, according to Paraguay's El Ministerio de Niñez y Adolescencia (Ministry of Children and Adolescents), 76 percent of the children affected by *criadazgo* are girls or adolescent women. They are typically put to work as maids or domestic servants. Their youth, gender, and separation from family and friends put them at particular risk for sexual exploitation. Bazán cited a 2021 Amnesty International report that found Paraguay's Public Health ministry received, on average, twelve reports of sexual violence against children and adolescents per day, while experts estimate that the real rate of sexual violence against minors and adolescents may be five times that.[151] Moreover, an average of two Paraguayan girls aged 10 to 14 give birth each day.

Bazán explained that the practice of *criadazgo* has its roots in Paraguay's deeply Catholic, patriarchal culture and in the economic deprivation of large sections of the population. But she pointed out that Paraguay's successive military dictatorships—particularly the authoritarian rule of strongman Alfredo Stroessner, who controlled the country from 1954 to 1989—also played a role in strengthening and normalizing the practice.

Paraguay is a party to several international agreements protecting the rights of children, including the United Nations Convention on the Rights of the Child. *Criadazgo* is a clear violation of the terms of those agreements. But the country has yet to adopt specific legislation to combat the practice. The United Nations has asked Paraguay to do more to curtail *criadazgo* and to make it a crime. International children's rights organizations such as PLAN International are also working to raise awareness about the issue.[152]

There has been no coverage of this story in US corporate media despite the fact that Bazán's reporting was funded in part by the US-based Pulitzer Center. However, the practice of *criadazgo* has gotten some coverage in Latin American news media over the years. The BBC's Spanish-language news outlet *BBC Mundo* published a report on *criadazgo* in 2016.[153] A 2022 article in Paraguay's *La Nación* explored the lives of low-income families in Paraguay and the reasons their children are forced to work.[154] Bazán's report on *criadazgo* was also published by Uruguay's *La Diara*.[155]

Israel-Linked Group Attempts to Censor Pro-Palestinian Artists on Spotify

Alan MacLeod, "Shadowy, Israel-Linked Group Attempts to Censor Pro-Palestinian Spotify Artists," *MintPress News*, June 12, 2023.

Student Researcher: Ashton Sidford (Diablo Valley College)

Faculty Evaluator: Mickey Huff (Diablo Valley College)

"We Believe in Israel," a subsidiary of Britain Israel Communications and Research Centre (BICOM) in the United Kingdom, has been attempting to remove Palestinian and pro-Palestinian artists from the music streaming giant Spotify. *MintPress News* senior staff writer Alan MacLeod reported that the group has been lobbying Spotify and the UK government.

The group's connections to the state of Israel remain obscure, MacLeod reported, noting that the group has "conceded that they work closely with the Israeli Embassy but insist they are not directed by them." The group is directed by former arms lobbyist and Labour Party operative Luke Akehurst.[156]

Rachel Blain, the campaign manager for We Believe in Israel, spearheaded the operation. "Spotify must take down songs promoting hatred," Blain wrote in an article for *The Times of Israel.*[157] "Before joining We Believe in Israel, Blain had worked at the Zionist Federation, the British Board of Deputies, and at an unnamed embassy in London," MacLeod reported, "Given her professional background, it is likely that that embassy was the Israeli one."

The campaign by We Believe in Israel sought to remove Arabic music that it believed was harmful to the state of Israel. In early 2023, after months of pressure from We Believe in Israel, Spotify removed several Arabic songs that contained lyrics critical of Israel, and "the group welcomed the decision but made clear that they saw this as only the first step in a much wider campaign of censorship," reported MacLeod. We Believe in Israel has accused Spotify of promoting violence by allowing these artists to have their music on the platform.

One artist specifically targeted was British-Iraqi rapper Lowkey, known for his pro-Palestinian activism and music. The group claimed Lowkey's music was "direct incitement of violence towards Jews and Israelis." There was an immediate pushback—with thousands signing a counter-petition in defense of the artist and his work—ultimately leading to the campaign's failure. MacLeod reported that the petition on behalf of Lowkey included "dozens of the most prominent Jewish individuals in the creative industries." We Believe in Israel has also been accused of seeking to censor Palestinian popstar Mohammed Assaf.

With a battered public image around the world, particularly in Western countries, Israeli officials—including former Israeli Justice Minister Ayelet Shaked and former Director General of the Ministry of Justice Emi Palmor—have resorted to attempting to remove Palestinian voices from radio, television, and the internet.[158] Shaked bragged that Facebook had removed 95 percent of the content she requested the platform to block. Palestinians' social media and financial accounts have been blocked as a consequence.[159]

As of May 2024, the censorship of Palestinian artists on Spotify has received no coverage by US corporate media. The only coverage since MacLeod's June 2023 piece has been from another independent outlet, the *Palestine Chronicle*.[160] Its story highlighted another pro-Israel group, the Board of Deputies of British Jews, that has lobbied Spotify to censor Palestinian voices. "The Board of Deputies badges itself as the representative body of British Jews," the *Palestine Chronicle* reported, "But as it makes clear in official filings, it collaborates closely with the Israeli government, including with the IDF Spokesperson's Office."

NICOLE MENDEZ-VILLARRUBIA is a senior at North Central College studying journalism, gender studies, and sociology. She is an experienced writer and public speaker, and also serves as co-president of OUTreach, a community for queer students on campus.

CAM LIPPINCOTT is a junior American studies major at UC Berkeley and previously studied at Diablo Valley College. His interests include contemporary US history, political journalism, and spending too much money eating out. He plans on attending graduate school after undergrad.

AMY GRIM BUXBAUM is a Professor of Communication at North Central College in Naperville, IL, where she teaches courses in organizational communication and rhetoric.

STEVE MACEK is a Professor of Communication and Media Studies at North Central College and serves as co-coordinator of Project Censored's campus affiliate program. He writes frequently about censorship and First Amendment issues for *Truthout*, *Common Dreams*, *The Progressive*, and other independent media outlets.

ANDY LEE ROTH, PHD, has edited or coedited the yearbook's Top 25 chapter since its 2014 edition. A coauthor of *The Media and Me*, the Project's guide to critical media literacy, he has also written for *Index on Censorship*, *YES! Magazine*, *The Progressive*, *Truthout*, and *In These Times*.

Notes

1.   Gaye Tuchman, *Making News: A Study in the Construction of Reality* (New York: The Free Press, 1978), 164.
2.   Todd Gitlin, *Media Unlimited: How the Torrent of Images and Sounds Overwhelms Our Lives* (New York: Henry Holt and Company, 2001); and, more recently, Jeffrey Gottfried, "Americans' News Fatigue Isn't Going

Away — About Two-Thirds Still Feel Worn Out," Pew Research Center, February 26, 2020.

3.	Carl Jensen, "Junk Food News: 1877–2000," in *Censored 2001: 25th Anniversary Edition*, eds. Peter Phillips and Project Censored (New York: Seven Stories Press, 2001), 252.

4.	Research suggests otherwise. See, e.g., Homero Gil de Zúñiga, Brian Weeks, and Alberto Ardèvol-Abreu, "Effects of the News-Finds-Me Perception in Communication: Social Media Use Implications for News Seeking and Learning about Politics," *Journal of Computer-Mediated Communication* 22, no. 3 (May 2017): 105–23.

5.	Jensen, "Junk Food News: 1877–2000," 252.

6.	See the Project Censored website for a complete archive of its annual "Censored" story lists, dating back to 1976.

7.	Tuchman, *Making News*, 209, see also 1.

8.	Tuchman, *Making News*, 180, 177.

9.	Tuchman, *Making News*, 196.

10.	Tuchman, *Making News*, 152. "In short," Tuchman summarized, "stories about issues raised by the women's movement are made into routine occurrences" by the news organizations that cover them (p. 153).

11.	E. Barbara Phillips, "Novelty without Change," *Journal of Communication* 26, no. 4 (December 1976): 92; quoted in Tuchman, *Making News*, 135.

12.	For information on how to nominate a story, see "How to Support Project Censored" at the back of this volume.

13.	Validated Independent News stories are archived on the Project Censored website.

14.	For a complete list of the Project's judges and their brief biographies, see the acknowledgments at the back of this volume.

15.	Special thanks to Olivia Rosenberg for research assistance during the final vetting of this year's top *Censored* stories.

16.	"National Census of Fatal Occupational Injuries in 2022," news release, Bureau of Labor Statistics, December 19, 2023.

17.	Jan Mirkowski, "The World's Most Dangerous Countries for Workers," Arinite Health and Safety, October 20, 2021.

18.	Mike Fitts, "Striking Union Claims Black Workers Being Injured at SC Jobsites That Go Uninspected," *Post and Courier*, April 4, 2023.

19.	Mary Joyce Carlson, Daniel M. Rosenthal, and Charlotte Schwartz, "Re: Civil Rights Complaint against the South Carolina Occupational Health and Safety Agency for Racial Discrimination in Programmed Inspections," Letter to Naomi Barry-Pérez, Director of Civil Rights, US Department of Labor, Union of Southern Service Workers, April 4, 2023.

20.	Fox 9 Staff, "Minnesota's Fatal Workplace Injuries Remain Steady in 2022, Report Finds," KMSP-Fox 9 (Minneapolis-St. Paul), December 20, 2023.

21.	Sean McGoey, "Workplace Fatalities on the Rise," WBAY (Green Bay, WI), April 12, 2024.

22.	Jordan Barab, "Failing to Protect Workers," *DC Report*, December 17, 2024.

23.	James Pollard, "Labor Union Asks Federal Regulators to Oversee South Carolina Workplace Safety Program," Associated Press, December 7,

2023; Bruce Rolfsen, "Union Asks OSHA to Strip South Carolina of Job Safety Powers," *Bloomberg Law*, December 7, 2023.

24. Carolyn Neunuebel, "What the World Bank's Country Climate and Development Reports Tell Us about the Debt-Climate Nexus in Low-Income Countries," World Resources Institute, April 11, 2023; see also, Lena Anderson and Mickey Huff, "Wealthy Nations Continue to Drive Climate Change with Devastating Impacts on Poorer Countries," in *Project Censored's State of the Free Press 2023*, eds. Mickey Huff and Andy Lee Roth (Fair Oaks: The Censored Press; New York: Seven Stories Press, 2022), 66–68, also archived on the Project Censored website.

25. See, for example, Cem İsmail Addemir and Steve Macek, "Debt Crisis Looms for World's Poorest Nations," in *Project Censored's State of the Free Press 2024*, eds. Andy Lee Roth and Mickey Huff (Fair Oaks: The Censored Press; New York: Seven Stories Press, 2024), 74–77, also archived on the Project Censored website.

26. Bob Buhr et al., "Climate Change and the Cost of Capital in Developing Countries," Imperial College Business School and SOAS University of London, 2018.

27. Kaamil Ahmed, "Rich Countries 'Trap' Poor Nations into Relying on Fossil Fuels," *The Guardian*, August 21, 2023.

28. See, for example, Joe Thwaites and David Ryfisch, "High Stakes for Climate Finance in 2024," *Climate Home News*, January 15, 2024.

29. Antony Sguazzin, Ronojoy Mazumdar, and Prinesha Naidoo, "Debt Crisis Looms for Poorer Nations Most Vulnerable to Climate Change," *Bloomberg*, May 29, 2023.

30. Alan Rappeport, "World Bank Warns Record Debt Burdens Haunt Developing Economies," *New York Times*, December 13, 2023.

31. Andrew Ross, "Climate Debt Denial," *Dissent*, Summer 2013.

32. Delaney Nolan, "Saltwater Threat to Louisiana Drinking Water to Grow across US, Experts Warn," *Earth Island Journal*, October 11, 2023; Marlowe Starling, Emily Driehaus, and Aarohi Sheth, "New Orleans's Saltwater Intrusion Scare Is a Reminder of a Nationally Looming Threat," *Sierra*, October 31, 2023.

33. Solcyré Burga, "What to Know about the Saltwater Threat to Louisiana's Drinking Water Supply," *Time*, September 24, 2023, updated October 16, 2023; Jen Christensen, "Louisiana Could See Months of High Salt Levels in Drinking Water, Threatening Residents' Health," CNN, October 5, 2023; Omar Villafranca and Analisa Novak, "New Orleans' Drinking Water Threatened as Saltwater Intrusion Looms," CBS News, September 26, 2023.

34. Andrew Wulfeck and Scott Sistek, "New Orleans No Longer under Current Threat of Salt Water Intrusion from Mississippi River," FOX Weather, September 30, 2023, updated October 13, 2023; Carlie Kollath Wells and Chelsea Brasted, "Salt Water Intrusion No Longer a Threat to New Orleans' Drinking Water," *Axios New Orleans*, October 12, 2023.

35. "A Study Reveals the Spread and Cost of Saltwater Intrusion in the US Mid-Atlantic," *Smart Water Magazine*, February 8, 2023; Don Rainey, "Saltwater Intrusion, an Emerging Water Quality Issue below Our Feet," *Florida Weekly Naples Edition*, January 25, 2024.

36. Monica Sanders, "Intruding Tides: Saltwater Intrusion's Threat to Louisiana and Beyond," *Forbes*, October 5, 2023.
37. Vox Staff, "The Fight over Gas Stoves," *Vox*, November 4, 2023.
38. Amanda Hoover, "The Gas Stove Culture Wars Have Begun," *Wired*, January 12, 2023.
39. Jeff Brady, "How Gas Utilities Used Tobacco Tactics to Avoid Gas Stove Regulations," NPR, October 17, 2023.
40. Rebecca Leber, "How the Fossil Fuel Lobby Weaponized Julia Child's Gas Stove," *Vox*, November 4, 2023; Rebecca Leber, "There's Something Different about the New Gas Stove Influencer," *Vox*, March 10, 2023.
41. Kate Yoder, "To Obscure the Risks of Gas Stoves, Utilities Borrowed from Big Tobacco's Playbook," *Grist*, October 18, 2023.
42. Alex Baumhardt, "Lawmakers, Advocates Ask Oregon to Investigate NW Natural for Misleading Claims about Natural Gas," OPB, December 13, 2023.
43. "Advocates Call on WA Department of Health to Counter Gas Industry Misinformation with Trusted Resources for Public," news release, Sierra Club, November 30, 2023; Elliott Negin, "The Gas Industry is Gaslighting Us," *The Equation* (blog), Union of Concerned Scientists, April 11, 2024.
44. Aaron Gell, "How Did Gas Stoves Ignite a Culture War?" *Bloomberg Businessweek*, March 9, 2023.
45. Michael J. Coren, John Farrell, and Alice Li, "Are Induction Stoves That Much Safer than Gas? We Tested Them," *Washington Post*, January 16, 2024; Rachel Wharton, "Worried about Your Gas Stove? Here's What to Do," *New York Times*, March 15, 2024; Mike Snider, "New York Bans Gas Stoves, Furnaces in New Buildings," *USA Today*, May 3, 2023, updated May 4, 2023; Elizabeth Elkind, "GOP Bill to Keep Biden's 'Hands Off' Americans' Home Appliances Passes House," Fox News, May 7, 2024.
46. Jonathan Levy, "Opinion: Gas Stoves Are Bad for Your Health. So Is the Industry's Big Tobacco-Style Coverup," *Los Angeles Times*, November 3, 2023.
47. Ashley Belanger, "Lawmakers Tell Facebook to Stop Deleting Abortion Posts for No Reason," *Ars Technica*, July 12, 2022.
48. Deidre McPhillips, "Telehealth Abortions Now Account for Nearly 1 in 5 in US, with Thousands Accessed under Shield Laws Each Month, Report Says," CNN, May 14, 2024.
49. "Profiting from Deceit: How Google Profits from Anti-choice Ads Distorting Searches for Reproductive Healthcare," Center for Countering Digital Hate, June 15, 2023.
50. Nikki McCann Ramirez, "Dems Demand Twitter, Meta Rein in Rampant Abortion Misinformation," *Rolling Stone*, December 7, 2023.
51. "Reproductive Rights and Justice Movement Leaders Respond to 'Big Tech' Suppression of Accurate Abortion Information," Reproaction, October 26, 2023.
52. Clare Duffy, "The Newest Content Moderation Minefield for Tech Platforms: Abortion Posts," CNN, June 29, 2022.
53. Susan Rinkunas, "22 Democrats Sponsor a Bill That Could Censor Abortion Info from the Internet," *Jezebel,* October 12, 2023; Kylie Cheung, "Abortion Rights Activists Get Creative to Challenge Big Tech

at SXSW: 'No Business as Usual'," *Jezebel*, March 12, 2024; Erin Matson, "Big Tech Is Failing to Allow Accurate Abortion Information," Reproaction (Medium), November 29, 2023.

54. Franziska Haupt et al., "2023 Forest Declaration Assessment: Off Track and Falling Behind," Forest Declaration Assessment, October 23, 2023.

55. Haupt et al. "2023 Forest Declaration," 79, 83.

56. Haupt et al. "2023 Forest Declaration," 83, 144.

57. Mary Gagen et al., "Forest Pathways Report 2023," World Wildlife Fund, October 2023.

58. Maxine Joselow, "Nations Made Bold Climate Pledges. They Aren't Close to Meeting Them," *Washington Post*, November 15, 2023.

59. "Global Efforts to Halt Deforestation Falling Short—Report," *DW*, October 24, 2023; "World 'Failing' on Pledge to Halt and Reverse Deforestation by 2030," France 24, October 24, 2023.

60. Manuela López Restrepo, "The U.S. Army Is Falling Short of Its Recruitment Goals. She Has a Plan for That," NPR, October 5, 2023.

61. Nan Levinson, "The Army Is Recruiting—Gen Z Just Isn't Biting," *The Nation*, April 20 2023.

62. Peter Swope, "Gridiron Imperialism: How the NFL Propagandizes for the US Military," *Brown Political Review*, November 22 2021.

63. Sam Wineburg et al., "Evaluating Information: The Cornerstone of Civic Online Reasoning," Stanford Digital Repository, November 22, 2016.

64. Shannon Liao, "Why the US Military's Engagement with Gen Z on Twitch Is Increasingly under Scrutiny," CNN, August 16, 2020.

65. Günseli Yalcinkaya, "The Girlbossification of Global Warfare," *Dazed*, October 27, 2023.

66. See also, Julia Karon et al., "Solving Stranded Credits: Assessing the Scope and Effects of Transcript Withholding on Students, States, and Institutions," Ithaka S+R, October 5, 2020.

67. In December 2023, after publishing our initial summary analysis of this story, Project Censored received email communication from a representative of Ashworth College, which stated: "We updated our transcript policy in January 2023 to allow for transcript access notwithstanding an outstanding balance owed, but due to the complexity of the change, our systems in some cases did not allow for access in accordance with the policy. We are in the process of accelerating the system's change to better allow for seamless access for learners with balances owed."

68. Danielle Douglas-Gabriel, "Government Moves to Protect Students When Colleges Are at Risk of Closing," *Washington Post*, October 24, 2023.

69. Sarah Wood, "College Transcript Holds: What to Know," *U.S. News & World Report*, January 30, 2023.

70. See Meredith Kolodner, "Withholding College Transcripts for Loan Payment Is 'Abusive,' Agency Says," *New York Times*, September 30, 2022, updated October 3, 2022; also published by *The Hechinger Report*, October 1, 2022.

71. "Hidden Debt Trap," *The Hechinger Report*, undated [accessed May 21, 2024].

72. "Commission Votes Unanimously to Pass Package of Reforms Including Limit on Use of Acquitted Conduct in Sentencing Guidelines," news release, United States Sentencing Commission, April 17, 2024; see also,

"2024 Amendments in Brief," United States Sentencing Commission, June 2024.

73. "Commission Votes Unanimously to Pass Package of Reforms Including Limit on Use of Acquitted Conduct in Sentencing Guidelines," news release, United States Sentencing Commission, April 17, 2024.

74. "About the Commission," United States Sentencing Commission, undated [accessed June 5, 2024].

75. Dennis A. Pangindian et al., "The U.S. Sentencing Commission's Pro-posed 2024 Amendments to the Federal Sentencing Guidelines Seek to Restore Consistency in Loss Calculations and Mitigate the Impact of Acquitted Conduct," *National Law Review*, April 1, 2024.

76. Ryan Nadeau, "Not Guilty, Sentenced to Life: Terence Richardson Granted Evidentiary Hearing by Va. Supreme Court to Prove Inno-cence," ABC 8 News (Richmond, VA), February 1, 2024.

77. Dean Mirshahi and Rolynn Wilson, "Judge Allows New Evidence in Innocence Petition Case for Terence Richardson, Who Was Found Not Guilty but Sentenced to Life," ABC 8 News (Richmond, VA), May 23, 2024.

78. Holly Barker, "US Sentencing Commission Hearing Focuses on Acquitted Conduct," *Bloomberg Law*, March 6, 2024.

79. Clay Cane, "Why Two Black Men in Va. Were Sentenced to Life after Being Found Not Guilty for Killing a White Police Officer," BET, March 23, 2023.

80. "Not Guilty, Sentenced for Life: The Case against Ferrone Claiborne and Terence Richardson," ABC 8 News (Richmond, VA), undated [accessed June 13, 2024].

81. Paul Kix, "His Clients Were Acquitted of Murder. Why Did They Get Life Sentences?" *The Atlantic*, May 27, 2022.

82. Anuj Mudaliar, "ChatGPT Leaks Sensitive User Data, OpenAI Suspects Hack," Spiceworks, February 1, 2024.

83. Jared Serbu, "NARA Sees 'Unacceptable Risks' from Using ChatGPT for Agency Business," *Federal News Network*, May 1, 2024.

84. Cade Metz, "How Could A.I. Destroy Humanity?" *New York Times*, June 10, 2023; "Does AI Pose an Existential Risk to Humanity? Two Sides Square Off," *Wall Street Journal*, November 8, 2023; Aaron Gregg, Cristiano Lima-Strong, and Gerrit De Vynck, "AI Poses 'Risk of Extinction' on Par with Nukes, Tech Leaders Say," *Washington Post*, May 30, 2023; Billy Perrigo, "Exclusive: U.S. Must Move 'Decisively' to Avert 'Extinc-tion-Level' Threat from AI, Government-Commissioned Report Says," *Time*, March 11, 2024.

85. Etay Maor, "Embrace GenAI without Exposing Your Data to Risk," *Forbes*, April 29, 2024.

86. "World News in Brief: Water Crisis for Children, Hunger in East Africa, New Yazidi Memorial," UN News, November 13, 2023.

87. "The Climate Crisis Is a Child Rights Crisis: Introducing the Children's Climate Risk Index," UNICEF, August 19, 2021.

88. "World News in Brief."

89. "UN Climate Change Conference—United Arab Emirates," United Nations Climate Change, November 30–December 12, 2023.

90. Sr. Titilayo Aduloju, "UNICEF: Millions of Children Globally Face Water Scarcity Due to Climate Change," *Vatican News*, November 13, 2023; "Unicef Warns of Vulnerable Children amid 'Worst' Water Scarcity in South Asia," *The News International*, November 13, 2023; "The Climate Changed Child: One in Three Children Exposed to Severe Water Scarcity," *The New Arab*, November 28, 2023; "1 in 3 Children Worldwide Exposed to Life-Threatening Water Scarcity: Unicef," *The Morung Express*, November 14, 2023.

91. "Panama President Signs into Law a Moratorium on New Mining Concessions. A Canadian Mine is Untouched," Associated Press, November 3, 2023.

92. Kathia Martínez and Juan Zamorano, "Panama's Supreme Court Declares 20-Year Contract for Canadian Copper Mine Unconstitutional," Associated Press, November 28, 2023.

93. See also Reagan Haynie and Mickey Huff, "Fossil Fuel Investors Sue Governments to Block Climate Regulations," in *Project Censored's State of the Free Press 2024*, eds. Andy Lee Roth and Mickey Huff (Fair Oaks: The Censored Press; New York: Seven Stories Press, 2023), 45–48, also archived on the Project Censored website.

94. Valentine Hilaire and Elida Moreno, "Election in Panama: Who Are the 5 Frontrunners in Sunday's Presidential Race?" Reuters, May 1, 2024.

95. "Panama President-Elect Rules Out First Quantum Talks until Arbitration Dropped," Reuters, May 9, 2024.

96. See, for example, Divya Rajagopal, "Future of First Quantum Mine Is for the People of Panama to Decide, US Official Says," Reuters, March 5, 2024; and Naimul Karim, "Impossible for Panama's Next Government to Ignore Mining, Says First Quantum CEO," *Financial Post*, February 12, 2024.

97. Andrea Salcedo, "Why Ordinarily Quiet Panama Has Erupted in Deadly Protests," *Washington Post*, November 7, 2023, updated November 8, 2023.

98. Leila Miller, "Panama's 2024 Election: What to Know," *New York Times*, April 4, 2024.

99. Dell Cameron, "Docs Show FBI Pressures Cops to Keep Phone Surveillance Secrets," *Wired*, June 22, 2023.

100. Joseph V. Cuffari, *Secret Service and ICE Did Not Always Adhere to Statute and Policies Governing Use of Cell-Site Simulators (REDACTED)*, Office of Inspector General, Department of Homeland Security, February 23, 2023.

101. Cuffari, *Secret Service and ICE*, 7.

102. Cuffari, *Secret Service and ICE*, 12–13.

103. For previous coverage by Project Censored of overbroad collection of private data by law enforcement agencies, see Samantha Bosnich et al., "Law Enforcement Surveillance of Phone Records," in *Censored 2018: Press Freedoms in a "Post-Truth" World*, eds. Andy Lee Roth and Mickey Huff with Project Censored (New York: Seven Stories Press, 2017), 67–71, also archived on the Project Censored website.

104. Thomas Claburn, "Secret Service, ICE Break the Law over and over with Fake Cell Tower Spying," *The Register*, March 4, 2023; Eric Priezkalns, "US Security Agencies Broke IMSI-Catcher Laws," *Commsrisk*, March 28, 2023.

105. "Net Zero Tracker," New Climate Institute, undated [accessed June 10, 2024].

106. "New Analysis: Half of World's Largest Companies Are Committed to Net Zero," Net Zero Tracker, November 5, 2023.

107. Michael Hiltzik, "Column: Big Oil Companies Are Already Reneging on Their Global Warming Promises," *Los Angeles Times*, February 9, 2023; Simon Jessop and Ross Kerber, "JPMorgan, State Street Quit Climate Group, BlackRock Steps Back," Reuters, February 15, 2024.

108. For example, "Holding Polluting Sectors Accountable for the Climate Crisis," *Economist Impact*, October 10, 2022; Peter Eavis and Clifford Krauss, "What's Really Behind Corporate Promises on Climate Change?" *New York Times*, February 22, 2021, updated May 12, 2021; Shashi Menon, "Greenwashing and Other Pitfalls on the Road to Net-Zero," *Forbes*, February 15, 2023.

109. Evan Halper, "Companies Made Big Climate Pledges. Now They Are Balking on Delivering," *Washington Post*, December 3, 2023.

110. "Press Release: Bottled Water Volume Growth Slows in 2022, Data from Beverage Marketing Corporation Show," news release, Beverage Marketing Corporation, May 23, 2023.

111. See Ryan Felton, "Should We Break Our Bottled Water Habit?" *Consumer Reports*, October 9, 2019.

112. Felton, "Should We Break?"

113. Carla Delgado, "Our Bottled Water Habit Stands in the Way of Universal Clean Drinking Water," *Popular Science,* March 24, 2023.

114. For previous coverage by Project Censored of inequalities in drinking water systems, see, for example, Jessie Eastman, Allison Kopicki, and Steve Macek, "Widespread Lead Contamination Threatens Children's Health, and Could Triple Household Water Bills," in *Censored 2018,* eds. Andy Lee Roth and Mickey Huff with Project Censored (New York: Seven Stories Press, 2017), and archived on the Project Censored website.

115. See, for example, Bryn Nelson, "The Water Crisis No One In America Is Fixing," *Time*, February 16, 2023; Robert Samuels and Emmanuel Martinez, "The Problems in the Pipes," *Washington Post*, February 18, 2023; Sarah Gibbens, "Is Tap Water Safe to Drink? Here's What You Really Need to Know," *National Geographic*, March 20, 2023; Dorany Pineda et al.,"'A Ticking Time Bomb': Why California Can't Provide Safe Drinking Water to All Its Residents," *Los Angeles Times,* September 27, 2023.

116. James O'Rourke, "Environmentalists Call on Insurance Companies to Stop Insuring the Fossil Fuel Industry," *Colorado Times Recorder*, March 1, 2024; Matt Dwyer, "Climate Activists in Hartford Urge Insurance Giant Travelers to Cut Ties with Fossil Fuel Companies," *Connecticut Public Radio*, May 15, 2024; Scott Harris, interview with Joanna Mallary, "Student Climate Campaign Targets CT-Based Insurance Companies for Fossil Fuel Investments," *Between the Lines*, May 13, 2024.

117. Sabrina Jacobs, interview with Risalat Khan and Nikki Reisch, "California's Climate and Insurance Crisis," KPFA (Santa Cruz, CA), May 3, 2024; Risalat Khan and Charles Slidders, "California's Climate and Insurance Crisis: Uninsurability Meets Industry Greed," CIEL (Center for International Environmental Law), April 3, 2024.

118. Consumer Watchdog, "Watchdog Renews Call to Mandate Insurance Companies Disclose the Fossil Fuel Projects They Insure as Insurance Commissioner Ricardo Lara Convenes Climate Summit," PR Newswire, April 9, 2024.

119. Jean Eaglesham, "Insurers Are in the Hot Seat on Climate Change," *Wall Street Journal*, July 13, 2023.

120. Maxine Joselow, "The Next Big Climate Test for Biden: Natural Gas Export Projects," *Washington Post*, October 17, 2023.

121. "Over One Hundred Days into the War, Israel Destroying Gaza's Food System and Weaponizing Food, Say UN Human Rights Experts," United Nations Office of Human Rights, January 16, 2024.

122. For example, Erika Solomon, "Aid Groups in Rafah Say Israel's Advance Is Pushing Them Out," *New York Times*, May 29, 2024.

123. "'So Much Blood on the Ground': Dangerous and Deadly Vehicle Pursuits under Texas' Operation Lone Star," Human Rights Watch, November 27, 2023.

124. Camilo Montoya-Galvez, "Texas Immigration Law Blocked Again, Just Hours after Supreme Court Allowed State to Arrest Migrants," CBS News, March 20, 2024,

125. See, for example, Alexander Ward, "GOP Embraces a New Foreign Policy: Bomb Mexico to Stop Fentanyl," *Politico*, April 10, 2023; and Adriana Gomez Licon, "Some GOP Candidates Want to Use Force against Mexico to Stop Fentanyl. Experts Say That Won't Work," Associated Press, October 9, 2023.

126. Joel Rose, "Who Is Sneaking Fentanyl across the Southern Border? Hint: It's Not the Migrants," NPR, August 9, 2023.

127. Sarah Dewberry and Rosa Flores, "Texas AG Sues Biden Administration for Cutting Razor Wire at the US-Mexico Border," CNN, October 24, 2023. See also, Erik Ortiz, "Influx of Migrants at Border Gains Renewed Attention as 'Crisis' Rhetoric Spreads," NBC News, October 4, 2023.

128. Marina Schauffler, "Compound Injustice: PFAS May Concentrate over Time in Landfills near the Penobscot Indian Reservation," *Maine Monitor*, September 10, 2022; Deena Winter, "Forever Chemicals Found in Tribal School Well on Leech Lake Reservation," *Minnesota Reformer*, September 1, 2023; Bennet Goldstein, "Great Lakes Pollution Threatens Ojibwe Treaty Rights to Fish," *Wisconsin Watch*, February 24, 2023; Liz McLaughlin, "'We Live off the Land': Indigenous Communities Say Pollution Is Cutting off a Vital Food Source," WRAL News (Raleigh, NC), August 3, 2023, updated August 5, 2023.

129. E.A. Crunden, "PFAS Testing Overlooks Tribal Systems," *E&E News* (*Politico Pro*), December 14, 2022.

130. Lisa Sorg, "Newsline Special Report: A Community Inundated with Industrial Waste," *NC Newsline*, May 27, 2023; Sebastián Rodríguez, "Forever Chemicals Are Disproportionately Polluting Black and Hispanic Neighborhoods," *The Verge*, May 16, 2023.

131. Hannah Norman and KFF Health News, "PFAS 'Forever Chemicals' Found in Freshwater Fish, Yet Most States Don't Warn Residents," *Scientific American*, December 12, 2023.

132. Dan Kraker, "Fond du Lac Band Sues 3M and Other Companies over PFAS Pollution," Michigan Public Radio, July 27, 2023.

133. Pam McFarland, "Tribes, Alaska Villages to Gain $278M for Water Infrastructure," *Engineering News-Record*, June 29, 2023.

134. Shantal Riley, "Lake Superior's Forever Chemicals," *Washington Post Magazine*, January 12, 2022.

135. Vaishnavi J, "Why Is KOSA So Popular and What Does It Mean for Child Safety Regulation in the US?" *Tech Policy Press*, March 20, 2024. For previous critical analysis by Project Censored, see Steve Macek, "Despite Its Popularity, the Kids Online Safety Act Won't Help Young People, It Will Hurt Them," Project Censored, February 22, 2024; and Shealeigh Voitl and avram anderson, "EARN IT Still Ignores Privacy, Censorship Concerns," Project Censored, June 29, 2023, updated February 19, 2024.

136. Kids Online Safety Act, S. 1409, 118th Congress (2023–2024).

137. Kids Online Safety Act, H.R. 7891, 118th Congress (2023–2024).

138. Cristiano Lima-Strong, "Senate Poised to Pass the Biggest Piece of Tech Regulation in Decades," *Washington Post*, February 15, 2024; Natasha Singer, "Bipartisan Bill Aims to Protect Children Online," *New York Times*, January 31, 2024.

139. Jason Kelley, "Thousands of Young People Told Us Why the Kids Online Safety Act Will Be Harmful to Minors," *Techdirt*, March 21, 2024.

140. Sino Esthappan and Victoria Lee, "Incarcerated Youth Deserve a Quality Education, and Many Don't Get One," Urban Institute, October 23, 2018.

141. James Rainey and James Queally, "California Is Closing Its Last Youth Prisons. Will What Replaces Them Be Worse?" *Los Angeles Times*, June 2, 2023.

142. Patrick Oakford et al., "Investing in Futures: Economic and Fiscal Benefits of Postsecondary Education in Prison," Vera Institute of Justice, January 2019. See also, Jacqueline Archie et al., "Studies Document Links between Education, Incarceration, and Recidivism," in *Project Censored's State of the Free Press 2021*, eds. Mickey Huff and Andy Lee Roth (New York: Seven Stories Press, 2020), 104–7, also archived on the Project Censored website.

143. See, for example, "Teachers Say Gov. Newsom's Proposed Budget Would 'Wreak Havoc' on School Funding," CBS News, May 17, 2024; and Dan Walters, "California's Budget Deficit Revives State's Everlasting Battle over School Funding," *Cal Matters*, May 21, 2024.

144. "FBI Releases 2022 Crime in the Nation Statistics," news release, Federal Bureau of Investigation, October 16, 2023.

145. Amanda Hernández, "Politicians Love to Cite Crime Data. It's Often Wrong," *Stateline*, October 27, 2023.

146. Ken Dilanian, "Most People Think the U.S. Crime Rate Is Rising. They're Wrong," NBC News, December 16, 2023; Zac Anderson, "FBI Data Shows America Is Seeing a 'Considerable' Drop in Crime. Trump Says the Opposite," *USA Today*, April 30, 2024.

147. Adam Gabbatt, "FBI Data Shows US Crime Plummeted in 2023 but Experts Warn Report Is Incomplete," *The Guardian*, March 19, 2024; Josh Renaud, "FBI Publishes Wrong Crime Numbers for St. Louis Again amid Technology Woes for City Police," *St. Louis Post-Dispatch*, October 4, 2023.

148. Marisa E. Marraccini and Zoe M.F. Brier, "School Connectedness and Suicidal Thoughts and Behaviors: A Systematic Meta-Analysis," *School Psychology Quarterly* 32, no. 1 (March 2017): 5–21.

149. See, e.g., Donna St. George, "In a Crisis, Schools Are 100,000 Mental Health Staff Short," *Washington Post*, August 31, 2023; Ellen Barry, "Are We Talking Too Much about Mental Health?" *New York Times*, May 6, 2024.

150. Rhitu Chatterjee and Christine Herman, "How a Hospital and a School District Teamed up to Help Kids in Emotional Crisis," NPR, June 11, 2021.

151. "A Maze with No Way Out: Sexual Violence, Pregnancy and Impunity for Girls in Paraguay," Amnesty International, December 1, 2021.

152. "The Normalization of 'Criadazgo' in Paraguay," Plan International, 2024.

153. Ángel Bermúdez, "Criadazgo, la Cuestionada Práctica de Los Paraguayos Que 'Adoptan' Niños Como Empleados Domésticos," BBC Mundo, June 16, 2016.

154. Lourdes Pintos, "Trabajo Infantil: El Enemigo Visible de la Educación en Paraguay," *La Nación*, September 18, 2022.

155. Jazmín Bazán, "Criadazgo: La Explotación Infantil en Paraguay Atrapada Entre Las Paredes Del Silencio," *La Diara*, January 31, 2024.

156. Asa Winstanley, "New Bombshell Film Exposes Israel Lobby Role in UK Labour Party," *Electronic Intifada*, September 22, 2022.

157. Rachel Blain, "Spotify Must Take Down Songs Promoting Hatred," *Times of Israel* (blog), April 21, 2022.

158. Glenn Greenwald, "Facebook Says It Is Deleting Accounts at the Direction of the U.S. and Israeli Governments," *The Intercept*, December 30, 2017.

159. For previous coverage of this topic by Project Censored, see the Déjà Vu News chapter in this volume.

160. David Miller and Paul Salvatori, "How Israeli Lobbyists Infiltrated Spotify to Censor Palestinian Music," *The Palestine Chronicle*, September 5, 2023.

CHAPTER 2

Déjà Vu News
What Happened to Previous *Censored* Stories

NICOLE MENDEZ-VILLARRUBIA, GRACE HARTY, OLIVIA ROSENBERG, and STEVE MACEK

Each year, Project Censored's Top 25 story list identifies and publicizes socially and politically significant, independently produced news stories that have gone underreported by major corporate news organizations.

Occasionally, previously ignored issues move to the forefront of public discourse because of political events or because the corporate media belatedly decide they might be of interest to audiences. Sometimes, independent news coverage even spurs corporate news outlets to cover issues and perspectives the big outlets might otherwise have ignored. When that happens, select stories from our annual lists begin to make larger headlines and enter into broader public conversations.

Yet even when previously ignored stories garner greater exposure, it is not uncommon for corporate media coverage to continue to omit important details and marginalize disfavored, typically critical, perspectives. Moreover, some stories from our Top 25 lists continue to be left off of the national news agenda entirely, regardless of how consequential they may be.

This Déjà Vu chapter delves into the fates of five

important stories from previous Project Censored story lists.

It starts with a review of story #14 from *State of the Free Press 2023*, which investigated the repression of Palestinian media. Next, it updates two stories from *State of the Free Press 2022*: story #6 about the role of the pro-Zionist website Canary Mission in doxxing and blacklisting pro-Palestinian activists and academics, and story #16 about the UK's femicide census, an attempt to track the incidence of gender-related murders of women. Following that, the chapter revisits story #11 from Project Censored's 2020 yearbook, which detailed connections between the Azov Battalion, a Ukrainian militia with well-documented neo-Nazi allegiances, and violent White supremacists in the United States. Finally, the chapter updates the #23 story from *Censored 2016: Media Freedom on the Line* about the causes and consequences of the nation's backlog of unprocessed rape kits.

Although some of these stories have received a modicum of establishment media attention since we first spotlighted them, they all merit reexamining, and the corporate news industry's ongoing coverage of them warrants continued scrutiny.

State of the Free Press 2023 #14

Repression of Palestinian Media

Yuval Abraham, "Israel Charges Palestinian Journalists with Incitement—for Doing Their Jobs," *The Intercept*, April 5, 2022.

Nadda Osman, "Sheikh Jarrah: Activists Raise Concerns over Deleted Social Media Content," *Middle East Eye*, May 7, 2021.

Ramzy Baroud, "How Israel's 'Facebook Law' Plans to Control All Palestinian Content Online," *Jordan Times*, January 18, 2022.

Student Researchers: Eli Rankin (Saint Michael's College) and Cem İsmail Addemir (Illinois State University)

Faculty Evaluators: Rob Williams (Saint Michael's College) and Steve Macek (North Central College)

As Project Censored reported in its 2023 yearbook, Palestinian journalists routinely face harassment by Israeli military personnel, and the world's leading social media platforms have been quick to suspend and restrict users who post pro-Palestinian content, including journalists.

Between 2020 and the time of the Project's original report, some twenty-six Palestinian journalists based in the West Bank had been imprisoned for attempting to cover Palestinian resistance to Israeli occupation. According to an April 5, 2022, report by Yuval Abraham in *The Intercept*, Palestinian journalists who posted footage or commented on Israel's use of force were often placed in administrative detention for months at a time without ever being charged and subjected to harsh interrogations.

Palestinian journalists' social media posts were often used against them by Israeli authorities. After reporter Hazem Nasser filmed Israeli troops operating in the West Bank in May 2021, Israeli soldiers detained and interrogated him repeatedly for a month. Israeli authorities ultimately charged Nasser with incitement based solely on some old Facebook posts.

Between May 6 and May 18, 2021, the Arab Center for the Advancement of Social Media, 7amleh, documented five hundred cases of digital rights violations targeting Palestinians.[1] These were cases in which social media platforms deleted stories, hid hashtags, and restricted or completely suspended accounts, often at the request of Israel's "Cyber Unit." Of those five hundred violations, half involved Instagram and a third involved Facebook—both owned by social media giant Meta.

During spring 2021, activists took to social media to condemn the evictions of Palestinian families from the Sheikh Jarrah neighborhood of Jerusalem. Subsequently, activists who condemned the evictions and journalists who covered them faced account suspensions and restrictions on social media, Nadda Osman reported for *Middle East Eye*. Mona Shtaya of 7amleh told Osman that these restrictions were part of a longstanding pattern: "Annually there are tens of thousands of requests that the Israeli cyber unit [sends] to social media companies in an attempt to silence Palestinians. The number of requests is increasing annually."

At the time of Project Censored's 2023 report, the systematic repression of Palestinian journalists and the silencing of Palestinian expression on social media had not been widely covered by US news outlets, especially the establishment press. The arrest of dozens of Palestinian journalists detailed in Abraham's *Intercept* article never made it onto the corporate news media's radar. There were scattered reports in the establishment press about censorship of Palestinian activists on social media. *The Washington Post* published a May 2021 article about Twitter and Facebook blocking or restricting Palestinian content.[2] The same month, NBC News reported on Palestinian accusations of censorship against social media platforms.[3] ABC News also ran an October 2021 story documenting Facebook employees' concerns about restrictions on the Instagram account of a well-known Palestinian activist.[4]

Update

As of June 25, 2024, Israel has killed at least 108 journalists and media workers as part of their war on Gaza, according to preliminary investigations by the Committee to Protect Journalists (CPJ). The CPJ's report found that "journalists in Gaza face particularly high risks . . . including devastating Israeli airstrikes, disrupted communications, supply shortages, and extensive power outages." Furthermore, a Palestinian Journalists' Syndicate volunteer told *Common Dreams* that "the group has evidence that at least 96 of the 109 Gaza reporters whose deaths it documented 'were deliberately and specifically targeted by surgical Israeli strikes against them.'"[5]

Israel's strategic internet blackouts cut off those in Gaza from essential news and emergency services and left the international community unable to observe the harm done to civilians. The timing of one such blackout coincided with the ICJ hearing on genocide, according to *Common Dreams*.[6] In fact, as *Common Dreams* reported, the case brought forth by South Africa stated, "Israel is deliberately imposing telecommunications blackouts on Gaza and restricting access by fact-finding bodies and the international media. At the same time, Palestinian journalists are being killed at a rate significantly higher than has occurred in any conflict in the past 100 years."

Global Voices called the repression of Palestinian media "digital apartheid" and interviewed Mona Shtaya, a digital rights defender based in Palestine.[7] She said, "Social media platforms should serve as a means for Palestinians to share their narrative. However . . . these platforms heavily censor Palestinian voices, shadowban Palestinians and their supporters, and infringe upon their rights to free speech."

Meta's censorship of Palestine-related media has dramatically increased since then, especially on Instagram. A November 27, 2023, article by the *Columbia Journalism Review* noted that 7amleh had received more than fourteen hundred reports of unjustified content moderation between October 7, 2023, and the date of publication alone, compared to eleven hundred claims in all of 2022.[8] They include "blocked comments, hidden hashtags, and Palestine-related Instagram stories that received markedly fewer views than other posts by the same person."

Al Jazeera and Access Now revealed that Meta's problematic auto-moderation and filters disproportionately targeted Arabic-language content, particularly any originating from Palestine, via deletion and shadowbans (limiting content's reach).[9] However, Hebrew language and official Israeli state communications promoting misinformation and explicitly calling for violence against Palestinian civilians were not deplatformed in the same way.

Furthermore, Meta's hate speech policy instructs the removal of content critical of "Zionists." According to Access Now, "While the company claims it only removes content where the word 'Zionist' is used as a proxy to attack Israeli or Jewish individuals and groups, this policy was widely criticized by human rights organizations and progressive Jewish and Muslim community groups in 2021." Meta considered expanding this policy in February 2024, and Access Now warns that a blanket ban could invite censorship and abuse.

YouTube also censors pro-Palestine content, according

to an April 2024 report by 7amleh.[10] Meanwhile, the platform carries Israeli government-sponsored ads inciting violence, some of which were pulled after criticism.

The Washington Post has published a few articles about journalists killed in Gaza, citing CPJ statistics.[11] Both the *Washington Post* and *New York Times* ran articles in May 2024 detailing the government-ordered shutdown of Al Jazeera's operations in Israel.[12] Israeli officials raided Al Jazeera's offices, confiscated its equipment, and blocked the distribution of its content via satellite, cable, and internet. The *Times*'s article included a brief quote from the Palestinian Journalists' Syndicate and noted that two Al Jazeera journalists had been "among at least 92 Palestinian journalists killed since the war began."[13]

A December 2023 *New York Times* article discussed the rise of watermelon imagery as a substitute for Palestine-related words to avoid censorship on platforms such as Instagram.[14] *Scripps News* and *The Hill* published full articles about a Human Rights Watch report accusing Meta of systemically censoring pro-Palestinian content; *Time* devoted a few sentences to it.[15] A March 2024 article from CNBC focused on how social media companies were rejecting claims of shadowbanning and censorship, with Meta dismissing the findings of the Human Rights Watch report.[16]

Canary Mission Blacklists Pro-Palestinian Activists, Chilling Free Speech Rights

Murtaza Hussain, "The Real Cancel Culture: Pro-Israel Blacklists," *The Intercept*, October 4, 2020.

Lex McMenamin, "Protecting Pro-Palestine Activists Can Feel Almost Impossible—but These Students Succeeded," *The Nation*, March 16, 2021.

Student Researcher: Miranda Morgan (Sonoma State University)

Faculty Evaluator: Allison Ford (Sonoma State University)

The Project's 2022 yearbook highlighted how Canary Mission, an anonymously-run digital database, was blacklisting pro-Palestinian activists. However, this was not being covered by corporate news media. Canary Mission labels activists, scholars, and students who criticize Israel as "terrorists" and "antisemites," according to an October 2020 report for *The Intercept* by Murtaza Hussain. Denouncing Israeli militarism online, in-person, or attending pro-Palestine protests can turn ordinary people into Canary Mission targets.

One activist interviewed by Hussain described Canary Mission as "very powerful in silencing people and making them think free speech is not their right. It instills a powerful sense of fear and paranoia." Others shared this sentiment, and their fear is not unfounded. The consequences of being blacklisted include loss of employment, travel restrictions, threats to immigration status, and consequent mental health struggles.

Reports published in 2018 by *The Intercept* and the Israeli newspaper *Haaretz* indicated that student activists have been questioned by the US and Israeli governments based on information from Canary Mission.[17]

Update

Since Project Censored first called out the corporate media's lack of reporting on Canary Mission, most coverage of the group has come from independent and student news media. A December 2023 article for *The Nation* by James Bamford and his subsequent interview appearance on *Democracy Now!* further documented Canary Mission's ties to Israeli intelligence.[18]

According to Bamford, the organization is a crucial asset for Israel's Ministry of Strategic Affairs, which primarily focuses on the United States. In his article for *The Nation*, he wrote that Canary Mission is "not only intended to silence anti-Israel dissent; its list of names is also used to prevent those individuals from entering Israel and attempting to visit family, including both Jews and Palestinians, and professors as well as students."

An August 2022 article in the *Philadelphia Inquirer* described how a young Palestinian American was fired from her job as a high school athletic trainer due to her Canary Mission profile. Her employers cited social media posts critical of Israel, some made when she was 14 years old.[19] Ultimately, she decided to file a federal discrimination charge against the school district.

Sahar Aziz, a Rutgers law professor quoted in the article, said, "This particular case is going to the heart of the American fundamental right to politically dissent, to express your beliefs ... And when you belong to a group that's not afforded those beliefs at equal levels as everyone else, that's evidence of discrimination against that group—but also a threat to those American values."

Similarly, legal commentary published in *Jurist* emphasized how Canary Mission sows distrust for academic thinking and factual discourse overall. Al Jazeera and the *Middle East Eye* briefly mentioned Canary Mission in broader articles discussing the censorship of pro-Palestinian views in classrooms and newsrooms.[20]

Student op-eds voicing concern about Canary Mission have appeared in the *Chicago Maroon*, *Massachusetts Daily Collegian*, and *Columbia Spectator*, among other campus newspapers.[21] They challenge university leaders' failure to protect students and faculty from doxxing.

Original reporting for *USC Annenberg Media* and *Her Campus* revealed that Accuracy in Media, a non-profit that purports to promote citizen activism, also publicized individuals' Canary Mission profiles at USC, Harvard, and elsewhere.[22] A January 2024 *Annenberg Media* article by Valeria S. Macias described how Accuracy in Media shared a petition via electronic billboards warning employers not to hire "antisemites," linking to Canary Mission profiles for students and professors at the University of Southern California. According to Macias, "Many of the people being highlighted have engaged in pro-Palestinian protests, have tweeted in support or are members of any student organizations speaking out against Israel's war in Gaza." The same thing happened at Harvard and Columbia, according to a November 2023 article in *Her Campus*. A targeted student, who characterized Accuracy in Media's campaign as "xenophobic, racist, and Islamophobic," said the group primarily singles out Black, Muslim, and undocumented students.

Her Campus reported that the president of Accuracy in Media, Adam Guillette, said they took names published in the *Harvard Crimson*—referring to a letter by the Palestinian Solidarity Committee co-signed by thirty-four student groups—and wouldn't know students' immigration status. He claimed they "target any organization that signs an antisemitic proclamation" and later added, "We would never dox anyone . . . it's morally outrageous."

A Columbia student is suing Accuracy in Media under New York civil rights law, which requires written consent to use an individual's name and photo in advertising. The student alleges defamation, noting that they were no longer a leader of a student organization that signed the open letter in support of Palestine published in the *Columbia Spectator*.[23]

According to *Documented*, an investigative watchdog group dedicated to immigration issues in New York State, Canary Mission has particularly targeted New Yorkers, second only to Californians.[24] New York City Councilwoman Shahana Hanif, the first Muslim woman elected to the position, was profiled by Canary Mission following her call for a ceasefire in Gaza and arrest at a rally. *Documented*'s coverage also cited a 2019 report issued to the United Nations by Palestine Legal, which found that Canary Mission "was disproportionately targeting Arab and Muslim students and faculty."

Corporate news media have not published detailed reporting on Canary Mission. Coverage has been limited to single-sentence mentions in the *Los Angeles Times* and *Forbes*, without follow-up.[25] The corporate media's lack of attention to Canary Mission and its McCarthyite tactics extends to the group's funders. Bamford's *Nation* article cited financial data obtained in 2018 by *The Forward*, an independent Jewish news site that exposed Canary Mission's origins and funding sources.[26] In reporting for *The*

Forward, Josh Nathan-Kazis uncovered tax data from 2016–2017, which revealed millions of dollars were funneled through nonprofit organizations to get tax breaks for Canary Mission donations. The Helen Diller Family Foundation, the Jewish Community Federation of San Francisco, and the Jewish Community Foundation of Los Angeles all had financial transactions linked to Megamot Shalom, an Israeli nonprofit reportedly serving as a front for Canary Mission. After Nathan-Kazis's original article was published, the foundations claimed they would pause funding to Megamot Shalom.

In his article, Bamford noted that "Americans who were financially supporting Canary Mission were potentially committing a serious crime, acting as agents of a foreign power," because Israeli intelligence organizations gather and act upon the site's information. Aside from reporting by independent outlets such as *The Nation*, *Democracy Now!*, and *The Forward*, there has been no significant coverage of Canary Mission's financial backers. *The Guardian* also covered the story in a January 2024 report about Canary Mission "establishing a foothold in Australia."[27]

State of the Free Press 2022 #16

Femicide Census Connects UK Killings with Global Wave of Violence against Women

Julia Long et al., "UK Femicides 2009–2018," Femicide Census, November 25, 2020.

Karen Ingala Smith, "Coronavirus Doesn't Cause Men's Violence against Women," Karen Ingala Smith (blog), April 15, 2020.

Karen Ingala Smith, "2020," Karen Ingala Smith (blog), April 14, 2020, updated January 9, 2021.

Karen Ingala Smith, "2021," Karen Ingala Smith (blog), February 8, 2021, updated June 7, 2021.

Yvonne Roberts, "'If I'm Not in on Friday, I Might be Dead': Chilling Facts about UK Femicide," *The Guardian*, November 22, 2020.

Student Researcher: Arden Kurhayez (North Central College)

Faculty Evaluator: Steve Macek (North Central College)

In 2021, the UK-based nonprofit Femicide Census measured an increase in fatal violence against women. Its 2020 report found that, on average, "a woman was killed by a male partner or ex-partner every four days" from 2009 to 2018. If the report included killings outside of romantic relationships, the frequency would increase to one murder every three days.

Despite femicide being "a leading cause of premature death for women" globally, Femicide Census reported that law enforcement and legislators have been treating cases as isolated incidents.

Out of 1,425 women killed by men from 2009 to 2018 in the UK, 62 percent were killed by a current or former intimate partner, while 38 percent were killed by a family member, friend, or recent acquaintance. Femicides committed by an intimate partner or family member often had a known history of abuse, accounting for 59 percent of such cases, with one-third of those killed having previously reported the abuse to police.

Femicide Census only records killings legally proven to have been committed by a man. Its counts omit femicides committed outside the UK, but another organization, Women Count USA, maintains comparable records, some dating back to the 1950s, for violence against women and girls in the United States.[28]

As Yvonne Roberts reported for the *Guardian*, the

seemingly isolated killings are, in fact, instances of a larger public health crisis. UN Women, a United Nations organization with a focus on gender equality, described the wave of violence against women amidst the COVID-19 pandemic as a "shadow pandemic."[29]

As of June 2021, there was a striking lack of corporate coverage about rising femicide rates. When corporate news outlets did cover the issue, they typically framed it as a problem in other countries but not in the United States.

Update

Since Project Censored spotlighted it in 2021, corporate coverage of femicide in the United States is still lacking. Women Count USA has gotten zero corporate coverage. However, this lack of coverage does not mean femicide is no longer a serious problem in the United States. According to the United States Bureau of Justice Statistics, in 2021, 34 percent of women murdered in the US were killed by an intimate partner.[30] UN Women reported that femicides in North America have increased by 29 percent since 2017.[31] Yet, when the nation's most prominent news outlets cover femicide, the reporting addresses either isolated incidents within the United States or international trends.

In both 2022 and 2024, for example, CNN ran stories about violence against women in Italy.[32] Its 2022 article covered incidents across Europe, specifically in Greece, the United Kingdom, France, and Spain, but did not mention the United States. The 2024 piece went into greater depth on femicide in Italy, citing the nation's entrenched patriarchal culture as a root cause. One other CNN story that mentioned femicide focused on a single incident that took place in 2023 in the United States, when a Colombian woman was murdered by her boyfriend in Wisconsin.[33] This article described femicide as a national issue in Colombia, despite the murder being committed by a US citizen in the United States.

The only other national news outlet to address the issue has been the Associated Press, which covered femicide in Kenya and Turkey, again with no mention of the United States.[34]

Data Against Femicide, a feminist data science group working out of the Massachusetts Institute of Technology (MIT), launched a project in 2019 to document killings in Latin America and the Caribbean.[35] MIT created the initiative in response to the lack of reliable official data about gender-related murders of women and girls and the need for feminist counter-data to supplement significantly limited official statistics. The founders of the organization also run a graduate seminar in which they teach about theoretical and historical perspectives on femicide and how to apply an intersectional feminist perspective to collecting and analyzing data about murders of women.

"If we could understand better how often [femicide] happens, where it happens, what are the motivations, then that would help the state to direct resources," Helena Suárez Val, co-founder of Data Against Femicide, explained. The "immediate allocation of support and services" could be dramatically improved, Val said, "if we really knew the scope and scale of the problem."

During the past year, international outrage surrounding femicide has grown, resulting in multiple protests in numerous countries. There has been significant independent news coverage of anti-femicide marches in France, Kenya, and Mexico in response to high rates of femicide in each of those nations. Protests in Italy have received coverage from *Time*, ABC News, and the Associated Press.[36] Despite a lack of stories about femicide in the United States, the conversation is growing louder internationally.

Censored 2020 # 11

Ukrainian Fascists Trained US White Supremacists

Max Blumenthal, "Blowback: An inside Look at How US-Funded Fascists in Ukraine Mentor US White Supremacists," *MintPress News*, November 19, 2018.

Whitney Webb, "FBI: Neo-Nazi Militia Trained by US Military in Ukraine Now Training US White Supremacists," *MintPress News*, November 9, 2018.

Rebecca Kheel, "Congress Bans Arms to Ukraine Militia Linked to Neo-Nazis," *The Hill*, March 27, 2018.

Student Researcher: Tanner J. Swann (Indian River State College)

Faculty Evaluator: Elliot D. Cohen (Indian River State College)

In 2018, although the Trump administration prohibited travelers and refugees from majority-Muslim countries from entering the United States for fear they might be terrorists, militant American White supremacists were meanwhile traveling freely between the United States and Ukraine, where they trained with the neo-Nazi Azov Battalion militia, according to reports from *MintPress News* and *The Hill*.

A federal criminal rioting complaint filed in Los Angeles in 2018 included an affidavit stating that four American White supremacists from the Rise Above Movement (RAM) trained with Ukraine's Azov Battalion, Max Blumenthal reported for *MintPress News*. The training took place after the White supremacist gang took part in violent riots in Huntington Beach and Berkeley, California, and in Charlottesville, Virginia, Blumenthal reported.

According to his report, although RAM's "crude neo-Nazi ideology" was on display at rallies and in well-publicized street battles, media coverage of RAM "glossed over the group's attraction to a burgeoning trans-Atlantic conglomeration of white supremacists" centered in Ukraine, including, specifically, the Azov Battalion.

As Whitney Webb reported for *MintPress News*, the Azov Battalion's prominence was "the direct result of U.S. government policy toward Ukraine." In the name of combatting "Russian aggression" following the 2014 annexation of Crimea, the United States supported Ukraine's military with hundreds of millions of dollars worth of weapons and programmatic and technical assistance. At least some of this aid "repeatedly found its way to the Azov Battalion," Webb wrote.

In March 2018, Congress banned arming the Azov Battalion, as *The Hill*'s Rebecca Kheel reported. Three previous House bills had included a ban on US aid to Ukraine funding the Azov Battalion, Kheel wrote, "but the provision was stripped out before final passage each year." In 2018, however, the $1.3 trillion omnibus spending bill expressly stipulated that "none of the funds made available by this act may be used to provide arms, training or other assistance to the Azov Battalion."

According to *The Hill*'s report, online posts from 2017 by the militia's news service showed Azov Battalion members testing US-made grenade launchers. Those posts were subsequently deleted, and the Ukrainian National Guard insisted that Azov did not possess the grenade launchers. Webb's article noted that, although US funds could no longer be used to purchase weapons for the Azov Battalion, the group continued "to receive arms from U.S. allies such as Israel."

At the time Project Censored first spotlighted this story, the Azov Battalion's connections with American neo-Nazi and White supremacist groups had received little coverage from the establishment media. In May 2019, MSNBC produced a three-minute report, "'Breaking Hate' Extreme Groups at Home and Abroad," which reported on the failed attempt by Andrew Oneschuk, a teen living at home with his parents, to join the Azov Battalion.[37] However, MSNBC provided scant detail about Azov and made no mention of prior reports on US White supremacists training with them.

Update

Since December 2019, the geopolitical situation in Ukraine has changed dramatically. On February 24, 2022, Russian troops invaded Ukraine, escalating a conflict that had been simmering since Russia annexed Crimea in 2014. The ensuing fighting claimed the lives of hundreds of thousands of soldiers and civilians and, by February 2024, had caused as many as ten million Ukrainians to flee their homes.[38] As Reuters and other news outlets reported, the number of displaced persons makes this catastrophe the largest refugee crisis since the Second World War.[39]

The Azov Battalion, which has been part of the

Ukrainian National Guard since 2014, played a key role in early resistance against the invasion and was the primary force defending Mariupol during the bloody three-month-long Russian siege of the city.[40] Almost overnight, establishment media in the United States and Europe began to whitewash the group's sordid, racist past. As Branko Marcetic explained in an April 2022 article for *Jacobin*, in the wake of the Russian attack, corporate news outlets such as CNN and the *Financial Times* began promoting the idea that Azov had "depoliticized itself" and no longer had anything to do with the far-right ethno-nationalist National Corps political party despite copious evidence to the contrary.[41] Even the typically anti-fascist *Guardian*, Marcetic observed, has downplayed the issue of Azov's neo-Nazi ideology in its war coverage. Marcetic highlighted the contrast between establishment press coverage before and after the Russian invasion of Ukraine:

> Before this war, Western media coverage presented a Ukrainian far right that was uniquely well-organized, well-connected to both the Ukrainian state and private benefactors, increasingly emboldened, violent, and threatening to democracy, and on the march in terms of its influence. Suddenly, this same media is now telling us all of this is simply lies and Russian propaganda, in line with the favored talking point of the neo-Nazis themselves. Calling this "Orwellian" doesn't do it justice.[42]

In a June 2023 article for *The Nation*, Lev Golinkin noted that by September 2022, members of Azov had toured the United States, met with members of Congress, and received favorable coverage from MSNBC and other establishment news outlets despite the fact that Azov's press officer for the tour operated a Twitter account brimming with neo-Nazi code words, swastikas, and other White supremacist symbols.[43]

Given the establishment news media's newfound reluctance to acknowledge the Azov Battalion's virulent politics, it is hardly surprising that connections between the Ukrainian militia and violent US White supremacists have still not received adequate coverage. In 2021, prior to the invasion, the *New York Times* ran a single story about Craig A. Lang, an American who fought for far-right groups in Ukraine and was now facing murder charges in Florida.[44] *The Washington Post* published a March 2022 op-ed by terrorism expert Rita Katz, who warned that neo-Nazis in the United States and Europe were leveraging the war in Ukraine for recruitment purposes.[45] Katz described "a surge in online activity by white nationalists and neo-Nazis in conjunction with the war in Ukraine," including recruitment efforts on behalf of Azov. She warned, "Extremists who successfully make it to Ukraine could return home with new weapons and combat experience under their belts." In June 2022, the independent outlet *The Intercept* ran a story about neo-Nazi foreign fighters in Ukraine but did not specifically discuss the involvement of American extremists.[46]

Unprocessed Rape Kits

Emily Homrok, "How Often Do Rape Kits Go Unprocessed?" *Truthout*, October 3, 2014.

Nora Caplan-Bricker, "The Backlog of 400,000 Unprocessed Rape Kits Is A Disgrace," *New Republic*, March 9, 2014.

Taylor Kate Brown, "New Hope for Rape Kit Testing Advocates," BBC, January 5, 2015.

Student Researchers: Jessika Bales (Indian River State College) and Nathan Bowman (College of Marin)

Faculty Evaluators: Jared Kinggard (Indian River State College) and Susan Rahman (College of Marin)

Rape and Sexual Assault: A Renewed Call to Action, a report issued by the White House Council on Women and Girls in January 2014, revealed that nearly one in five US women had experienced rape or an attempted rape in their lifetimes. Furthermore, the report indicated that although the testing of rape kits—forensic exams that collect evidence of rape or sexual assault, including the perpetrator's DNA—can be "vital for the prosecution of cases," a backlog of untested rape kits may factor into low rape prosecution rates.

The White House report cited a 2011 study of more than two thousand law enforcement agencies, which found that 44 percent of the agencies did not send forensic evidence to a laboratory because the suspect had not been identified; another 15 percent said they did not submit the evidence because the prosecutor did not request it; and 11 percent cited the labs' inability to produce timely results. The White House report described a DNA Backlog Reduction Program administered through the National Institute of Justice, which would fund 120 state and local crime labs to conduct DNA testing.

Writing for *Truthout*, Emily Homrok reported that a

five-month study conducted by CBS News in 2009 had found a minimum of at least twenty thousand unprocessed rape kits across the United States.[47] Part of the reason for this, according to the White House report, is because too many police officers and departments continue to hold outdated misconceptions regarding sexual assault, including, for example, "that many women falsely claim rape to get attention." Additionally, "if victims do not behave the way some police officers expect (e.g. crying) an officer may believe she is making a false report," when, in fact, only a small percentage of reported rapes turn out to be false.

In March 2014, the White House announced that its fiscal year 2015 budget would provide $35 million for a new grant program to "inventory and test rape kits, develop 'cold case' units to pursue new investigative leads, and support victims throughout the process."[48] As Nora Caplan-Bricker reported for the *New Republic*, the Department of Justice estimated that as many as four hundred thousand rape kits were currently going unexamined because local authorities could not afford to analyze them. Testing a rape kit costs between $500 and $1,500, so, Caplan-Bricker wrote, "the administration's proposed investment is only enough to make a moderate-sized dent in the issue."

Update

On November 2, 2023, the US Senate voted to renew the Debbie Smith Act, legislation that provides critical funding to speed up the rate of DNA processing at public crime laboratories. Since the Act's first reenactment in

2004, it has helped process over 860,000 DNA cases, including rape kits. Prior to this, the last reauthorization of the Act had been in 2019.

Rape, Abuse & Incest National Network (RAINN), the largest anti-sexual violence organization in the United States, hailed the government's renewal of the Debbie Smith Act as a step toward addressing the rape kit backlog. According to RAINN, "Reauthorization will be vital to ending the backlog of the still nearly 90,000 untested sexual assault kits in 37 states and Washington, DC, as of January 2022. These untested kits are a major obstacle to effectively prosecuting perpetrators and protecting communities."[49] The federal affairs, appropriations, and national coalitions director for RAINN, Samantha Cadet, said completing a rape kit is a long and invasive process. Many victims choose not to complete a kit due to the trauma surrounding their experience of assault. That so many kits go untested adds insult to injury. Cadet said, "When a survivor decides to obtain a rape kit it is imperative that the kit is tested and processed in a timely manner."

Also in 2023, Nancy Mace (R-SC), a sexual assault survivor, introduced the Rape Kit Backlog Progress Act in Congress with substantial bipartisan support. As the *HuffPost* reported, the Backlog Act sought to penalize police departments that fail to process kits or neglect to add DNA information taken from rape kits to the National DNA Database by making them ineligible for certain Department of Justice grants.[50] Unfortunately, then-Speaker of the House Kevin McCarthy (R-CA) did not allow the Backlog Act to come up for a vote despite having promised Mace he would permit it. McCarthy's failure to honor this agreement was the main reason Mace subsequently voted to remove McCarthy as House Speaker, according to Reuters.[51]

Since Project Censored first highlighted this under-reported story in its 2014 yearbook, the backlog of rape kits has received increased attention from corporate news outlets, including *U.S. News & World Report* and *USA Today*.

Despite earmarked government funding, many states are still struggling with backlogged kits. According to a June 2023 *U.S. News & World Report* article, the Justice Department has spent more than $1.3 billion since 2011 towards backlog programs. The article claimed that law enforcement and crime labs across thirty states and Washington, DC, were in possession of some twenty-five thousand untested rape kits. The news outlet investigated changes in the number of unprocessed kits from 2018–2022. As of 2022, Alaska and Connecticut reported no kits, whereas New Hampshire reported only one backlogged kit. On the other hand, Maryland and Massachusetts each had over two thousand kits backed up in their law enforcement systems.[52]

In September 2023, *USA Today* reported that Congressional lawmakers estimated the United States still had more than a hundred thousand untested rape kits. The backlog allowed alleged rapists, some with prior convictions or facing multiple accusations, to avoid accountability and potentially commit additional violent acts. The sheer number of untested kits underscored the need for further legislation to end what has been called an "interstate serial rapist problem," *USA Today* reported.[53]

Despite the persistence of rape kit backlogs in some states, as of September 2023, survivors in most states can now track the status of their rape kits. According to a September 2023 report from the *Virginia Mercury*, new tracking systems in a number of states "aim to address historical challenges, such as inadequate forensic evidence handling, delays in case processing and underreporting of assaults. The systems can streamline communication among law enforcement agencies, forensic laboratories, and survivors." Amanda Hernandez reported that forty states and Washington, DC, have implemented or committed to establishing their own rape kit tracking systems, while Alaska and Florida launched online tracking portals in summer 2023, and Colorado and Louisiana enacted legislation to establish tracking systems of their own.[54]

With a new Speaker in the House of Representatives and more news outlets paying attention to the issue, there is a chance that the Backlog Act can be reintroduced and—with pressure from the public—passed, finally giving rape survivors opportunities to pursue justice in their cases, if not peace of mind.

NICOLE MENDEZ-VILLARRUBIA is a senior at North Central College studying journalism, gender studies, and sociology. She is an experienced writer and public speaker, and serves as co-president of OUTreach, a community for queer students on campus.

GRACE HARTY recently graduated from North Central College with a bachelor's degree in communication studies and a minor in writing.

OLIVIA ROSENBERG is a senior at North Central College studying communication and sociology with particular interests in storytelling and news reporting. She has experience in institutional communication and public relations as well as research writing for the *Encyclopedia of Domestic Violence*.

STEVE MACEK is a Professor of Communication and Media Studies at North Central College and serves as co-coordinator of Project Censored's campus affiliate program. He writes frequently about censorship and First Amendment issues for *Truthout, Common Dreams, The Progressive,* and other independent media outlets.

Notes

1. "7amleh Issues Report Documenting the Attacks on Palestinian Digital Rights," 7amleh, May 21, 2021.
2. Elizabeth Dwoskin and Gerrit De Vynck, "Facebook's AI Treats Palestinian Activists Like It Treats American Black Activists. It Blocks Them," *Washington Post,* May 28, 2021.
3. Olivia Solon, "Facebook Battles Reputation Crisis in the Middle East," NBC News, May 29, 2021.
4. Chris Looft, "Facebook Employees Questioned Apparent Restrictions on Palestinian Activist's Account: Documents," ABC News, October 29, 2021.
5. "Journalist Casualties in the Israel-Gaza War," Committee to Protect Journalists, October 7, 2023 [accessed June 25, 2024].
6. Jessica Corbett, "Gaza Internet Blackout Conceals Israel's Human Rights Violations—and Is Itself One," *Common Dreams,* January 18, 2024.
7. Seerat Khan, "Digital Apartheid and the Use of Social Media Algorithms in Humanitarian Crises," *Global Voices,* November 14, 2023.
8. Yona TR Golding, "Tracking Lost Pro-Palestinian Posts," *Columbia Journalism Review,* November 27, 2023.
9. Priyanka Shankar, Pranav Dixit, and Usaid Siddiqui, "Are Social Media Giants Censoring Pro-Palestine Voices amid Israel's War?" Al Jazeera, October 24, 2023; Marwa Fatafta, "It's Not a Glitch: How Meta Systematically Censors Palestinian Voices," Access Now, February 19, 2024.
10. "Youtube's Impact on Palestinian Digital Rights during the War on Gaza," 7amleh, April 25, 2024.
11. See, for example, Jennifer Hassan et al., "Journalists Killed in the Israel-Gaza War: A Look at the Lives Lost," *Washington Post,* October 19, 2023, updated January 7, 2024.
12. Erik Wemple, "Israel's Shameful Ban on Al Jazeera," *Washington Post,* May 10, 2024; Vivian Yee, Emma Bubola, and Liam Stack, "Israel's Shutdown of Al Jazeera Highlights Long-Running Tensions," *New York Times,* May 9, 2024.

13. Yee, Bubola, and Stack, "Israel's Shutdown"; see also, Vivian Yee and Ameera Harouda, "Two More Journalists Killed in Gaza, Including Son of Al Jazeera Reporter," *New York Times*, January 7, 2024.

14. Callie Holtermann, "Images of Watermelons Signal Support for Palestinians," *New York Times*, December 27, 2023.

15. Alex Arger, "Meta Systemically Censors Pro-Palestinian Content, Report Claims," *Scripps News*, December 26, 2023; Julia Shapero, "Human Rights Watch Finds 'Systemic Censorship' of Palestinian Content on Meta Platforms," *The Hill*, December 22, 2023; Chad de Guzman, "What to Know about Meta's 'Political Content' Limit—and How to Turn It off on Instagram," *Time*, March 26, 2024, updated March 27, 2024.

16. Emma Graham, "Social Media Firms Reject 'Shadow Banning' Allegations on Palestinian-Related Content," *CNBC*, March 6, 2024.

17. Alex Kane, "The FBI Is Using Unvetted, Right-Wing Blacklists to Question Activists about Their Support for Palestine," *The Intercept*, June 24, 2018; and Noa Landau, "Official Documents Prove: Israel Bans Young Americans Based on Canary Mission Website," *Haaretz*, October 4, 2018.

18. James Bamford, "Who Is Funding Canary Mission? Inside the Doxxing Operation Targeting Anti-Zionist Students and Professors," *The Nation*, December 22, 2023; Amy Goodman, interview with James Bamford, "Who Funds Canary Mission? James Bamford on Group That Doxxes Students & Profs for Palestine Activism," *Democracy Now!*, December 27, 2023.

19. Massarah Mikati, "She Was Fired for Being Publicly Pro-Palestine. One Year Later, No One Is Hiring Her," *Philadelphia Inquirer*, August 23, 2022.

20. L. Ali Khan, "Academic Freedom under Attack: The Chilling Effect of Surveillance Sites on US Professors Who Criticize Israel," *Jurist*, November 20, 2023; Rami G. Khouri, "Watching the Watchdogs: Fear in Newsrooms Silences Pro-Palestine Voices," Al Jazeera, November 1, 2023; and MEE Staff, "Palestine at the Centre of Free-Speech Battle on US Campuses, Academics Say," *Middle East Eye*, August 25, 2023.

21. UChicago Jews for a Free Palestine, "The Campus Antisemitism Crisis Is a Distraction," *Chicago Maroon*, January 26, 2024; Owen Ray, "The Canary Mission's Doxxing Needs to Stop," *Massachusetts Daily Collegian*, November 1, 2023; Jewish Voice for Peace and Students for Justice in Palestine, "Columbia, You Are Failing Your Palestinian, Muslim, Arab, Black, Brown, and Jewish Student Activists," *Columbia Spectator*, October 16, 2023, updated October 24, 2023.

22. Valeria S. Macias, "Accuracy in Media Truck Seen near USC Advertising 'Check Your Hate' Petition," *USC Annenberg Media*, January 31, 2024; Lia Freeman, "We Spoke to a College Student Who Ended up on a 'Doxxing Truck' for Her Activism," *Her Campus*, November 14, 2023, updated January 24, 2024

23. Sarah Huddleston and Shea Vance, "Columbia Student Sues Group behind 'Doxxing Truck'," *Columbia Spectator*, November 13, 2023, updated November 14, 2023.

24. Amir Khafagy, "Secretive Organization Targets City Council Member for Pro-Palestinian Comments," *Documented*, March 20, 2024.

25. Teresa Watanabe, "Pro-Palestinian UC Students Feel They Are Not Supported. Some on the Faculty Are Organizing to Change That," *Los Angeles Times*, December 21, 2023; and Brian Bushard, "Billion-

aire Ackman Calls on Harvard to Suspend Students Who Allegedly Removed Jewish Student from Protest," *Forbes*, November 2, 2023, updated November 4, 2023.

26. Josh Nathan-Kazis, "REVEALED: Canary Mission Blacklist Is Secretly Bankrolled by Major Jewish Federation," *The Forward,* October 3, 2018; Josh Nathan-Kazis, "Following Forward Report, Federation Says It Will No Longer Fund Canary Mission," *The Forward,* October 4, 2018; Josh Nathan-Kazis, "Second Major Jewish Charity Admits Funding Group Tied to Canary Mission Blacklist," *The Forward,* October 11, 2018.

27. Christopher Knaus and Ariel Bogle, "Pro-Israel 'Surveillance' Group Turning Attention to Australia, Leaked Posts Show," *The Guardian*, January 29, 2024.

28. "Femicide Accountability Project," Women Count USA, undated [accessed May 9, 2024].

29. "The Shadow Pandemic: Violence against Women during COVID-19," UN Women, undated [accessed June 6 2024].

30. Erica L. Smith, "Female Murder Victims and Victim-Offender Relationship, 2021," Bureau of Justice Statistics, December 2022.

31. "Press Release: More Women and Girls Killed in 2022 Even as Overall Homicide Numbers Fall, Says New Research from UNODC and UN Women," news release, UN Women, November 22, 2023. This report acknowledged that the increased rate of femicides in North America was "in part due to improved recording practices."

32. Mia Alberti and Sophie Tanno, "More than 100 Women Murdered in Italy So Far This Year," CNN, November 25, 2022; Barbie Latza Nadeau and Antonia Mortensen, "Italy Grapples with Its Patriarchal History as Femicide Cases Shock the Nation," CNN, March 9, 2024.

33. Elizabeth Plaza, Fernando Ramos, and Heather Chen, "US Citizen Charged over Alleged Killing of DJ in Colombia," CNN, January 28, 2023.

34. Tom Odula, "Thousands March against Femicide in Kenya Following the January Slayings of at Least 14 Women," Associated Press, January 27, 2024; Ayse Wieting and Suzan Fraser, "Turkey Struggles to Stop Violence against Women. At Least 71 Have Been Killed This Year," Associated Press, March 7, 2024.

35. "About Data against Femicide," Data Against Femicide, undated [accessed June 6, 2024].

36. Antonio Vanuzzo, "Killing of Female Student Sparks Mass Protests in Italian Cities," *Time*, November 25, 2023; Maggie Rulli et al., "Italian Woman's Death, Allegedly at the Hands of Ex-boyfriend, Sparks Outcry against Femicide," ABC News, December 16, 2023; Giada Zampano, "Thousands Rally in Italy over Violence against Women after Woman's Killing That Outraged the Country," Associated Press, November 25, 2023.

37. Christian Piccolini, "'Breaking Hate': Extreme Groups at Home and Abroad," video, 02:45, MSNBC, May 10, 2019.

38. "Full-Scale Ukraine War Enters Third Year, Prolonging Uncertainty and Exile for Millions of Displaced," UNHCR, February 20, 2024.

39. "Worst Refugee Crisis Since WW2 as Ukrainians Flee Country," Reuters, March 9, 2022.

40. Roman Goncharenko, "The Azov Battalion: Extremists Defending Mariupol," DW, March 16, 2022.

41. Branko Marcetic, "Whitewashing Nazis Doesn't Help Ukraine," *Jacobin*, April 7, 2022.

42. Marcetic, "Whitewashing Nazis."

43. Lev Golinkin, "The Western Media Is Whitewashing the Azov Battalion," *The Nation*, June 13, 2023.

44. Andrew E. Kramer, "U.S. Prosecutors Call Him A Murderer. To Ukraine He's An Asylum Seeker," *New York Times*, March 3, 2021.

45. Rita Katz, "Neo-Nazis Are Exploiting Russia's War in Ukraine for Their Own Purposes," *Washington Post*, March 14, 2022.

46. Seth Harp, "Foreign Fighters in Ukraine Could Be a Time Bomb for Their Home Countries," *The Intercept*, June 30, 2022.

47. Laura Strickler, "Rape Kits Data, By The Numbers," CBS News, November 9, 2009.

48. "FACT SHEET: Combatting Violence against Women," news release, The White House, March 5, 2014.

49. "Senate Moves to End Rape Kit Backlog," news release, RAINN, November 3, 2023.

50. Alanna Vagianos, "An Unlikely Alliance in Congress Has a Plan to Fix the Nationwide Rape Kit Backlog," *HuffPost*, September 27, 2023.

51. Moira Warburton, Richard Cowan, and David Morgan, "Kevin McCarthy Ousted as House Speaker in Historic Vote," Reuters, October 4, 2023.

52. Chris Gilligan, "States Struggle with Rape Kit Backlogs despite Funding Efforts," *U.S. News & World Report*, June 20, 2023.

53. Doc Louallen, "New Bill Seeks to Pressure Police Nationwide to Take Inventory of Untested Rape Kits or Lose Funding," *USA Today*, September 27, 2023.

54. Amanda Hernandez, "Sexual Assault Survivors Can Now Track Their Rape Kits in Most States," *Virginia Mercury*, September 13, 2023.

CHAPTER 3

Just Barbie Girls in a Corporate Media World
Saying Kenough to Patriarchal Junk Food News

REAGAN HAYNIE, SIERRA KAUL, GAVIN KELLEY,
JEN LYONS, MARCELLE SWINBURNE, and MICKEY HUFF

> *Either you're brainwashed, or you're weird.*
> —BARBIE (MARGOT ROBBIE), *Barbie* (2023)

> *When the going gets weird, the weird turn pro.*
> —HUNTER S. THOMPSON, *Fear and Loathing in Las Vegas* (1971)

Political trends from liberal to conservative cycle in historical waves, fashion trends reappear every twenty to thirty years (give or take), and even gender roles shift to reflect the norms of a given historical period. For women, there were many transformations in the twentieth century, from the Flappers of the 1920s to Rosie the Riveter in WWII, and from Barbie of the 1950s to, well, Barbie in the twenty-first century! In the marketing industry, the reprise of such patterns and how they are adapted for the public is known as "rebranding." That is exactly what the Mattel toy company has done with one of its most famous products, Barbie.

As it turns out, the doll who once inspired the song lyric "life in plastic, it's fantastic" has reemerged in the past year as a feminist icon (and the plastic now resides

149

in our organs and archeological digs, but that's another matter).[1] Of course, there have been classic rebrands over the decades—Doctor Barbie, Astronaut Barbie, and even Stereotypical Barbie. The 2023 Hollywood blockbuster *Barbie* even showed audiences that it was okay to be "Weird Barbie." In a surge of performative wokeness, including co-opting the slogans of recent social justice movements, the corporate world was ready to rebrand and exploit Barbie feminism.

In this day and age, anyone can be Barbie. And if we look around at our culture and what's happening today, we mean *anyone*. There's International Superstar Barbie, Taylor Swift. She transformed from the humble daughter of a Merrill Lynch vice president to a global celebrity. Talk about pulling yourself up by your bootstraps (Benjamin Franklin Ken not included)! Then, we have Hip-hop Barbies, Megan Thee Stallion and Nicki Minaj. These two have been trading raps and going toe-to-toe in the music world, proving you really can be (and say) anything. Heck, there's even a raft of Congressional Barbies and Kens among politicos in the nation's capital, with talking head pundits in hot pursuit. And we can't forget Warmonger Barbie, also known as Hillary "We Came, We Saw, He Died" Clinton. She transitioned from Mistress Shaming Barbie, following her stint as First Lady Barbie, and has now re-emerged as Election Cheerleader Barbie, though she has also reverted to Shaming Barbie when it comes to telling young people they know nothing about history.[2] Clinton persists in becoming First Female President Barbie, but Mattel refuses to produce this model (they're just not "with Her") . . . and word on the street is that she is just not *Kenough*.

The growth of this Barbie universe would not be possible without the help of the Junk Food News universe. "Junk Food News," a term originally coined by Project Censored's founder Carl Jensen in 1983, refers to frivolous or inconsequential news stories that receive substantial coverage from corporate media outlets. Stories regarding celebrity music tours, rap and hip-hop artist battles and beefs, and trivial political hoopla that constantly fill the corporate media headlines and airwaves serve to distract audiences from more serious topics, including the rollback of women's rights in states such as Texas, the costs of the ongoing Israeli siege of Gaza, and the horrific impact the Department of Defense [sic] has had on the modern climate crisis, to name just a few.

News Anchor Barbie needs ratings, and when, on rare occasions, she actually does cover these more controversial topics, viewers tune out, causing Corporate Media Producer Barbies to promote Junk Food News instead. As it turns out, the media, like much else in capitalist America, is a business—if a specific Barbie doesn't sell, it is discontinued. Similarly, stories that do not draw and retain audiences get the ax, so News Anchor Barbie can play along or clear the way for next season's new model: Influencer Barbie! Citizens in the land of the free just won't be able to see them on TikTok.[3]

Unfortunately, the establishment media's infatuation with Junk Food News and consistent camouflaging of significant stories only continues to grow. And with the US government working to ban the hugely popular social media app TikTok by the end of the year, legacy media will only extend its influence over audiences, continuing to control what stories—and whose—make the news and which do not. As Barbie herself, played by Margot Robbie, notes in the *Barbie* movie, "Either you're brainwashed or you're weird," and we certainly know which option the corporate media world prefers. But as the late great Gonzo journalist Hunter S. Thompson once quipped, "When the going gets weird, the weird turn pro." Let's take a look at this year's Junk Food News professionals and what the corporate media could have been reporting to the public instead.

WAP BARBIE HISS AND DISS: HER MINAJESTY IS OUT, PEDOPHILE-PROTECTOR BARBIE IS IN

This year, we're covering something that might be making a comeback: women's beef in the hip-hop industry. Nicki Minaj, whose alter ego is Harajuku Barbie (and the fashion she promotes), decided to go toe-to-toe with Megan Thee Stallion after Megan released her song "Hiss" in which she dissed rap star Drake (now under rapid fire from Compton-based artist Kendrick Lamar).[4] Minaj seemed to have taken one line in particular personally: "These hoes don't be mad at Megan, these hoes mad at Megan's Law."

For anyone who needs a quick refresher, Megan's Law is the federal law that requires information about sex offenders to be made public. So, why would Nicki be mad about it? Well, her husband and her brother are both registered sex offenders, and Nicki, being the family woman she is, decided it was her duty to defend them in the public eye (even though Megan was never attacking them specifically, but the shoe was a perfect fit).

In a Twitter tirade (sorry Elon, calling it X feels as wrong as defending sex offenders), Nicki did her best to provoke Megan into responding and eventually even made her own diss track response called "Bigfoot," referencing Megan being shot in the foot in 2020 by rapper Tory Lanez, who was later sentenced to ten years in prison for the assault.[5] Unfortunately for Nicki, the self-proclaimed Queen of Rap, her song never beat Megan's in the charts. In fact, she had to make multiple remixes and never got within range of "Hiss," which stayed at #1 on the Billboard 100 for almost two weeks.[6]

Even though Nicki's song was failing, she was getting plenty of support from her fans, the Barbz. Some were stalking and doxxing people who defended Megan; at the same time, others were producing their own rap music, like right-wing commentator Ben Shapiro (thank goodness the *Washington Post* took the time to cover this breaking story).[7] If that sentence just gave you whiplash, then sorry, but we won't be bigfooting the bill. Ben Shapiro was, in fact, featured on conservative rapper Tom MacDonald's song "Facts," and Nicki Minaj complimented it.[8] We know what you must be thinking: Are we in *The Twilight Zone*?

However, Nicki and Megan's feud isn't new: It has been around since Megan collaborated with rapstress Cardi B for "WAP" ("wet a** p*ssy"). You remember that song, right? If not, better hop a ride in Megan's Barbie SUV back to the 2022 Junk Food News chapter![9] It was the song that famously horrified Ben Shapiro. Apparently, Ben hates hearing about women getting turned on. This feud ended up all over the corporate news media as *Forbes*, the *Washington Post*, NPR, and even the *Los Angeles Times* covered it.[10] Of course, why wouldn't two women fighting via hip-hop not make news when the media regularly capitalize on clicks and likes at the expense of women? They even decided to chronicle how the feud was connected to Cardi B because Megan collabed with her back when we were all concerned with what WAP meant and not whose WAP it was. Anyways, Minaj has beef with Cardi B, which means she has beef with Megan. At this point, Minaj is the walking embodiment of that infamous quote from Greta Gerwig's summer blockbuster of 2023, *Barbie*, "Everyone hates women. Men hate women and women hate women. It's the one thing we can agree on."

Say what you will about *Barbie*, that quote is undeniably true. Over the years, there have been many news stories in multiple editions of Project Censored's yearbook illustrating deep-rooted, systemic hostility toward women. To name a few, we noted in the Junk Food News chapter a few years ago how everyone thought it was funny that Kanye West was stalking his ex-wife Kim Kardashian (instead of recognizing it as a form of abuse) or back when Gorilla Glue Girl was teased mercilessly for her honest mistake of confusing hair spray and glue, causing a viral sensation and exemplifying the term "humilitainment."[11] Now, we are talking about a music industry beef between Nicki Minaj and every female rapper that has ever existed. It is almost as if the only thing that keeps people together is a mutual hatred of women (and of hockey mascot Gritty; we don't even know what the "bleep" he is, but we don't like it).

Unfortunately, our old pal Ye, formerly known as Kanye West, is a recurrent character in the Junk Food News universe. So, how is Ye connected to this sad story of everyone hating women? Well, he currently is feuding with most of the key players in this piece (Ye has a beef with Drake, meaning he has a beef with Minaj, etc.), which *Forbes* delightfully decided to cover under "business" for some reason.[12] Ye also announced that he has decided to make his own adult film company called Yeezy Porn.[13] Interestingly, this happened just one month after the state of Texas restricted its citizens' access to PornHub because the internet's most popular porn-sharing platform did not want to institute age verification as required by Texas state law.[14]

It's funny how Texas is concerned with teens being able to access porn when two years ago, the state overturned *Roe v. Wade*. Reports since then show an increase in teenage pregnancy after twelve years of declining rates leading up to the state's repeal of fundamental abortion rights.[15] Perhaps Texas legislators heard and took to heart Japanese myths that blame Japan's declining birth rate on women who choose to focus on careers instead of finding husbands.[16] In Texas, it seems the best course of action is to allow (read: force) women to become pregnant before they even have a chance to start a career—hell, before they even start getting ready for prom. Is it too tongue-in-cheek to say everything is bigger in Texas, including the forced birth rates among teens and new potential job opportunities with Yeezy Porn? No, we don't think so.

THE SNUB HEARD AROUND THE WORLD AND WESTERN FEMINISM'S SELECTIVE OUTRAGE

In summer 2023, Greta Gerwig's *Barbie* made waves, becoming a record-breaking box office hit thanks to its star-studded cast and strategic collaboration between Gerwig, the Mattel toy company, and their iconic blonde-haired, blue-eyed fantastic plastic toy.

Despite its success, the film and Margot Robbie were "snubbed" for Best Picture and Best Actress at the 2024 Academy Awards. This oversight ignited selective outrage from figures like former presidential candidate Hillary Clinton. Clinton's tweet, "Greta & Margot, While it can sting to win the box office but not take home your gold, your millions of fans love you. You're both so much more than Kenough," drew criticism for its tone-deafness, particularly from pro-Palestinian activists and feminists.[17] One user on the social media platform Twitter (X), Hania Tayara, highlighted the disparity in attention that powerful women like Clinton were giving to wealthy Hollywood A-listers while supporting wanton violence harming women abroad, stating, "Women and girls in Gaza are using tent scraps as period products, but let's talk about Barbie! White feminism is gross [...] so is Hillary Clinton saying 'kenough.'"[18] Coincidentally, *Barbie*'s Oscar snub occurred around the same time that reports emerged of sexual violence committed by Israel Defense Forces personnel against Palestinian women. These reports are in addition to the Palestinian Ministry of Health's current death count of nearly thirty-five thousand Palestinians, half of whom are women and children.[19]

According to a United Nations investigation conducted in February 2024, there have been reports of hundreds of Palestinian women and girls arbitrarily detained by Israel Defense Forces since Hamas attacked an Israeli music festival on October 7, 2023. The UN found instances of inhumane treatment, denial of basic necessities, and allegations of sexual assault, including rape and strip searches by Israeli army officers.[20] The report also detailed how Palestinian women and children were deliberately targeted "in places where they sought refuge, or while fleeing," some of whom were "carrying white pieces of cloth when they were killed."

A March 2024 report from *The Guardian* titled "'My Period Has Become a Nightmare': Life in Gaza without Sanitary Products" detailed how sanitary products, along with toilets, baths, and showers, are nearly impossible to access.[21] The shortage of menstrual products has forced some women to resort to washing and reusing them, putting many at risk of infection. Additionally, there is currently only one shower for every 4,500 people and one toilet for every 220 people in Gaza, according to the World Health Organization.[22] Other sources reported that more than six hundred people have been forced to share a single toilet.[23]

Many have argued that the sanitation crisis in Gaza will lead to a rise in preventable deaths. According to Doctors Without Borders (MSF), nearly 30 percent of patients under five coming to the MSF Shaboura clinic and Al-Mawasi health post died of diarrhea or skin diseases.[24]

Independent documentation of sexual violence against Palestinian women and severe lack of sanitary products has been widely ignored by corporate media, except for a single CNN article.[25] Otherwise, nearly every major corporate news outlet, including the *New York Times*, NBC, NPR, AP News, MSNBC, and CNN, covered *Barbie*'s Oscar snub.[26] The corporate media's prioritization of pop culture stories highlights its preference for Junk Food News rather than credible reports of fundamental human rights violations.

Additionally, Clinton, a.k.a. so many Barbies, has been very outspoken about the recently disproven claims that Hamas committed widespread sexual violence on October 7. On November 21, 2023, Clinton responded to a video from Sheryl Sandberg on social media repeating the claims that Hamas routinely raped women during the raid.[27] In her response, Clinton stated, "I agree with @SherylSandberg. Rape is never acceptable."[28] Without noting the lack of evidence regarding these claims, the outrage towards rape as a weapon of war is justified. It is a violent, indefensible act that deserves attention and condemnation—but we wonder why Sandberg, best known for urging women to "lean in" as leaders, has also remained noticeably silent when it comes to condemning Israel's violent assaults on Palestinian women and girls.

The stark truth is that Clinton's outrage at violence against women has never been consistent—just ask the women of Libya. These "feminist" elites have little to say about Palestinian suffering. Hillary Clinton's outrage over *Barbie*'s Oscar snub, juxtaposed with her silence on the ongoing atrocities in conflict zones like Gaza, lays bare the disturbing "worthy" and "unworthy" victims debate perpetuated by the American political and media establishment.[29] This narrative reinforces the lie that violence against women and children in "enemy" territories becomes acceptable when committed by an ally. It seems that Clinton's feminism, like that of many Western neoliberals, extends to wearing pantsuits and pussyhats but stops short of condemning the routine abuse and murder of Palestinian women.

This same criticism applies to much of America's political establishment. As of May 8, 2024, only ninety-four of the 535 members of Congress have called for a ceasefire in Gaza.[30] Moreover, the staggering toll of nearly thirty-five thousand Palestinians dead, seventy-eight thousand reported injuries, and thousands more trapped under rubble is not merely a consequence of seven months of horrific war but also a testament to America's complicity in Israel's ongoing, genocidal assaults.[31] This failure to uphold social justice and human rights is driven by political and economic gain, serving to maintain the interests of the American empire.

The failure of elected officials to unequivocally condemn Israel's war crimes, especially when they serve American imperialism, perpetuates a vicious cycle of violence. We need to demand accountability and genuine advocacy for the rights and dignity of all people.

HATERS GONNA HATE, HATE, HATE SWIFT'S IMPACT ON THE NFL (AND THE ENVIRONMENT)

Taylor Swift owned 2023. From country singer to global pop phenomenon, the 34-year-old cemented herself as the modern International Superstar Barbie. Her "Eras Tour," which consisted of 152 shows across five continents, maintained a massive following. On the tour's first leg, including the first sixty shows across North America, Swift grossed more than $1 billion in ticket revenue, with 4.35 million tickets sold.[32] Beyond that, she has already sold more than $200 million in merchandise, and the documentary of her ongoing tour has earned more than $250 million in sales, making it the highest-grossing concert film of all time.[33] Accordingly, Swift was named *Time Magazine*'s Person of the Year, Apple Music's Artist of the Year, and Spotify's Most Streamed Artist globally.[34] These milestone achievements tell us Swift is far from going "out of style."

But all of that success is forgotten when it comes to her new beau, Sport Ken. It's a "Love Story," baby, just say yes! Taylor Swift, the it-girl of 2023, became half of the it-couple in 2024 after going public with Kansas City Chiefs's tight end (a.k.a. Tight End Ken), Travis Kelce (his job is Sport). Despite her undeniable successes and general likability, Swift proved to be too much for NFL fans, as she averaged twenty-five entire seconds of screen time at each Chiefs game she attended this past season.[35] How dare an adult woman support her partner in a public manner? Mobs of NFL fans were furious over the flicker of Swift interrupting their views of adult men in shiny spandex pants trying to injure each other every Sunday, taking to Facebook and other social media platforms to complain about this travesty. Nancy Armour of *USA Today* explains, "It's funny—and by funny I mean tiresome and lazy—how a high-profile female fan wrecks the game, while the prominent visibility of male celebrities or team owners at sporting events is accepted without complaint. Celebrated, even."[36] Fascinating that these are the same fans who obsess over the fake stats of their fantasy football team and improbable ten-leg parlay bets but are offended at the image of a successful woman supporting her partner.

But time out. Perhaps there is more to it than that. Some NFL purists do not like the influx of Swiftie Barbies into their Sport Ken gridiron world, despite the additional whopping $331.5 million Swift brought to the league, particularly benefitting the Chiefs, last season. Swift's presence also seems to have boosted sales of Travis Kelce jerseys by 400 percent and is arguably responsible for bringing record numbers of female viewers to the game, something the NFL leadership has been trying and failing to do for years.[37] But even more perturbing to conservative, jingoistic American football fans, more than the paltry half-minute on average of screen time television cameras give her during a three-hour game constantly interrupted by commercials, could be Swift's positive encouragement of young people to vote (she is pro-choice, an outspoken supporter of LGBTQ rights, and referred to Trump's presidency as an "autocracy").[38] This spawned wild conspiracy theories among some NFL fans (with the help of Fox News) who believed Swift was a CIA or "deep state" asset secretly working for Team Blue to re-elect Biden. Given the number of "uncommitted" voters in the primaries this past spring, the Democrats couldn't be so lucky. A Pentagon spokesperson shot back at the claims on Fox News, saying, "As for this conspiracy theory, we are going to *shake it off*."[39]

Meanwhile, in a Barbenheimer explosion of misogyny, the Chiefs's 28-year-old kicker Harrison Butker, who was, for some inexplicable reason, giving the commencement address at Benedictine College, told the graduating class that the women receiving their diplomas had been lied to about the importance of education and career and that their only true vocations were to be wives and mothers.[40] Come on, are women supposed to support their partners at games, or aren't they? Chiefs' fans say no, but the man who kicks a ball for a living says it's the only thing they should do! Even the nuns at Benedictine rebuked Butker's remarks, calling them "divisive." But wait, there's more! Butker's own mother is an accomplished academic and medical physicist at Emory University School of Medicine.[41] Irony abounds. One wonders if Butker's mom stayed at home, then maybe he wouldn't be such a misogynist. Just kidding, that's on him, even if he's not fond of his mother's life choices to be a successful professional (or any other woman's, for that matter). And let's remember, a woman's success seems to always come at the expense of her likability and image—just ask the *Barbie* movie.

Further, Swift's commitment to her man does not only come at the expense of her personal image. The environment cries each time she boards her private plane. Experts estimate that her flights to thirteen NFL games over the 2023 season have dumped 138 tons of carbon into the atmosphere, the equivalent of what eighty-three households produce in a year.[42] But that's just the tip of the melting iceberg. As part of her exceptionally successful Eras Tour, Swift flew an estimated seven times around the globe in her private plane throughout 2023, emitting an estimated 1,200 tons of CO_2 in the process.[43] Swift's travels gained so much attention that several Twitter (X) accounts were created to track her carbon footprint. However, it didn't take long for International Superstar Barbie's legal team to shut that down, accusing the account owners of "harassing and stalking behavior."[44]

But, let's be real, Taylor Swift flying to visit her dazzling beau, Sport Ken . . . sorry, Travis Kelce . . . is not the central problem here. It's the other billionaires (besides Swift herself) and CEOs who have spent a combined total of eleven years in the air from the comfort of their private planes since the start of 2022. Accordingly, "the carbon footprint of all those flights [by private planes]—a jaw-dropping 44,739 journeys—would be the equivalent of the total emissions of almost 40,000 people."[45] An estimated 40 percent of all private flights do not even have passengers on board. They are simply traveling to pick someone up.[46] So, instead of being afraid of a popstar, it is time to start paying attention to some of the biggest carbon footprints by billionaires who blame Swift and company alone for air pollution.

Interestingly, the biggest global polluter is neither Taylor Swift nor the other billionaires flying around in their private jets. It is the US Department of Defense (DOD), the Pentagon, that remains the most carbon-intensive polluting institution in the world, responsible for more annual emissions than most countries.[47] How is this even possible? Well, according to Ruqaiyah Zarook of *Mother Jones*, the DOD "maintains more than 560,000 buildings on about 500 bases around the world, making up a large portion of its emissions." The DOD has an extensive network of fossil-fueled ships, trucks, planes, and other vehicles to support its operations, further adding to the alarming rates of pollution and contributing to the climate crisis.[48] Since 2001, the DOD has consistently consumed between 77 and 80 percent of all US government energy consumption.[49]

Where are the Twitter (X) accounts tracking the Pentagon's carbon footprint? Maybe Sport Ken could host a game show to see if contestants can guess where the largest emissions will be next, likely coming soon to a warzone near you. Give us a break, GI Joe. International Superstar Barbie certainly isn't the only one to blame for the climate crisis, so let's not give her a bad *Reputation*.

MAKE ME WALK, MAKE ME TALK, DO WHATEVER YOU PLEASE: RACE TO THE DREAMHOUSE 2024

Much like the lead-up to a championship boxing match, the folks vying to lead the free world know that you have to feed the junk beast if you want headlines. Whether that's through bravado or blunders, the more outlandish, the more you or your opponent trend, and if it means offering up a sacrificial lamb, the media is more than happy to "pause" for the juiciest clickbait.

As the rebrands of Uncle Joe and Combover Ken were running (again) to be the next rich White guy to live in Barbie's Democracy Dreamhouse for another four years, certain vice-presidential hopefuls went on book tours to see who could churn up the most meme-able headlines. Surely this year's winner must be South Dakota Governor Kristi Noem's putting a cap in her own puppy.[50] Hours upon hours of interviews, and then coverage of those interviews, produced exactly the sort of sensational, headline-grabbing distraction that legacy media just loves.

Meanwhile, Trump pulled a page right out of Mattel's marketing bag: While Barbie may have a whole line of pink-themed products, his supporters could grab their very own Golden High Tops for just $399. Or, if ditching the separation of church and state is more up your alley, you can grab your very own Trump-endorsed God Bless the USA Bible for $59.99, which comes branded with Old Glory itself on the cover.[51] Not to be outdone, as blood continued to stain the sands of the Middle East, you could rest assured that the leader of the free world, Joe Biden, would have a strong stance on what flavor of ice cream he was having on his sugar cone as he sugarcoated any talk about ending the war in Gaza.[52] Apparently, ceasefire wasn't one of the thirty-one flavors on the menu.

But that doesn't mean those are the only headlines coming out of the Biden administration. There's always Kamala Harris with meme-grabbing one-liners, like "My mother used to—she would give us a hard time sometimes, and she would say to us, 'I don't know what's wrong with you young people. You think you just fell out of a coconut tree?' (Laughs.) You exist in the context of all in which you live and what came before you."[53] Her ability to go full viral meme probably peaked when she was greeted by Spanish-speaking protesters while visiting a community center in Puerto Rico. Harris began happily clapping along to a protest song she didn't understand was actually directed at her. One protester sang, "We want to know, Kamala, what did you come here for? We want to know. The vice president is here making history. We want to know what she thinks of the colony."[54] It's almost as if she had just . . . fallen out of a coconut tree.

Meanwhile, regarding a woman's fitness to run for higher office, according to "the most trusted name in news," let's not forget that CNN's Don Lemon weighed in early in the 2024 presidential race, asserting that GOP candidate Nikki Haley was "past her prime." She was barely fifty at the time, while both Trump and Biden are considerably older (if that's going to be a thing). Noting that the media's obsession with age is "*a battle as old as time* that women have been fighting forever," media scholar Allison Butler called out Lemon's nonsense: "It is time to stop judging women by their age and presuming that their assumed ability to reproduce (or at least be sexually available) is their defining, or most valuable, characteristic."[55] Barbie would be well into her eighties today, clearly past her prime. Someone should alert Don Lemon to get on the case.

While the talking heads behind the legacy media desks often give male political figures a pass on their gaffes—"What will he say next?"—the reaction to the words and actions of their female counterparts are far less forgiving. Legacy media's double standard treatment reminds us that there isn't just a pay gap that exists between the sexes, but a heavy undercurrent of misogyny.

CONCLUSION

Well, Barbies and Kens, we hope you enjoyed the Junk Food News party. A punch bowl laced with beefs, snubs, carbon emissions, and double standards from Washington, DC—what more could you have asked for? Sure, maybe you wanted actual news coverage from corporate media, but who needs that when there is an opportunity to make Taylor Swift look like the planet's archnemesis or a CIA asset working to reelect Joe Biden while destroying the NFL? Obviously, Swift is an easier target than the male billionaires flying around in their own private planes, not to mention the Department of Defense. But that's the thing: The main difference between powerful men and powerful women taking up airtime is that women inevitably risk something most men usually do not—their likability. As America Ferrera's character, aptly referred to as "mom," expounded in *Barbie*, "It's literally impossible to be a woman."

It's crucial to confront neoliberal feminism, epitomized by women like Hillary Clinton, as we acknowledge the nuances surrounding powerful women. Despite her accomplishments, Clinton remains steadfast in defending and promoting policies that harm women across the globe, such as her hawkish foreign policy on Libya, which has stripped Libyan women of precious rights and led to the death or displacement of thousands within the region, or her advocacy of her husband's 1994 crime bill, which disproportionately harmed marginalized communities, including women of color.[56] Clinton's lack of concern and support for Palestinian women isn't shocking: There seems to be little space in neoliberal feminism when the safety and interests of (non-Western) women are at odds with Western imperialism.

Still, despite ongoing disparities, authentic feminist women are running this world more than ever before.[57] And if the corporate media would ditch the negative narratives that inevitably form around successful women, the public just might shift its attention from rap battles and diss tracks to stories that address the teetering global imbalances we see today. Society expects women to wear an infinite number of hats. We live in a country where a viral college graduation speech explains that a woman's most important roles are as a homemaker and a mother, but in the same breath, condemns alternative routes to motherhood, specifically citing the evils of IVF and surrogacy, and where more women earn bachelor's degrees than men but make up only 16 percent of CFOs in Fortune 500 companies (which is an all-time high, by the way).[58] We live in a culture that creates the façade that gendered differences are shrinking, but men still out-earn women, with a pay gap that ranges between 8 to 27 percent depending on age, industry, and race (how's that for some intersectional oppression?). Where everything is an oxymoron and where womanhood is ... literally impossible.

In Barbie-land, everything appears like an all-around good time: fun, flawless, and free from patriarchy. But just as Barbie-land offers a manufactured utopian fantasy, so too do the corporate media and their peddling of Junk Food News. Headlines are sensational, distracting, and packed with humilitainment, often at the expense of women. Establishment media present a sanitized, simplified version of reality, in which intricate issues are reduced to viral-ready video clips and soundbites, and the latest celebrity hit piece exposés masquerade as multi-part, in-depth investigations that we just call Junk Food News. Beyond the clickbait glamor lies a stark reality in which the complexities of gender, power, and inequality continue to fester. It's time we all said *Kenough* to patriarchy once and for all.

REAGAN HAYNIE is Project Censored's social media manager. She holds a BA in communication arts from Loyola Marymount University and has a strong commitment to freedom of expression and anti-imperialist journalism.

SIERRA KAUL is a current graduate student in pursuit of her Master's of Library and Information Sciences degree. She has spent over half a decade working with Project Censored as both an editor and author. She enjoys horror movies for their calming effects and Rockstar energy drinks for their health benefits.

GAVIN KELLEY is a Cal State Long Beach graduate with a degree in creative writing. He wields his pen as an arts organization administrator and is currently the interim administrative director for the Colburn School's dance program. A kung fu practitioner and a martial arts movie podcaster and fan, Gavin developed a keen eye for Junk Food News after years of studying straight-to-video B movies. He co-hosts the *Martial Arts Mania Podcast.*

JEN LYONS is an instructor of history for several college campuses throughout the San Francisco Bay Area and Northern Nevada. Lyons earned both her BA and MA in history from the University of Nevada, Reno. She spends her free time stressing out over the Las Vegas Raiders and other professional sports teams. She currently resides in Denver, CO.

MARCELLE LEVINE SWINBURNE teaches California, US, and women's history at Diablo Valley College and Solano Community College. Current research interests include the history of clothing and fashion and the history of family life. In her free time, Marcelle enjoys scrapbooking and entertaining her infant son.

MICKEY HUFF is director of Project Censored and president of the Media Freedom Foundation. He has co-edited and contributed to Project Censored's annual books since 2009. Junk Food News analysis has long been one of his guilty pleasures.

Notes

1.   Jack Guy, "Archeologists Are Now Finding Microplastics in Ancient Remains," CNN, March 25, 2024.
2.   Livia Albeck-Ripka, "Hillary Clinton Accuses Protesters of Ignorance of Mideast History," *New York Times*, May 9, 2024.
3.   Bobby Allyn, "TikTok Ban Expected to Become Law, but It's Not So Simple. What's Next?" NPR, April 22, 2024.
4.   Conor Murray, "What We Know about the Nicki Minaj-Megan Thee Stallion Feud—from 'Hiss' to 'Big Foot'," *Forbes*, January 30, 2024.
5.   Anastasia Tsioulcas and Chloe Veltman, "Tory Lanez Sentenced to 10 Years for Megan Thee Stallion Shooting," NPR, August 8, 2023.
6.   Chris Deville, "Megan Thee Stallion's 'Hiss' Debuts at #1," *Stereogum*, February 5, 2024.
7.   Herb Scribner and Anne Branigin, "Ben Shapiro's New Song Hit No. 1 on iTunes: How Did That Happen?" *Washington Post*, January 31, 2024.

8. Conor Murray, "Nicki Minaj and Ben Shapiro Form Unlikely Alliance as 'Big Foot' and 'Facts' Look for Billboard Chart Debuts," *Forbes*, February 1, 2024.

9. Nardos Haile, "A History of Nicki Minaj's Rap Beefs with Other Black Female Artists," *Salon*, February 4, 2024; see Jen Lyons et al., "TikToking Our Return to Normalcy," in *Project Censored's State of the Free Press 2022*, eds. Andy Lee Roth and Mickey Huff (Fair Oaks: Censored Press; New York: Seven Stories Press, 2021), 167–72.

10. Murray, "What We Know"; Olivia McCormack and Herb Scribner, "The Nicki Minaj and Megan Thee Stallion Feud, Explained," *Washington Post*, January 29, 2024; Sidney Madden, "Explaining the War of Words between Nicki Minaj and Megan Thee Stallion," NPR, January 29, 2024; Alexandra Del Rosario, "In Nicki Minaj-Megan Thee Stallion Feud, Nods to Megan's Law Become Diss Track Fodder," *Los Angeles Times*, January 30, 2024.

11. For more on humilitainment, see Lyons, et al., "TikToking Our Return," 159–92.

12. Conor Murray, "Everyone Involved in the Drake and Kendrick Lamar Beef—as Kanye West Says He's Energized for the 'Elimination of Drake'," *Forbes*, April 22, 2024.

13. Charisma Madarang, "Kanye West Announces 'Yeezy Porn' amid Reports of Adult Film Company," *Rolling Stone,* April 24, 2024.

14. William Melhado, "Pornhub Suspends Site in Texas Due to State's Age-Verification Law," *Texas Tribune*, March 14, 2024, updated April 30, 2024.

15. Lise Olsen, "After Abortion Ban, Texas Teen Birth Rate Rises," *Texas Observer,* January 30, 2024.

16. Alana Semuels, "The Mystery of Why Japanese People Are Having So Few Babies," *The Atlantic*, July 20, 2017.

17. Hillary Clinton (@HillaryClinton), "Greta & Margot, While it can sting to win the box office but not take home the gold, your millions of fans love you," X, January 24, 2024.

18. The New Arab Staff, "Barbie or Barbarism? Oscar Snub Stirs More Outrage than Plight of Gaza Women, Activists Say," *The New Arab,* January 26, 2024; Hania | هانياة (@HaniaTayara), "Women and girls in Gaza are using tent scraps as period products, but let's talk about Barbie," X, January 24, 2024.

19. United Nations Office for the Coordination of Humanitarian Affairs, "Hostilities in the Gaza Strip and Israel—Reported Impact | Day 215," OCHA, May 8, 2024.

20. "Israel/oPt: UN Experts Appalled by Reported Human Rights Violations against Palestinian Women and Girls," news release, United Nations, February 19, 2024.

21. Aseel Mousa, "'My Period Has Become a Nightmare': Life in Gaza without Sanitary Products," *The Guardian*, March 5, 2024.

22. "Lethal Combination of Hunger and Disease to Lead to More Deaths in Gaza," World Health Organization, December 21, 2023.

23. "Hostilities in the Gaza Strip and Israel | Flash Update #32," OCHA, November 7, 2023.

24. "Lack of Clean Water Brings Disease and Suffering in Gaza," Medecins Sans Frontieres (Doctors Without Borders), February 8, 2024.

25. Richard Roth, Kareem El Damanhoury and Richard Allen Greene, "UN Experts Demand Investigation into Claims Israeli Forces Killed, Raped and Sexually Assaulted Palestinian Women and Girls," CNN, February 20, 2024.

26. Joseph Bernstein, "For 'Barbie' Fans Online, a Bitterly Ironic Oscar Snub," *New York Times*, January 23, 2024; Daysia Tolentino, "Who Got Snubbed by the Oscar's? Barbie, but Not Ken," NBC News, January 23, 2024; Neda Ulaby, "'Barbie' Receives 8 Oscar Nominations, but Was That Kenough?" NPR, January 24, 2024; Jake Coyle, "'Barbie' Oscars Snubs Prompt a Backlash, Even from Ken (and Hillary)," Associated Press, January 24, 2024; Zeeshan Aleem, "The 'Barbie' Snub Discourse Has Lost the Plot," MSNBC, January 25, 2024; and Sara Stewart, "Opinion: Why the 'Barbie' Oscars Snubs Are So Enraging," CNN, January 24, 2024.

27. Sheryl Sandberg (@sherylsandberg), "No matter what you believe should happen in the Middle East, what marches you're attending, or what flag you're flying," Instagram, November 20, 2023.

28. Hillary Clinton (@HillaryClinton), "I agree with @sherylsandberg: Rape is never acceptable," X, November 21, 2023.

29. The concepts of "worthy" and "unworthy" victims are derived from chapter 2 of the now classic work by Edward S. Herman and Noam Chomsky, *Manufacturing Consent: The Political Economy of the Mass Media* (New York: Pantheon Books, 1988).

30. "Ceasefire Tracker," Working Families Party, May 8, 2024.

31. United Nations Office for the Coordination of Humanitarian Affairs, "Hostilities in the Gaza Strip and Israel - Reported Impact | Day 215," OCHA, May 8, 2024.

32. Maria Sherman, "Taylor Swift's Eras Tour Is the First Tour to Gross over $1 Billion, Pollstar Says," Associated Press, December 8, 2023.

33. Sherman, "Taylor Swift's Eras Tour."

34. Sherman, "Taylor Swift's Eras Tour."

35. Jeanna Kelley, "Taylor Swift's Real NFL Screen Time Is So Much Lower than You Think," *SB Nation*, February 11, 2024.

36. Nancy Armour, "The Thin-Skinned Men Triggered by Taylor Swift at Chiefs' NFL Games Need to Get a Grip," *USA Today*, January 20, 2024, updated January 21, 2024.

37. Emily Dozier, "How Much Money Has Taylor Swift Made for the NFL? Explaining How the Singer Has Generated Millions in Revenue for the Chiefs?" *Sporting News*, February 11, 2024.

38. Caitlin O'Kane, "Taylor Swift Posts Message about Voting on Super Tuesday," CBS News, March 5, 2024; Kirsten Spruch, "A Timeline of Taylor Swift's Political Evolution," *Billboard*, May 29, 2020.

39. Olivia Alafriz, "Haters Gonna Hate: Pentagon Pushes Back against Fox News Conspiracy Theory Involving Taylor Swift," *Politico*, January 10, 2024.

40. Cindy Boren, "In Commencement Speech, Chiefs Kicker Targets 'Diabolical Lies' Told to Women," *Washington Post*, May 14, 2024.

41. Charles Curtis, "FYI: Harrison Butker's Mom Is an Accomplished Medical Physicist," *For The Win (USA Today)*, May 16, 2024; Clarissa-Jan Lim, "Benedictine College Nuns Call Out Harrison Butker for Sexist Commencement Speech," MSNBC, May 18, 2024.

42. Tarryn Giebelmann, "Taylor Swift: Climate Hypocrite or Just the Scapegoat?" LinkedIn, February 20, 2024.

43. Laura Collins, "Taylor Swift Flew Her Private Jets 178,000 Miles Last Year for Her Eras Tour - And to See Lover Travis Kelce," *Daily Mail*, April 25, 2024.

44. Collins, "Taylor Swift Flew."

45. Michael Goodier and Niels de Hoog, "The Jet Set: 200 Celebrities' Aircraft Have Flown for Combined Total of 11 Years since 2022," *The Guardian*, November 21, 2023.

46. Goodier and de Hoog, "The Jet Set."

47. Alliyah Lusuegro, "Pentagon Pollution Is a Global Embarrassment," *The Progressive*, December 14, 2023; see also Fabiola Gregg and Jennifer Levinson, "US Military—A Massive, Hidden Contributor to Climate Crisis," in *Project Censored's State of the Free Press 2021*, eds. Mickey Huff and Andy Lee Roth (New York: Seven Stories Press, 2020), 37–39, also archived on the Project Censored website.

48. Ruqaiyah Zarook, "Why the Pentagon Is the World's Biggest Single Greenhouse Gas Emitter," *Mother Jones*, October 7, 2022; Jangira Lewis, "US Military Pollution: The World's Biggest Climate Change Enabler?" Earth.org, November 12, 2021.

49. Neta C. Crawford, "Pentagon Fuel Use, Climate Change, and the Costs of War," Watson Institute for International and Public Affairs (Brown University), November 13, 2019, 4.

50. Martin Pengelly, "Trump VP Contender Kristi Noem Writes of Killing Dog – And Goat – In New Book," *The Guardian*, April 26, 2024.

51. Claudia Lauer and Jill Colvin, "Trump Hawks $399 Branded Shoes at 'Sneaker Con,' a Day after a $355 Million Ruling against Him," Associated Press, February 17, 2024; Jill Colvin, "Trump Is Selling 'God Bless the USA' Bibles for $59.99 as He Faces Mounting Legal Bills," AP News, March 26, 2024.

52. Armani Syed, "Biden Expresses 'Hope' for Gaza Ceasefire While Eating Ice Cream with Seth Meyers," *Time*, February 27, 2024.

53. "Remarks by Vice President Harris at Swearing-in Ceremony of Commissioners for the White House Initiative on Advancing Educational Equity, Excellence, and Economic Opportunity for Hispanics," The White House, May 10, 2023.

54. Lucy Leeson, "Kamala Harris Unknowingly Claps along to Spanish Song Protesting against Her on Visit to Puerto Rico," *The Independent*, March 25, 2024.

55. Allison Butler, "No, Don, It's *Patriarchy* That's 'Past Its Prime'," *Ms. Magazine*, February 17, 2024.

56. Sharon Donovan, "Clinton's Actions in Libya Took Rights for Women," *Des Moines Register*, January 8, 2016; Udi Ofer, "How the 1994 Crime Bill Fed the Mass Incarceration Crisis," ACLU, June 4, 2019.

57. "Women in Power in 2023: New Data Shows Progress but Wide Regional Gaps," news release, UN Women, March 7, 2023.

58. Register Staff, "Full Text: Harrison Butker of Kansas City Chiefs Graduation Speech," *National Catholic Register*, May 16, 2024; Kevin Brewer, "The Number of CFOs Who Are Women Hits an All-Time High," *Journal of Accountancy*, February 2, 2023.

CHAPTER 4

Bolstering Genocide

News Abuse in Corporate Media Coverage of Israel's Attack on Gaza

ROBIN ANDERSEN

In 2002, Peter Phillips, the director of Project Censored at the time, introduced the term *News Abuse* to identify how big media distort public understanding of significant news events. He recognized the need to look closely at news about the most serious topics in order to identify specific ways that coverage of them deflects criticism of the status quo and ultimately reinforces systems of injustice. Since then, Project Censored has documented how News Abuse helps mold public discourse in favor of corporate agendas at the expense of working people's perspectives and actions. Starting with the 2021 yearbook, the News Abuse chapters I've written have highlighted how, more and more, News Abuse by corporate media outlets enables the exploitation of people and the environment while multiplying racial, social, and economic inequalities. In addition, the most recent News Abuse chapters have documented how corporate media privilege the perspectives of military leaders and weapons producers while distorting or silencing the voices of those who call for de-escalation, peace, and a new world vision.

This year, the practice of news abuse entered new, ever

more dreadful territory. This chapter examines the many ways that US establishment media spectacularly failed to represent the suffering of Palestinians for whom Gaza is home. Since October 7, when Hamas attacked Israel, big media coverage has provided more propaganda than information, leaving the public bereft of even the most fundamental facts about Israel's subsequent assault on Gaza and its Palestinian inhabitants.

Public exposure to propaganda best explains how—at a time when the official death toll in Gaza stood at thirty-two thousand Palestinians, compared with 1,200 Israelis killed—nearly half of Americans did not know which side had suffered a greater death toll.[1] It was a casualty ratio of roughly 26 to 1, which almost certainly underestimated the numbers of Palestinians killed even then.[2]

Additionally, corporate media eschewed narratives necessary for understanding the history of Israeli violence against Palestinians and the long genesis of the conflict, what historian Rashid Khalidi has called *The Hundred Years' War on Palestine*.[3] By doing so, coverage eliminated the context for understanding the October 7 attacks by Hamas. In fact, on May 15, 2023, less than five months before the October 7 attack, the UN commemorated for the first time the Nakba of 1948, which displaced Palestinians during the establishment of the state of Israel.[4]

As Al Jazeera reported, "Between 1947 and 1949, at least 750,000 Palestinians from a 1.9 million population were made refugees beyond the borders of the state. Zionist forces had taken more than 78 percent of historic Palestine, ethnically cleansed and destroyed about 530 villages and cities, and killed about 15,000 Palestinians in a series of mass atrocities, including more than 70 massacres."[5]

Since October 7, 2023, the strikingly biased coverage consistently presented a pro-Israeli frame. Corporate media deflected blame and justified Israel's relentless bombing campaign. As big media engaged in News Abuse, some reporting used familiar tropes and rhetorical language, but other news featured verbal constructions that were less easy to recognize. As we will see, coverage was influenced by Israeli directives and internal newsroom memos that shaped the language and tone and led to mystifications that deliberately blurred the vision of the realities on the ground in Gaza.

From the start, establishment media reported unverified atrocity propaganda, accepting the demonization of Hamas and Palestinians, and uncritically repeated the proclamations of Israeli officials who characterized Hamas and Gazans as subhuman animals.[6] Defense Minister Yoav Gallant openly declared, "There will be no electricity, no food, no fuel, everything is closed." He added, "We are fighting human animals and we are acting accordingly."[7] Within days, the conditions were set for Israel's genocide in Gaza. The rapid timing and the severity of the destruction should have set off early warning signals. Still, the killing persisted as establishment media engaged in News Abuse that facilitated and normalized Israel's crimes of war.

Readers and viewers need to evaluate how media language, frames, and characterizations create meaning and define what is significant and what is not. Editorial choices can distort, illuminate, confirm, or deny our impressions and understanding of facts and events. With this in mind, a News Abuse analysis outlines how to recognize and evaluate misleading terms and verbal constructions.

TERMS, LANGUAGE, AND REPETITION

Media bias in favor of Israel may have been obvious from the start, but how do we identify bias and verify the claims? Let's start by examining news content for terms, language, and repetition, using a systematic analysis of news content from a sampling of establishment news outlets.

Examining three of the most influential US newspapers—the *New York Times*, *Washington Post*, and *Los Angeles Times*—Adam Johnson and Othman Ali of *The Intercept* analyzed more than 1,100 articles from the first six weeks of the assault on Gaza.[8] They identified the key terms used by the papers to describe those killed. In addition, they recorded the context of those terms' use. They found that the papers disproportionately emphasized Israeli deaths, which were reported sixteen times more frequently than those of Palestinians. Of course, this was a complete reversal of the actual proportions of Israeli and Palestinian casualties, with much larger numbers of Palestinians killed than Israelis. This slanted coverage also explains the public's misunderstanding of the disproportionate nature of the killing, as previously noted.

Moreover, the papers reserved outrage and apathy for Israeli casualties. Israeli victims were "slaughtered" and "massacred" by Hamas, and their deaths were "horrific." But Palestinian victims were reported without emotion, often in the language of abstract numbers, through body counts. In addition, Palestinians were rarely "killed" and certainly never "murdered." Most often, they simply "died," and journalists infrequently identified the Israeli military as the perpetrator.

These findings were confirmed in another content

analysis done by University of California researcher Holly Jackson, who also cited the marked difference in newspaper language and tone. One murdered Palestinian was referred to as the "bloodied corpse of a presumed terrorist." By contrast, Israeli victims were humanized, frequently named, and described in relationship to family members and professions, while Palestinians remained anonymous.[9] Overall, research has found that newspaper reporting heavily favored Israel.

Only later would evidence emerge that the double standard in coverage at the *New York Times* was produced by design. In April 2024, *The Intercept* published an internal memo leaked by a *Times* journalist that confirmed the paper had been directing journalists to blatantly skew reporting on Gaza.[10] Written by Standards Editor Susan Wessling, with the help of International Editor Philip Pan and their deputies, the *New York Times* memo laid out rules listing which words were to be used and which were not acceptable. Staff frequently updated these directives. The words "carnage," "slaughter," and "massacre" were deemed too emotive for reporting on Palestinian deaths. Such terms, the memo advised, were used to "convey more emotion than information."

Leadership at the *New York Times* couched the rules as the best way to present the conflict fairly, but what the list exposed, instead, was the paper's lack of fairness and egregious imbalances in its coverage. Looking more closely at the *Times*'s reporting between October 7 and November 14, the newspaper used the word "massacre" fifty-three times when it referred to Israelis being killed by Palestinians but only once to refer to Palestinians killed by Israel.[11] The word *slaughter* is another example, used to describe Palestinian attacks on Israelis, but not Palestinians killed by the IDF, by a ratio of 22 to 1.[12] By that time, nearly fifteen thousand Palestinians had perished from Israeli attacks on the Gaza Strip, Al Jazeera reported.[13] In the "Cruelty of Language," journalist Ramzy Baroud lamented the lost "humanity of 120 thousand dead and wounded Palestinians" who did not figure in the "calculating" agendas of the US news media.[14]

A separate study produced by the media watch group Fairness and Accuracy in Reporting (FAIR) examined the use of the word "brutal" in the *Washington Post*, *Wall Street Journal*, and *New York Times*. The FAIR study found that reporters overwhelmingly used the word to describe violence committed by Palestinians rather than by Israelis.[15] "In doing so, journalists helped justify US support for the assault on Gaza and shield Israel from criticism," the report found. And the designation of the word "terrorist," according to the *Times* memo, was only to be used to refer to Hamas fighters when "describing attacks on civilians."[16] However, Israel's actions against Palestinians were not to be described as "terrorism" even as extensive evidence showed that Israeli forces were consistently targeting and killing civilians, including women and children.[17]

Previously, in January 2024, a CNN directive had also been leaked to *The Intercept*. This one revealed the role Israel Defense Forces (IDF) played in shaping the US network's coverage of the IDF's war on Gaza.

CONTROLLING THE NARRATIVE

The internal CNN directive disclosed that all the network's news on Gaza and Israel was being sent to CNN's

Jerusalem bureau, where it was being shaped by IDF personnel.[18] Quoting a CNN staff member who called it "journalistic malpractice" (another term used for News Abuse), the *Guardian* wrote that CNN was "facing a backlash from its own staff" over the policies that had led to "a regurgitation of Israeli propaganda" and the silencing of Palestinian voices and perspectives in the network's coverage of Gaza.[19] Pressure from the top had resulted in the uncritical acceptance of Israeli claims and a "pro-Israel slant" in coverage.

Though one CNN spokesperson downplayed the revelations, asserting that CNN "does not share news copy with the censor" and that its interactions with the IDF were "minimal," another CNN staffer, who spoke on condition of anonymity, confirmed that "every single Israel-Palestine-related line" was subjected to approval from the Jerusalem bureau.[20] In the aftermath of October 7, CNN also hired a soldier from the official IDF Spokesperson Unit to assist in its coverage of Israel's war on Gaza, *The Intercept* reported. The terms "war crime" and "genocide" were considered "taboo," and reporters were under intense pressure to question anything they learned from Palestinian sources.[21] As David Lindsay, CNN's director of news standards and practices, told journalists in a November 2 memo, "Hamas representatives are engaging in inflammatory rhetoric and propaganda ... We should be careful not to give it a platform."[22]

Additionally, as civilians were killed indiscriminately by Israeli saturation bombing, the IDF insisted that CNN report Israeli bombs as "blasts" attributed to nobody until the Israeli military weighed in "to either accept or deny responsibility."[23] Across the media spectrum, newspapers and broadcasters used the passive voice to conceal where the bombs were coming from and who was dropping them. These revelations confirmed what independent journalists and many others had noticed—that Israel was controlling the war's narrative, especially as it was being presented to the American public by the nation's most prominent news outlets. As Professor Sunny Singh at London Metropolitan University pointed out, "Western media—not just CNN—has been pushing Israeli propaganda all through" Israel's attacks.[24]

As "blasts" and "explosions" turned up frequently in media coverage, identifying this passive language became widespread on social media, with Alan MacLeod of *Mint-Press News* excelling in posts "correcting" news headlines that failed to identify Israeli responsibility for deadly attacks on Palestinians.[25] This pattern became glaringly apparent in the *New York Times*'s coverage of Israel's bombing of the Jabalia refugee camp on Halloween.[26] *The New York Times* ran this headline, "Photos Show an Explosion Has Caused Heavy Damage in Gaza's [Jabalia] Neighborhood."[27] The mysterious "explosion," its destruction, and the crater left in its wake had come from nowhere. Only later, following Israeli confirmation, did the *Times* identify Israel as the perpetrator of the bombings.

By contrast, independent and international news and online footage showed the huge bomb crater, ruined buildings, and stunned, wounded civilians frantically trying to find loved ones still alive under the rubble. *Common Dreams* reported that the "Israeli bombing" left the "Jabalia refugee camp completely destroyed."[28] An Al Jazeera Arabic correspondent describing the scene said, "The massacre is huge ... Peoples' limbs are scattered around everywhere."[29] Alternative media quoted human-itarian actors such as Aicha Elbasri, a researcher at the Arab Center for Research & Policy Studies, who said that "what we are watching today is one of the darkest hours of our time . . . We are watching genocide live."[30]

OMITTING THE CONTEXT OF ISRAELI VIOLENCE AND SUBJUGATION

Instead of offering relevant background and context, US establishment media preferred to repeat official Israeli characterizations of October 7. As Jeremy Scahill reported for *The Intercept*, "U.S. media outlets and politicians have promoted and laundered Israel's claims."[31] While US news outlets, including CNN, called the Hamas attack "unprec-edented," Sanjana Karanth reported for the *HuffPost* that it was "inaccurate for officials and media to call the attacks unprovoked."[32] Consequently, the narrative promoted by the establishment press reinforced the demonization of Palestinians as *others* outside of the human commu-nity.[33] It denied what was actually happening in Gaza by ignoring the long history and ongoing reality of Israel's violent repression of Palestinians.

This "othering" narrative was achieved by eliminating historical context when reporting on Gaza, as the *New York Times* has consistently done. The *Times* memo on how to cover events in Gaza restricted use of interna-tionally-recognized terms and phrases best able to convey what happened before and after October 7. Phrases such as "genocide" were to be avoided despite affirmation by scholars and advocates around the world of the term's applicability in this case. Another contested term, "ethnic cleansing," also accurately describes Israel's intentions in Gaza.[34]

In fact, as Marjorie Cohn, a legal scholar, wrote in February 2023, Israel was moving toward "cleansing" all Palestinians from Palestine, as the new "fascist" government had increased the "collective punishment of Palestinians," which she identified then as a "war crime."[35] Additionally, Israeli leaders openly stated the policy of collective punishment—to make all Gazans pay for what Hamas had done—as Maj. Gen. Ghassan Alian announced, "Hamas has turned into ISIS, and the residents of Gaza, instead of being appalled, are celebrating . . . Human animals must be treated as such. There will be no electricity and no water [in Gaza], there will only be destruction. You wanted hell, you will get hell."[36]

As Project Censored's Andy Lee Roth and Mickey Huff noted in a December 2023 report for *Truthout*, "For decades, U.S. corporate media have treated Gaza's inhabitants as nonpersons, and daily life in Gaza as nonnews," resulting in coverage of Palestine marred by "slant, marginalization and outright censorship" on a range of issues from the repression of Palestinian media, to Israel's detention of Palestinian children, and other human rights violations.[37] The "daily realities of state violence and ethnic subjugation are not typically deemed newsworthy by U.S. corporate media outlets," Roth and Huff reported.[38]

The New York Times also advised its reporters to avoid the use of the term "refugee camp" in favor of other terms such as "neighborhood," as was used in an October 2023 headline that read "Photos Show an Explosion Has Caused Heavy Damage in Gaza's Jabaliya Neighborhood."[39] This substitution runs contrary to extensive

UN documentation of eight recognized refugee camps in Gaza.[40] Before October 7, Gaza housed hundreds of thousands of Palestinian refugees, many displaced from their homes during the Nakba, and UNRWA was tasked with providing aid to some 1.7 million refugees living in Gaza.

KILLING THOSE WHO BEAR WITNESS

While establishment media relied on Israeli messaging, Palestinian journalists doggedly bore witness to the slaughter, even as they were being targeted and murdered by Israel. Their work allowed global publics to grasp the horrors of the killing, which eventually led to international demands for an immediate ceasefire to stop the genocide.

As Israel sought to control the ground narrative, the military targeted journalists and their family members, along with press centers in Gaza.[41] The family of Al Jazeera's Gaza bureau chief Wael al-Dahdouh was killed by an Israeli airstrike that hit their house in the Nuseirat camp where his wife, daughter, and son had lived.[42] Yet Wael al-Dahdouh stayed to cover Gaza. His cameraman, Samer Abudaqa, was wounded by an Israeli drone attack while reporting on the bombing of a school; he died five hours later after the IDF blocked ambulances from reaching him. Al Jazeera filed suit in the International Criminal Court (ICC) for Abudaqa's assassination.[43] In January, a targeted Israeli strike hit the car of Hamza al-Dahdouh, Wael's eldest son, killing him and two other journalists.[44]

Many more Palestinian journalists persevered, despite personal pain, to continue what al-Dahdouh had identified as the journalist's duty to bear witness, to carry "this human message, we are carrying this noble message."[45]

Palestinian photojournalist Motaz Azaiza filmed the death of his fifteen family members, who were killed in an Israeli attack just a few days after the war began.[46] Yet he stayed for 108 days, living under Israeli siege in order to document similar scenes of carnage. In December 2023, he wrote, "Our situation is tragic beyond imagination. Remember, we are not just content for sharing; we are a people being killed, a cause trying not to be erased from existence. Oh, how alone we are!"[47] Motaz evacuated from Gaza in late January 2024.[48]

In December 2023, when *Common Dreams* reported on the call by Reuters, Agence France-Presse, Human Rights Watch, and Amnesty International for a probe into IDF attacks on journalists, it quoted journalist Abby Martin: "They don't want us to see the truth," she said, "That's why they're taking out the journalists."[49]

Journalists killed by Israel were honored on World Press Freedom Day, May 3, 2024.[50] By then, the Committee to Protect Journalists had officially counted ninety-seven journalists and media workers killed in Gaza since October 7.[51] Reporters Without Borders (RSF) reported that "more than 105 journalists have been killed since 7 October, including at least 22 killed in the course of their work," raising the question, "Where is the international community?"[52]

STARVATION, MASSACRES, AND CRIMES OF WAR

By the end of February 2024, as the genocide entered its fifth month, Israel's refusal to allow aid into Gaza resulted in what *Electronic Intifada* called an "engineered famine."[53] This was after the International Court of Justice had ordered Israel "to protect Palestinians in the occupied Gaza Strip from the risk of genocide by ensuring sufficient humanitarian assistance and enabling basic services."[54] As the most vulnerable Gazans—infants, children, the sick, wounded, and elderly—began to starve to death, establishment media used extreme linguistic gymnastics to cloak Israeli war crimes in ambiguity. When outlets twisted headlines to hide Israeli culpability, online platforms erupted in outrage.[55]

For example, on February 29, 2024, more than a hundred Palestinians were killed and hundreds wounded when Israeli snipers opened fire on people approaching an aid convoy carrying desperately needed flour in what came to be known as the Flour Massacre.[56] *The New York Times* published this contrivance as the headline for its coverage of the incident: "As Hungry Gazans Crowd a Convoy, a Crush of Bodies, Israeli Gunshots and a Deadly Toll."[57] Assal Rad, author and research director at the National Iranian American Council, called the *Times*'s headline "a haiku to avoid saying Israel massacres Palestinians that they're deliberately starving in Gaza."[58]

Alan MacLeod of *MintPress News* flagged the term "food aid–related deaths" and also noted that "virtually the entire Western media pretend they don't know who just carried out a massacre of 100+ starving civilians."[59] Linguistic gymnastics were so popular in news headlines reporting the massacre that Caitlin Johnstone compiled a list of them, including CNN's characterization of the "chaotic incident" and the *Washington Post*'s wording, "chaotic aid delivery turns deadly."[60] All these twisted terms were written in service to Israeli denials of the massacre and its deliberate policies to deny Gazans food.

By contrast, independent and international media identified the incident as an Israeli massacre. An Al Jazeera journalist at the scene reported, "After opening fire, Israeli tanks advanced and ran over many of the dead and injured bodies. It is a massacre, on top of the starvation."[61] *Democracy Now!* began its coverage with a clear statement and the relevant context, quoting a UN expert accusing Israel of the war crime of intentional starvation.[62] *Common Dreams* quoted UNICEF saying, "The child deaths we feared are here."[63]

THE USES OF A MYTHIC NARRATIVE, ATROCITY PROPAGANDA, AND NEWS ABUSE

Journalist Jonathan Cook asked what US establishment journalists should have been asking all along, "Is Hamas really so evil, so cunning, so much of a threat that it requires mass slaughter?"[64] In the face of mass starvation, the October 7 narrative of justification and claims that Israeli bombs were targeting Hamas, not killing civilians, had become hard to swallow. Israeli aid blockades designed to starve Gazans to death gradually lacked any apparent military purpose, Cook wrote, "beyond inflicting a savage vengeance on Palestinian civilians." Israel had begun to lose control of the narrative.

As starvation set in and genocide persisted, Caitlin Johnstone's early reflection on the role of Israeli atrocity propaganda remained pertinent. She said the October 7 attacks needed to be framed in "the most shocking and rage-inducing light possible" in order to make Israel's murder of civilians in Gaza look appropriate.[65] Soon after October 7, press reports of atrocities perpetrated by Hamas were so nightmarish that they seemed beyond belief. The demonization of Hamas was bolstered by stories spread across corporate media that Hamas had slit the throats of forty Israeli babies, decapitating many of them.[66] Visceral baby slaughter is classic war propaganda, and similar stories convinced skeptical Americans to support the 1990–1991 Gulf War.[67] Atrocity propaganda about Iraqi soldiers tossing more than three hundred Kuwaiti babies out of their incubators was roundly debunked only after the war.[68] But journalists published the original story uncritically, just as they eagerly circulated the unverified decapitated babies story.

The beheaded baby story was discredited by independent journalists, including Alan MacLeod, who determined that it originated from an anonymous Israeli military source, which the IDF would not verify.[69] Yet President Biden continued to repeat the unsubstantiated claims well into December 2023.[70] In a terrible trajectory from fiction to fact, Israel was exposed for truly committing atrocity crimes against infants. When the Israeli military forced the evacuation and closure of Al Nasr hospital in Gaza, premature babies left in intensive care unit cribs died there, "starving, cold and alone."[71] Seventeen days later, Palestinian TV journalist Mohammed Baalousha captured the ghastly footage of the tiny, decomposed corpses.[72] Baalousha was later targeted by an Israeli sniper.[73] After being shot, he, like Al Jazeera's Samer Abudaqa, was denied medical treatment for more than six hours as Israeli tanks blocked his evacuation.

THE TIMES'S MASS RAPE STORY

In late December, as South Africa was filing charges at the ICJ in the Hague, the *New York Times* bolstered its atrocity reporting, publishing a piece filled with lurid descriptions and what it called evidence of systematic, mass sexual violence by Hamas on October 7.[74] *The Times* immediately came under intense scrutiny, which has developed into sustained criticism.[75] In addition to its reliance on an organization called ZAKA, widely exposed as one of Israel's official propaganda sources, the piece titled "Screams without Words ..." was called a "disgraceful 'investigation'" and shamed for claiming to provide readers with definitive evidence while actually offering no evidence at all of mass rape.[76] But when investigative journalists at *The Intercept* revealed that one of the three authors of the *New York Times* report, Anat Schwartz, was a former Israeli Air Force intelligence official with little journalistic experience who had liked a social media post calling for Israel to turn Gaza into a "slaughterhouse," the piece was met with internal newsroom criticism at the *Times* that shook up its editorial staff.[77]

Criticism of the story from internal and external sources soon reached a fever pitch, with critics highlighting major discrepancies in the reporting. Even a *Times* editorial staffer admitted that "basic standards" had not been applied to the story and it "deserved more fact-checking."[78] With no public editor since 2017, the paper remained silent.[79] But by April 30, 2024, scholars and professors across the country wrote an open letter demanding that the *Times* "immediately commission a group of journalism experts to conduct a thorough and full independent review of the reporting, editing and publishing processes for this story and release a report of the findings."[80]

WHAT REALLY HAPPENED ON OCTOBER 7

A fundamental problem with the *Times*'s mass rape story—and, more generally, most corporate coverage of Gaza—was the unquestioned acceptance of the original Israeli narrative of October 7. But the narrative began to unravel soon after October 7, when investigative reporters uncovered evidence from victim testimony revealing that the Israeli army killed many of its own citizens. During the Hamas attack, the commander of the base at Erez called in an airstrike on his own position.[81] Further, Yasmin Porat, the Kibbutz Be'eri survivor, told the Israeli state broadcaster Kan that when Israeli special forces arrived, "They eliminated everyone, including the hostages . . . There was very, very heavy crossfire."[82] As Hamas operatives fled with Israeli hostages, many Israelis were killed by fire from Israeli helicopters. As Gareth Porter wrote, "No one knows how many were killed by each side, but the 28 Israeli helicopters were firing rounds of 30-millimeter cannon mortars, without any intelligence to guide their shooting."[83]

Additionally, many of those killed during the Al-Aqsa Flood Operation on October 7 were "soldiers or armed police on active duty, not civilians," Mnar Adley reported for *MintPress News*.[84] And as Ramzy Baroud pointed out, Western media rarely reported that many of those "slaughtered" by Hamas had been directly involved in the Israeli siege and previous massacres in Gaza.[85] Such actions are consistent with an Israeli military practice termed the

Hannibal Directive, which does not spare any Israeli who might be taken hostage by the enemy.[86] As Colonel Nof Erez told *Haaretz*, the Hannibal Directive "was apparently applied," and October 7 was "a mass Hannibal."[87]

CONCLUSION

Reviewing establishment media coverage, Chris Hedges observed in March 2024, "The start of Operation of Al-Aqsa Flood on Oct. 7 was accompanied by a deluge of Israeli propaganda."[88] Claims of beheaded babies, mass rape, and other heinous atrocities allegedly committed by Hamas "circulated far and wide," Hedges noted. Months later, experts have debunked the most outrageous claims, but the damage has already been done. Israel's propaganda campaign provided cover for Israel in Gaza, and US corporate media have done similarly, making them complicit in these crimes. The egregiously imbalanced coverage of the genocide stands as a major indictment of US establishment media.

Most of the information and visual documentation that served to counter the establishment media's hegemonic coverage of the genocide originates from sources on the ground in Gaza, including intrepid journalists and the people of Gaza themselves. Without their courage and tenacity, and the information and perspectives they have made available via websites, social media, and independent news outlets, global publics would have remained in the dark, ignorant of what has happened in Gaza and who is responsible for it.

ROBIN ANDERSEN is a writer, commentator, award-winning author, and Professor Emerita of Communication and Media Studies at Fordham University. She edits the Routledge Focus Book Series on Media and Humanitarian Action. Her latest books include *Investigating Death in Paradise: Finding New Meaning in the BBC Mystery Series*, and *Censorship, Digital Media, and the Global Crackdown on Freedom of Expression*. She writes for a variety of online publications including Fairness and Accuracy in Reporting (FAIR) and is a columnist for Al Jazeera *Arabic*. She is also a Project Censored judge.

Notes

1. Brendan Rascius, "Have More Palestinians or Israelis Died in War? Half of Americans Don't Know, Poll Says," *Miami Herald*, March 22, 2024. According to a March 2024 Pew Research poll, 34 percent of Americans were "not sure" about the number of Palestinians and Israelis killed, 7 percent believed they were "about the same," and another 7 percent believed that deaths were higher among Israelis. See Laura Silva, et al., "Majority in U.S. Say Israel Has Valid Reasons for Fighting; Fewer Say the Same About Hamas," Pew Research Center, March 21, 2024.
2. Ralph Nader, "Stop the Worsening Undercount of Palestinian Casualties in Gaza," Nader.org, March 5, 2024.
3. Rashid Khalidi, *The Hundred Years' War on Palestine* (New York: Metropolitan Books, 2020).
4. Emma Bowman and Daniel Estrin, "The U.N. Is Marking the 75th Anniversary of Palestinians' Displacement," WAMC (NPR), May 15, 2023.
5. "The Nakba Did Not Start or End in 1948," Al Jazeera, May 23, 2017.
6. Robin Andersen, "How Big Media Facilitate Israeli War Crimes in Gaza," Project Censored, October 18, 2023, updated December 14, 2023.
7. MEE Staff, "Israel-Palestine War: 'We Are Fighting Human Animals', Israeli Defence Minister Says," *Middle East Eye*, October 9, 2023.
8. Adam Johnson and Othman Ali, "Coverage of Gaza War in the *New York Times* and Other Major Newspapers Heavily Favored Israel, Analysis Shows," *The Intercept*, January 9, 2024.
9. Jackson studied reports published in the *New York Times*, *Washington Post*, and *Wall Street Journal* from October 7 to October 22; also cited in Andy Lee Roth and Mickey Huff, "How Corporate Media Helped Lay the Groundwork for Israel's Genocide in Gaza," *Truthout*, December 2, 2023.
10. Jeremy Scahill and Ryan Grim, "Leaked NYT Gaza Memo Tells Journalists to Avoid Words 'Genocide,' 'Ethnic Cleansing,' and 'Occupied Territory'," *The Intercept*, April 15, 2024.
11. Scahill and Grim, "Leaked NYT Gaza Memo."
12. Johnson and Ali, "Coverage of Gaza War."

13. "Israel Pounds Gaza Ahead of Truce, Killing and Injuring Dozens," Al Jazeera, November 24, 2023.

14. Ramzy Baroud, "Cruelty of Language: Leaked NY Times Memo Reveals Moral Depravity of US Media," *The Palestine Chronicle*, April 28, 2024.

15. Luca Goldmansour, "'Brutal' Is a Word Mostly Reserved for Palestinian Violence," Fairness and Accuracy in Reporting (FAIR), April 17, 2024.

16. Johnson and Ali, "Coverage of Gaza War."

17. Sharon Zhang, "Report: Israeli Army Uses AI to Produce Palestinian Targets for Assassination," *Truthout*, April 3, 2024.

18. Daniel Boguslaw, "CNN Runs Gaza Coverage past Jerusalem Team Operating under Shadow of IDF Censor," *The Intercept*, January 4, 2024.

19. Chris McGreal, "CNN Staff Say Network's Pro-Israel Slant Amounts to 'Journalistic Malpractice'," *The Guardian*, February 4, 2024.

20. Julia Conley, "CNN Admits 'Disturbing' Israel-Palestine Coverage Policy 'Has Been in Place for Years'," *Common Dreams*, January 5, 2024.

21. Boguslaw, "CNN Runs Gaza Coverage;" Conley, "CNN Admits."

22. Boguslaw, "CNN Runs Gaza Coverage."

23. Boguslaw, "CNN Runs Gaza Coverage."

24. Conley, "CNN Admits."

25. See, for example, Alan R. MacLeod (@alan.r.macleod), Instagram, February 6, 2024.

26. Robin Andersen, "NYT Runs Interference for IDF as It Bombs Jabalia Refugee Camp," FAIR, November 15, 2024.

27. Matthew Mpoke Bigg and Karen Zraick, "Photos Show an Explosion Has Caused Heavy Damage in Gaza's Jabaliya Neighborhood," *New York Times*, October 31, 2023.

28. Brett Wilkins, "Gaza Death Toll Climbs as Israeli Bombing Leaves Jabalia Refugee Camp 'Completely Destroyed'," *Common Dreams*, October 31, 2023.

29. "At Least 400 Killed or Wounded in Jabalia Refugee Camp," *Middle East Eye*, October 31, 2023.

30. Wilkins, "Gaza Death Toll Climbs."

31. Jeremy Scahill, "Netanyahu's War on Truth," *The Intercept*, February 7, 2024.

32. Hadas Gold et al., "Hamas Has Launched an Unprecedented Attack against Israel. Here's What to Know," CNN, October 9, 2023; Sanjana Karanth, "Media Calls the Attack on Israel Unprovoked. Experts Say That's Historically Inaccurate," *HuffPost*, October 8, 2023, updated October 9, 2023.

33. Ralph Nader, "Palestinians as 'The Others'," *CounterPunch*, April 22, 2024.

34. Stefan Moore, "Israel's Architect of Ethnic Cleansing," *Consortium News*, April 23, 2024; originally published as Stefan Moore, "Israel's Original Sin: The Legacy of Yosef Weitz," *Pearls and Irritations*, February 18, 2024.

35. Marjorie Cohn, "New Israeli Regime Moves Toward 'Cleansing' All Palestinians from Palestine," *Truthout*, February 12, 2023.

36. Gianluca Pacchiani, "COGAT Chief Addresses Gazans: 'You Wanted Hall, You Will Get Hell'," *The Times of Israel*, October 10, 2023.

37. Roth and Huff, "How Corporate Media Helped Lay the Groundwork."

38. Roth and Huff, "How Corporate Media Helped Lay the Groundwork."

39. Bigg and Zraick, "Photos Show an Explosion Has Caused Heavy Damage."
40. "Where We Work: Gaza Strip," United Nations Relief and Works Agency for Palestine Refugees in the Near East (UNRWA), undated [accessed May 7, 2024].
41. Ari Paul, "Israeli Attacks on Journalists Stifle Reporting on Gaza Horrors," FAIR, October 19, 2023.
42. "Family of Al Jazeera Gaza Bureau Chief Killed in Israeli Air Raid," Al Jazeera, October 25, 2023.
43. "Al Jazeera to Refer Journalist Samer Abudaqa's Killing to ICC," Al Jazeera, December 16, 2023.
44. Al Jazeera Staff, "Hamza, Son of Al Jazeera's Wael Dahdouh, Killed in Israeli Attack in Gaza," Al Jazeera, January 7, 2024.
45. "Al Jazeera to Refer Journalist Samer Abudaqa's Killing to ICC."
46. Menna Osama, "Relentless Palestinian Journalism Brings Gaza to the World," *Ahram Online*, January 14, 2024.
47. For an English translation of one of Motaz Azaiza's social media posts, see Leyla Hamed (@leylahamed), "The latest posts from Motaz, Bisan, Ismail Jood and more Palestinian journalists are heartbreaking," X, December 2, 2023.
48. The New Arab Staff, "Motaz Azaiza Evacuates Gaza after 108 Days under Israeli Siege," *The New Arab*, January 23, 2024.
49. Cited in Brett Wilkins, "Groups Demand Probe of 'Apparently Deliberate' IDF Attack on Journalists," *Common Dreams*, December 7, 2023.
50. Jessica Corbett, "Gaza Journalists Killed by Israel Honored on World Press Freedom Day," *Common Dreams*, May 3, 2024.
51. "Journalist Casualties in the Israel-Gaza War," Committee to Protect Journalists, October 7, 2023 [accessed May 3, 2024].
52. "More than 100 Journalists Killed in Six Months in Gaza – Where Is the International Community?" Reporters Without Borders (RSF), May 4, 2024.
53. Maureen Clare Murphy, "Palestinians Seeking Food Aid Killed as Israel Starves Gaza," *Electronic Intifada*, February 29, 2024.
54. "Israel Defying ICJ Ruling to Prevent Genocide by Failing to Allow Adequate Humanitarian Aid to Reach Gaza," Amnesty International, February, 26, 2024.
55. Robin Andersen, "Flour Massacre Called 'Aid-Related Deaths'—Rather than Part of Israel's Engineered Famine," FAIR, March 22, 2024.
56. Andre Damon, "Israel Massacres Palestinians Seeking Flour: A War Crime Made in Washington," World Socialist Web Site, February 29, 2024.
57. "As Hungry Gazans Crowd a Convoy, a Crush of Bodies, Israeli Gunshots and a Deadly Toll," *New York Times*, February 29, 2024, updated March 4, 2024.
58. Assal Rad (@AssalRad), "The *New York Times* wrote a Haiku to avoid saying Israel massacres Palestinians," X, March 1, 2024.
59. Alan MacLeod (@AlanRMacLeod), "It's absolutely surreal to see," X, February 29, 2024.
60. Caitlin Johnstone, "How the Imperial Media Report on an Israeli Massacre," *Consortium News*, March 1, 2024.

61. Al Jazeera staff, "'Massacre': Dozens Killed by Israeli Fire in Gaza While Collecting Food Aid," Al Jazeera, February 29, 2024, updated March 1, 2024.

62. Amy Goodman, interview with Michael Fakhri, "Israel Kills 104 Palestinians Waiting for Food Aid as U.N. Expert Accuses Israel of Starving Gaza," *Democracy Now!*, February 29, 2024.

63. Jake Johnson, "'The Child Deaths We Feared Are Here,' Says UNICEF," *Common Dreams*, March 3, 2024.

64. Jonathan Cook, "How Western Media Built the Case for Genocide," *Consortium News*, March 22, 2024.

65. Caitlin Johnstone, "People Have a Serious Case of 9/11 Brain Right Now, And It's Scary," *Caitlin's Newsletter* (Substack), October 12, 2023.

66. Alice Speri, "Beheaded Babies' Report Spread Wide and Fast, But Israel Military Won't Confirm It," *The Intercept*, October 11, 2023.

67. Phillip Knightly, "The Disinformation Campaign," *The Guardian*, October 4, 2001.

68. Aziz Abu-Hamad, "The Kuwaiti Incubator Hoax," *Washington Post*, February 25, 1994.

69. Alan MacLeod, "Propaganda Blitz: How Mainstream Media Is Pushing Fake Palestine Stories," *MintPress News*, October 13, 2023.

70. Jeremy Scahill, "Joe Biden Keeps Repeating His False Claim That He Saw Pictures of Beheaded Babies," *The Intercept*, December 14, 2023.

71. Nora Barrows-Friedman, "Israeli Military Left Palestinian Infants to Die," *Electronic Intifada*, November 29, 2023. Also, Our Correspondent, "Infant Corpses Discovered in Vacated ICU in Gaza Hospital," *Sunday Guardian*, December 10, 2023.

72. Wayne Lee (@leerocka), "The journalist Mohammed Balousha documents horrific footage," Instagram, November 29, 2023.

73. Osama, "Relentless Palestinian Journalism."

74. Wendell Roelf and Toby Sterling, "South Africa Files Genocide Case against Israel at World Court," Reuters, December 29, 2023; Jeffrey Gettleman, Anat Schwartz, and Adam Sella, "'Screams Without Words': How Hamas Weaponized Sexual Violence on Oct. 7," *New York Times*, December 28, 2023, updated March 25, 2024.

75. See, for example, my own article, "Investigating the *New York Times* 'Investigation' of Hamas Mass Rape: Narratives of Demonization," *CounterPunch*, February 11, 2024; Max Blumenthal and Aaron Maté, "Screams Without Proof: Questions for NYT About Shoddy 'Hamas Mass Rape' Report," *The Grayzone*, January 10, 2024; and "The Unravelling of the *New York Times* 'Hamas Rape' Story," The Listening Post (Al Jazeera), March 2, 2024.

76. See "NYT's Disgraceful 'Investigation': Weaponizing Sexual Violence against Women for Occupation Propaganda," Speak Up, December 30, 2023; and Corbin Bolies, "*New York Times* 'Reviewing' Reporter Who Liked Gaza 'Slaughterhouse' Tweet," *Daily Beast*, February 25, 2024.

77. Jeremy Scahill, Ryan Grim, and Daniel Boguslaw, "'Between the Hammer and the Anvil': The Story behind the *New York Times* October 7 Exposé," *The Intercept*, February 28, 2024; see also James North, "Extraordinary Charges of Bias Emerge Against NYTimes Reporter Anat

Schwartz," *Mondoweiss*, February 25, 2024; and Bolies, "*New York Times* 'Reviewing' Reporter."

78. Daniel Boguslaw and Ryan Grim, "*New York Times* Puts 'Daily' Episode on Ice Amid Internal Firestorm Over Hamas Sexual Violence Article," *The Intercept*, January 28, 2024.

79. Daniel Victor, "*New York Times* Will Offer Employee Buyouts and Eliminate Public Editor Role," *New York Times*, May 31, 2017.

80. "A Call from the Journalism Academy for an External Review at the *New York Times*," *Literary Hub*, April 30, 2024.

81. Amos Harel, "Failures Leading up to the Hamas Attack That Changed Israel Forever," *Haaretz*, October 20, 2023; Chris Hedges, "What Really Happened in Israel on October 7? w/ Max Blumenthal | The Chris Hedges Report," The Real News Network, YouTube video, 41:52, November 17, 2023. See also Jonathan Cook, "What the BBC Fails to Tell You About October 7," *Jonathan Cook* (Substack), November 2, 2023.

82. Ali Abunimah and David Sheen, "Israeli Forces Shot Their Own Civilians, Kibbutz Survivor Says," *Electronic Intifada*, October 16, 2023.

83. Gareth Porter, "How Israel Leverages Genocide with Hamas 'Massacres'," *Consortium News*, January 6, 2024.

84. Mnar Adley, "The Hannibal Directive: What Really Happened on October 7?" *MintPress News*, October 27, 2023.

85. Baroud, "Cruelty of Language."

86. Adley, "Hannibal Directive."

87. Asa Winstanley, "We Blew up Israeli Houses on 7 October, Says Israeli Colonel," *Electronic Intifada*, December 5, 2023.

88. Chris Hedges, "Oct. 7 and Israel's Propaganda War w/Ali Abunimah | The Chris Hedges Report," The Real News Network, YouTube video, 1:01:49, March 15, 2024.

CHAPTER 5

Media Democracy in Action

Contributions by KIRBY THOMAS WEST
(INSTITUTE FOR JUSTICE), SARAH LEAH WHITSON
(DEMOCRACY FOR THE ARAB WORLD NOW), DOROTHY
KIDD (UNIVERSITY OF SAN FRANCISCO), CASSANDRA
KUNERT (*WEAVE NEWS*), and JEJE MOHAMED
(AEGIS SAFETY ALLIANCE)

Introduction by MISCHA GERACOULIS

Freedom is something that dies unless it's used.
—HUNTER S. THOMPSON

Introducing this chapter during a key election year, in the wake of the thirty-first World Press Freedom Day and the annual release of the Reporters Without Borders (RSF) World Press Freedom Index, the contradiction between the Index's results and the meaning of the celebrated day is hard to miss. Each year since 1993, the third of May reminds governments of their duty to protect press freedom. Ironically, the Index's findings have determined political pressures to be press freedom's most grievous threat. In the United States, this pressure manifests in the concentration of corporately owned and partisan media and the expanse of news deserts. Of the 180 nations ranked by the index, the United States fell from forty-fifth place in 2023 to fifty-fifth in 2024, revealing the combined political and economic deterrents to the democratic functioning of the press and the public's right to know.

With high-stakes elections taking place around the world in 2024, political pressures are testing the limits of press freedom. The hyper-partisan media framing of the 2024 US presidential election campaign is a case in point, though not an unprecedented one.

When American journalist Hunter S. Thompson (1937–2005) hit the campaign trail in 1972, he went "gonzo." He believed that accurately reporting events meant actively participating in whatever scenario he encountered. While covering the Nixon and McGovern presidential campaigns, Thompson felt that realistic reporting on then-president Richard Nixon required subjectivity. Granted, Thompson's subjective lens was often blurred by intoxicants; still, he insisted there's no such thing as objective journalism. The phrase itself, he asserted, is a "pompous contradiction in terms."[1] Given that approximately 90 percent of media in the US is owned by just six corporations and that reporting consequently skews toward one partisan agenda or another, Thompson made a valid observation. In a 1997 interview with *The Atlantic*, he went further, explaining, "Objective journalism is one of the main reasons American politics has been allowed to be so corrupt for so long."[2]

The obvious check on said corruption is free, independent, ethical journalism that holds power to account and upholds the public's right to be informed. Kirby Thomas West, an attorney specializing in constitutional rights, explains in this chapter that the right to information is a foundational right that underpins all others. Describing the purpose of the Freedom of Information Act (FOIA) to protect the public interest, she discusses how journalists and public advocacy lawyers help check government officials' power through FOIA records requests. West gives the example of a case in which her nonprofit law firm assisted a news outlet in exposing egregious abuses of power that voters and taxpayers deserved to know. Public records, she asserts, while not always readily handed over, make FOIA indispensable to democratic processes.

Sarah Leah Whitson, executive director of Democracy for the Arab World Now, addresses the effect that Israel's war on Gaza has on democratic principles presumed sacrosanct in the United States. She points out that despite deep-reaching pro-Israel efforts in the US Congress, in American work-places, and on college campuses that seek to silence calls for ceasefire and divestment, public support for Palestine only continues to grow. Speaking to social media's power to make visible the popular movements advocating for peace and jus-tice in Palestine, Whitson examines the citizen pushback concerning attacks on US First Amendment rights.

Thompson's political reporting in *Fear and Loathing on the Campaign Trail '72* emerged from a violent era awash in abuses of power by the Nixon Administration, the Vietnam War, political assassinations, race riots, and the Kent State massacre. He refuted the era's prevailing notion that "kids are turned off from politics" and wouldn't bother to vote. Thompson wrote that the "youth vote [held] the fate of the nation in the palms of their hands." Similarly recognizing the agency of today's youth vote, Whitson posits the impact that youth-led demonstrations and social media movements may have on the outcome of the US presidential election.

At present, college students, independent journal-ists and media outlets, and citizen voices of conscience are uniting to hold the Biden Administration and the nation's universities accountable for aiding Israel's war on Gaza. Not unlike in Thompson's day, the very political and university leaders alleged to be guardians of press and academic freedoms instead exert their power to suppress those rights. Resisting that trend is Dorothy Kidd, professor of media studies at the University of San Francisco. Her essay describes how contemporary students' access to an array of digital tools allows for greater participation in movements to counter systemic problems, such as racism and gender violence, and to conduct anti-war protests. Bringing critical media analysis to her courses through "media-active dojo" practices, Kidd challenges dominant media structures and political narratives and assists students in learning how to organize for social change. With these skills, digital citizens and media creators have the potential to rival the power of the corporate media.

Commenting on the media environment of his time, Thompson speculated that between the fine line of "democratizing journalism and every man a journalist is some spectrum of reliability" not always evident in so-called straight reporting by the establishment press.[3] Cassandra Kunert, editor and writer with *Weave News*, describes the organization's grassroots journalism in comparable terms. Not full-on gonzo, per se, reporters with *Weave News* are nevertheless encouraged to incorporate their own perspectives and experiences into their reporting. Kunert elaborates on how this tack sheds light on viewpoints and subjects often overlooked by the corporate press. Under no obligation to conform to corporate mandates or political forces, citizen journalism has a democratizing effect on the "spectrum of reliability."

Much to the disservice of American democracy, newsroom layoffs and closures increase news media partisanship and decrease the public's access to a plurality of reliable news and information. Add to this the proliferation of content generated by artificial intelligence, and the need for ethical journalism, freedom of information, online safety, and critical media literacy has never been starker.

Jeje Mohamed, co-founder of Aegis Safety Alliance, addresses these issues in an article that connects the protection of journalists with the protection of democracy. Protection of each requires expanding diversity, equity, and inclusivity in the fields of journalism and safety and security. Mohamed's work to equip journalists, newsrooms, and human rights groups with online and in-the-field safety training helps ensure that journalists and others can safely do their jobs and defend press freedom.

If freedom, as Thompson pronounced, dies from lack of use, then the 2025 Media Democracy in Action chapter pays homage to those committed to keeping it alive. The individuals and organizations featured here exemplify journalism as an exercise in freedom, and they reaffirm the resilience of media in service to democracy.

FOIA IS AN INSTRUMENT FOR DEMOCRACY

KIRBY THOMAS WEST

In September 2018, Carter Walker, then working as a reporter for *LNP,* a daily newspaper based in Lancaster, Pennsylvania, submitted a public records request to the Lancaster County District Attorney's Office under Pennsylvania's Right-to-Know Law, the state's equivalent to the federal Freedom of Information Act (FOIA). He sought various records related to the office's use of civil asset forfeiture, a process by which the government can permanently take property allegedly connected to criminal activity—often without regard to the guilt or innocence of the actual property owner. Problematically, civil forfeiture also often involves a perverse financial incentive for law enforcement, with offices keeping forfeiture proceeds. Carter wanted to investigate this process, including what kind of property the Lancaster DA's office obtained through forfeiture, how much money the office generated from forfeitures, and what the office ultimately did with those funds. The DA's office denied Carter's request, citing an array of exceptions to the Right-to-Know Law. Carter successfully appealed to the Pennsylvania Office of Open Records, but the DA's office appealed in return, stonewalling Carter's attempts to shed light on the civil forfeiture process.

Carter's experience is one familiar to too many journalists. When holding government officials accountable, few tools in a journalist's toolbelt are as crucial as public records requests. They can provide a look behind the curtain at how the government really functions and insight into key decision-makers' behaviors (and misbehaviors). Despite this critical importance—or perhaps more accurately, because of it—obtaining government records is rarely as easy as submitting a simple request. Government agencies and officials often balk at releasing records and come up with creative arguments about why they should not have to.

Few outside the world of journalism appreciate this frustration as much as my organization, the Institute for Justice—a nonprofit public interest law firm focused on defending constitutional rights. Our strategic research department relies on records requests for numerous reports and projects that provide transparency into government processes and make sense of data. Records requests are also valuable to our litigation team. We rely on the reports and data our strategic research team compiles in litigation. We are also sometimes alerted to abuses of constitutional rights through the work of journalists relying on public records requests. Their investigations connect us to clients whose rights we can vindicate through litigation. We became interested in Carter's case in 2019 for all these reasons and because his reporting sought to shine a light on the process of civil forfeiture—the many abuses of which the Institute for Justice has documented and combatted for a decade. We agreed to take on Carter and LNP as clients and help them win the records in court.

Soon after the Institute for Justice stepped in, the DA's office backtracked and handed over most of the documents Carter requested. However, they still refused to provide one category of documents identifying who purchased forfeited property at public auctions, citing the right to privacy protected by the Pennsylvania Constitution. The Pennsylvania Commonwealth Court, Pennsylvania's intermediate court of appeals, ultimately rejected the office's argument. The decision weighed the minimal privacy intrusion of identifying individuals who attended public auctions against the "significant public interest in ensuring that law enforcement officials not participate as bidders in the auction to their personal benefit" and ordered that the office turn over the requested records. Carter finally obtained the full array of requested records in 2021, nearly three years after his initial request.

The full value of Carter's perseverance became evident two years later, in 2023. During the litigation for the forfeiture documents, the District Attorney at the time had testified that Lancaster's Drug Task Force kept almost no records related to its seizures of cash, though he "presume[ed] that they put it in some secure location."[4] This lax policy led to the disappearance of $28,000 in 2020.[5] In the wake of this disappearance, and Carter's legal win in his public records case, the new District Attorney opened an investigation into how the Drug Task Force maintained seized cash. That investigation ultimately concluded that the officer in charge of the Lancaster County Drug Task Force had been stealing seized cash from the agency's safe. In March 2023, the officer pleaded guilty to stealing approximately $171,000 over six years.[6] Carter's work showed how essential transparency is in civil forfeiture. The case also demonstrated how sometimes the records that *don't* exist reveal the whole story.

For journalists and public interest lawyers alike, public records requests are a valuable way to find and expose abuses of power. Ideally, the knowledge that they are being watched encourages government officials to behave in a way befitting their offices. More importantly, the information produced as a result of records requests can reveal when government officials fall short of the public's expectations. Obtaining these public records is often difficult, but it is worth the fight. As Justice Louis Brandeis famously said, "Sunlight is ... the best of disinfectants."[7] Sometimes a little litigation helps, too.

KIRBY THOMAS WEST is an attorney at the Institute for Justice (IJ), where she litigates cases defending First Amendment rights, property rights, and educational choice. She is also the co-director of IJ's National Initiative to End Forfeiture Abuse.

EXPANDING PUBLIC SUPPORT FOR PALESTINIAN RIGHTS AND THE COUNTEROFFENSIVE TO QUASH IT

SARAH LEAH WHITSON

Since the start of the war in Gaza, the unprecedented out-pouring of public support for Palestinians, in both major urban centers and small towns across the United States, has taken experts on Israel/Palestine politics—and likely Israel and its backers—by surprise. Across the world, there have been approximately ten thousand protests and actions demanding a ceasefire and urgent aid to Palestin-ians, a wholesale reevaluation of fixed support for Israel, and recognition of Israel as an apartheid settler-colonial state. On the heels of explosive numbers of pro-Palestine posts on social media and exposés in the alternative and independent press, journalists, artists, musicians, writers, actors, athletes, and celebrities have joined the ground-swell of support.

As of May 2024, Israel has killed at least 34,735 Pales-tinians—including more than 14,500 children and 9,500 women—according to the UN Office for the Coordina-tion of Humanitarian Affairs.[8] To put these numbers into perspective, in the first three weeks of the war, the number of children Israel had killed in Gaza surpassed the annual number of children killed in all global conflict zones for every year since 2019. Today, millions of Gazans face imminent starvation due to Israel's deliberate obstruction of humanitarian aid as it continues to bomb the hospitals, schools, churches, mosques, and residential homes still standing in the south of the tiny territory.

As the unavoidable facts of Israel's war in Gaza flood

social media hour by hour, day by day, sympathy for Palestinians among mainstream America has grown. A majority of Americans support an immediate ceasefire despite persistent opposition from the Biden administration, reflected in its first three vetoes against UN Security Council ceasefire resolutions and push for $14 billion more in weapons to Israel to support its war effort.[9]

It's most curious that the shift in opinions on Israel is happening *despite* the well-documented establishment media bias against Palestinians that has downplayed or ignored their suffering and abuse at Israeli hands and highlighted Israeli suffering in gross disproportion to the number of victims on each side. Though pro-Israeli media bias has been a long-standing trend in the Western mediascape, it has become more apparent since October 2023. From October 7 to November 7, for example, major US news channels mentioned Israelis and Israeli victims almost four times as often as Palestinians, even though "Palestinian casualties far surpassed Israelis."[10] Establishment media have buried information about child victims, mentioning them in "only two out of more than 1,100 news articles published from October 7 to November 25, a period in which the Israeli military killed 6,000 children in Gaza."[11] And centrist news talk shows have overwhelmingly featured only pro-Israeli guests.

In contrast, Palestinian eyewitnesses on the ground, citizen journalists, progressive analysts commenting on social media, and alternative and independent news media stations have shared a stream of information and advocacy in support of Palestinians. Instagram, Facebook, and Twitter (X) have seen a profusion of calls for a ceasefire and an end to Israel's apartheid rule, but TikTok is where the outpouring of youth support has been overwhelmingly pro-Palestine. Independent media publications, such as *Middle East Eye*, Al Jazeera, and *The Intercept*, have also operated free of the controls and restrictions routinely used to silence criticism of Israel and have produced investigations that expose Israeli atrocities and disassembled the official Israeli narratives.

These media outlets have provided necessary platforms for unfiltered facts and unmediated Palestinian and pro-Palestinian voices—from the victims of this latest war to marginalized experts critical of Israel—to share information and analysis directly to, and engage in dialogue with, global media consumers. They demonstrate a growing gap between the opinions of the general public, on the one hand, and establishment media that has traditionally served as a mouthpiece for the United States and Israel, on the other. This gap illustrates the importance of independent media and citizen journalism in reflecting and shaping public opinion.

Multi-Pronged Attack against Advocacy for Palestinian Rights

In response to the diminishing support for Israel among Americans, the Israeli government and its backers have pushed back aggressively to mixed results. Wielding Israeli state propaganda termed *hasbara*, they have tried to saturate the media with partisan views about the war, pinning blame for the shocking Palestinian death toll on Hamas and promulgating false allegations about Hamas atrocities, such as beheaded babies, babies baked in ovens, unborn babies cut from wombs, and mass systematic rape of women.[12]

Recognizing its faltering efforts to persuade the public, the Israeli regime has stepped up tactics to suppress pro-Palestine voices. In a desperate gambit to contain the shifting cultural tide, existing legislative and regulatory efforts have been bolstered to sanction pro-Palestine speech as "antisemitic" and to censure, censor, and punish students, academics, artists, and even employees in non-political industries.

The legal strategy to stifle pro-Palestine speech has relied on the passage and enforcement of anti-Boycott, Divestment and Sanction laws in at least thirty US states to punish those who advocate for a boycott of Israel. Those who refuse to sign a pledge to never advocate for a boycott of Israel can face personal retribution, employment terminations, and denial of jobs or contracts.[13] This strategy has also focused on expanding an official adoption of the International Holocaust Remembrance Alliance's "working definition" of antisemitism as a means to censor speech critical of Israel.[14] Even before the war in Gaza, the federal government, many states, and several public and private universities had adopted the expanded definition to chill criticism of Israel.

The naked exercise of power and control by pro-Israel university board directors and industry leaders has forced the heads of two leading universities, Harvard and the University of Pennsylvania, to resign, essentially for failing to curb student protests of the war in Gaza.[15] Celebrities critical of the war have been fired by their agencies or lost roles in film and television, and students have been attacked in elaborate public campaigns to discredit them individually.[16] Law students have lost opportunities from major law firms; movie industry executives, doctors, tech workers, writers, editors, artists, and musicians have lost their jobs, performance engagements, and representation for taking a pro-Palestinian stance.[17] Displays of cultural symbols associated with Palestine, such as a scarf known as the *keffiyeh*, have also led to bans and punishments.[18]

Under pressure from groups such as the pro-Israel Anti-Defamation League, Meta and its subsidiaries, Facebook and Instagram, have censored hundreds of pro-Palestine accounts and shadowbanned posts about Gaza. As a Chinese-owned company, TikTok has largely been immune to this pressure. Now facing a total ban in the United States, TikTok's refusal to censor posts supportive of Palestinian rights may be the motivation.

The implications of these censorship efforts go well beyond limiting support for Palestinians. They represent the most widespread, severe attack on First Amendment rights ever seen in this country, far exceeding the McCarthyite campaign both in scope and scale and reaching further than the current efforts to ban books on race and gender.

Suppose there's a silver lining in all this. In that case, it is witnessing the resistance and courage of a whole new generation of people around the world, including Americans nationwide and journalists and media organizations, who refuse to be bullied and silenced, and insist on standing for what they believe in despite the costs.

SARAH LEAH WHITSON is the Executive Director of Democracy for the Arab World Now and served as the executive director of Human Rights Watch's Middle East and North Africa Division from 2004 to 2020. Sarah Leah has led dozens of advocacy and investigative missions throughout the region, focusing on issues of armed conflict, accountability, legal reform, migrant workers, and human rights. She is widely published on human rights and foreign policy in the Middle East in international and regional media, including the *New York Times*, *Foreign Affairs*, the *Washington Post*, *Foreign Policy*, the *Los Angeles Times*, and CNN, and appears regularly on Al Jazeera, BBC, NPR, MSNBC, and CNN.

THE MEDIA-ACTIVE DOJO APPROACH TO MEDIA STUDIES

DOROTHY KIDD

I have long faced a conundrum in the media studies classroom. If enrolling students want to create their own media stories, they often expect to get job training, and almost always bring imaginations shaped by the neoliberal logic and capitalist production practices of Silicon Valley, Hollywood, K-pop, and TikTok. Their expectations are, of course, understandable, as students are responding to both the high cost of tuition and basic living expenses and our university administration's neoliberal focus and promotion of our programs as vocational training for corporate workplaces.

Nevertheless, I have noticed a shift since the COVID-19 lockdown of 2020. More students are open to critical discussions about the corporate media industries and capitalism. They want to apply their media-making skills to critique and construct alternatives to the dominant mediascape. If the COVID crisis sped up the incursion of communicative capitalism into all of our lives, it also allowed students to take greater advantage of a wide range of digital tools and communicative possibilities and to learn from the increased visibility of movements against racism and gender violence, and for ecological concerns, labor organizing, and anti-war protests.

I have taught media studies at a Jesuit university in San Francisco for more than two decades and have long employed many of the cardinal elements of critical media literacy. During the first days of the COVID pandemic, I re-read Lori Bindig Yousman's call to advocate for critical media literacy by using *intellectual judo* with neoliberal administrators.[19] Playing with her idea, I have been experimenting with what I call the *media-active dojo* approach in my courses to address the conundrum. Briefly, the approach consists of creating a collaborative learning space where we build skills that address students' current and future situations and contradictions as digital consumers, media-makers, and citizens in the contemporary capitalist media ecology.

The Shift to a New Media-Historic Era

When I began teaching in the United States two decades ago, we lived in a very different global mediascape. The capitalist digital platforms of Silicon Valley were not yet ascendant, and we had far less media-making capacity and less access to the reams of critical information we now take for granted, including sites for social movement mobilization. In that earlier media-historic era, I addressed students more as citizens and designed lessons and exercises to consider the openings and closings of the democratic public sphere. Teaching in the San Francisco Bay Area during a historical upswing of media reform, we drew from those media reforms and connected to the exemplary work of alternative and citizen media activists, and media policy advocates and reformers through the classroom, field visits, and collaborative research projects.

Most students became good at media criticism. They learned how to critique the capitalist mandates of media industries, deconstruct media texts, and discern targeted consumerist, racist, sexist, and gender-biased messages. Students discovered alternatives in the media-making and social justice fields. Our discussions, however, often seemed too abstract to engage every student.

The COVID-19 Emergency

Fast-forward to March 2020 when campuses shut down, forcing most students to return home. Rather than learn the new corporate educational software recommended by my administration, I picked up a much older yet more useful text, *A Pedagogy for Liberation*. In a section titled, "Starting with Reality in Order to Overcome It," Paulo Freire and Ira Shor discussed Freire's critical pedagogical praxis, which started by listening to learners, asking about their everyday encounters with capitalist domination and discerning their central problems with power.[20] Taking students' realities as the object under investigation, Freire would then design a space for collaborative problem-posing with the goal of developing actions to confront those realities.

The Media-Active Dojo

In the traditional martial arts *dojo*, students train in a combination of classical skills and tactical moves, learning how to visualize, find cracks in an opponent's power, and improvise to redirect an attacker's movements and turn their energy against them. In the *media-active dojo*, students learn critical analysis to assess capitalist media power, workshop classical tactics derived from alternative and activist media movements and advocates for change, and experiment with new adaptations. The aim is for students to reflect on and analyze their own mediated experiences and contradictions as producers, consumers, and citizens, and to gain new strategies to better act individually and collectively in their current and future mediatized lives.

The COVID-19 emergency made the *media-active dojo* approach even more necessary. Although the capitalist platforms—Google, Facebook, Apple, and Amazon—have dominated the global mediascape for more than a decade, the scope and scale of their control increased dramatically when millions, including and especially our students, migrated online in 2020. In this new mediascape, young people are finding most of their news and information via social media sites.[21] They are not only targeted by advertisers, as in the old media economy, but have become the principal targets of the platform capitalist corporations that depend on them to create and circulate valuable content and to recruit others in order to supply the data to sell to advertisers, brands, and many other companies.

For these reasons, each course I teach is designed to collectively consider current case studies from ongoing contests over power within the media ecology based on those that students bring forward from their own experiences and interests. We consider the varying values, goals, strategies, and practices of the dominant media and information corporations, as well as public service media, and alternative and citizens' media and social movement communicators. The students then produce research projects in their choice of media formats that include an analysis of the problem and a consideration of the community, citizen, and social justice groups that are organizing to make change with respect to those political, economic, and cultural problems. Finally, everyone shares their findings in a class showcase.

As I write this in spring 2024, we face many urgent mediated political and economic crises. I remind myself of Freire's words: The transforming teacher needs to realize that changing education and society is a very long haul. Critique alone—understanding how society works and how power operates—is not enough to navigate the material and digital power of capitalist systems and ideologies. We need to learn how to organize and construct change. To that point, I am heartened by my students' embrace of the media-active dojo approach, their curiosity about the historic and contemporary media practices of social change groups, and especially their enthusiasm for building community as they search for just and sustainable openings as media-makers and citizens.

Acknowledgment

I respectfully acknowledge that I live and work on the traditional territory of the Ramaytush Ohlone in San Francisco, California. Today, the San Francisco Bay is the meeting place of many Indigenous people from across Turtle Island, and I am grateful to have the opportunity to live on this land.

DOROTHY KIDD has been teaching media studies for more than thirty years in San Francisco, USA, and Vancouver, Canada, to which she brings a background of alternative media production, feminist popular education, Indigenous broadcast training, and transnational media activism.

WEAVING THE STREETS: DEMOCRATIZING MEDIA THROUGH GRASSROOTS JOURNALISM

CASSANDRA KUNERT

Weave News was founded in 2007 by John Collins, professor of global studies at St. Lawrence University (SLU), and his students with the mission of empowering citizen journalists to fill gaps left by establishment media coverage. Since its inception as an investigative group blog at a small liberal arts college in northern New York, *Weave News* has grown into a global network of journalists committed to upholding democratic principles through grassroots media-making. At its heart, *Weave News* is an organization of independent writers, editors, podcasters, photographers, activists, and other media practitioners whose voices and perspectives are woven into a storied tapestry that strengthens journalism's democratic function.

Although establishment media coverage may perpetuate social differences and alienating information silos, independent media organizations like *Weave News* remind us—across borders, whether real or imagined—of our shared struggles and experiences. By foregrounding grassroots perspectives from around the world, independent media empower readers and writers alike to identify with their common humanity and examine the motives of divisive and oppressive systems, including governments, corporations, non-profit and non-governmental organizations (NGOs), and social norms.

At *Weave News*, contributors position themselves as citizen journalists aiming to understand how complex global structures and relationships function in their own lives. The organization's do-it-yourself model has empowered both experienced and novice writers to publish on issues meaningful to them and the communities they serve that are often overlooked by the establishment press. Rather than simply critiquing a corporate environment that prioritizes a top-down, profit-based model, *Weave News* is committed to democratizing the news media space by offering independent journalism unbeholden to a prescribed narrative.

Weaving the Streets: Mobilization and Democratization

One of the organization's longest-running series, *Weaving the Streets*, illustrates *Weave News*'s ongoing commitment to highlighting citizen-led voices.[22] Launched in 2013 in collaboration with SLU gallery director Catherine Tedford, the series focuses on the creative ways that people use public spaces to express themselves. This overarching theme is designed to elicit a variety of responses. Contributors have examined public street art, sociopolitical stickers, cultural festivals, park gatherings, protest movements, and museums to write about such topics as identity politics, gentrification, environmental issues, and colonialism in locations including Madrid, Valencia, New York City, Copenhagen, Amman, and Beirut.

While maintaining an open submission policy, *Weaving the Streets* has mobilized and trained novice writers to become citizen journalists through a training guide and one-on-one mentoring sessions. The series received initial funding in 2012 from an Andrew W. Mellon Humanities grant to SLU called "Crossing Boundaries: Re-envisioning the Humanities for the 21st Century" and additional support in 2021 from the Patti McGill Peterson Grant through SLU's Center for International and Inter-cultural Studies. Both have funded research and travel for off-campus students contributing to *Weaving the Streets*.

Throughout their semester-long projects, students are expected to write three articles for *Weaving the Streets* that incorporate their own digital photographs. Student portfolios may also feature related objects, such as flyers, posters, buttons, street cards, and stickers, for a sister project titled "People's History Archive," a digital image collection of hundreds of items representing what the project organizers refer to as "street culture artifacts."[23] Another option offers contributors the opportunity to curate and catalog ten to twelve born-digital photographs published in the JSTOR image collection, "The Streets Are Talking: Public Forms of Creative Expression from Around the World."[24]

Before traveling, student authors research what they might write about; however, the nature of citizen jour-nalism necessitates flexibility. Once situated in their chosen locations, student journalists decide what to write about and how to structure their projects. Students' focus may shift, especially as they step out of their academic frames of reference and acclimate to the community. *Weaving the Streets*' editorial team works closely with writers throughout this process to create high-quality, publishable work that is true to the author's intentions and the community in focus.

Grassroots journalists are encouraged to include themselves in their stories to help ensure that the work is grounded in responsible representation and fair treatment of evidence. Editors advise novice writers to be upfront with readers about their social locations and positionalities in relation to the places and topics they are covering. At *Weave News*, we believe it is essential to understand whose perspectives we are reading and how that might influence what is (and is not) being said. By situating media practitioners within the context of the stories they write, readers and writers may gain greater empathy for the lived experiences of others and insight into their own lives.

As a media organization, *Weave News* promotes social justice through grassroots journalism and encourages media practitioners to explore global issues in hyperlocal contexts. The organization seeks to add context to public discussions by showcasing alternative perspectives and viewpoint transparency in our work. By facilitating public engagement, on-the-ground reporting, independent storytelling, and media production, projects such as *Weaving the Streets* exemplify the democratizing power of journalism.

CASSANDRA KUNERT is a contributing editor and writer for the *Weaving the Streets* project at *Weave News* and an early childhood educator. Since joining the Street Team in 2019, her topics of focus have been street art, American militarism, and the American far-right. Cassandra graduated from St. Lawrence University in 2021 with a major in global studies and government and a minor in Arabic studies.

IDENTITY-AWARE SAFETY & SECURITY TRAININGS PROTECT JOURNALISTS AND DEMOCRACY

JEJE MOHAMED

According to the Committee to Protect Journalists (CPJ), 2023 witnessed a record number of journalist killings, the highest since 2015, with hundreds more jailed.[25] The risks and threats that journalists around the world face are only increasing, with impacts on freedom of the press, democracy, and diversity in a field already hemorrhaging great talent.[26]

When I became a journalist and decided to focus on exposing human rights abuses and social injustices, I witnessed firsthand how those in power—whether governments, organized groups, or prevailing social dynamics—often disregard the collective welfare of others. I felt that being a journalist was the best thing I could do to serve my communities and try to move the needle toward a more just and equitable world.

My idealistic perception of journalism as critical to upholding democracy—holding those in power to account and protecting the universal rights of those most vulnerable and historically marginalized—is deeply entwined with my personal experiences and commitment to human rights, equity, and justice. Being a journalist in Egypt unexpectedly pushed me into the realm of safety and security, where it became part of my daily responsibilities to teach myself and trust my instincts to keep myself and others safe in an environment that is extremely hostile towards the press, where journalists have been targeted and attacked, and human rights violations are rampant.[27]

Now, my focus is on safety and security, where I train journalists and human rights activists to navigate the inherent risks and occupational hazards associated with their work. Much like the journalism industry, the safety and security field suffers from a lack of diversity and largely fails to recognize the necessity of a trauma-informed and identity-centric approach to safety and risk mitigation to build resilience in the journalism industry.

Hostile Environment First Aid Training (HEFAT) was developed in the late 1990s by primarily white, male British ex-military personnel and has been the benchmark ever since despite the rapidly changing journalism field. With more diversity in newsrooms and threats constantly emerging across borders, exacerbated by online and tech-facilitated threats, the safety and security field has yet to catch up, especially regarding the representation of experts from different gender, racial, sexual, and religious identities. As individuals, we do not walk through life the same way; our actual and perceived identities affect our experiences, and safety is an extension of that. Thus, the response cannot be one-size-fits-all. Risk assessment and mitigation planning must be unique, flexible, and different from one person to another.

For example, what comes to mind when we think about censorship, lack of access to information, suppression of speech, and attacks on the press? The answer will vary from one place to another, from one country to another, and maybe even from one journalist to another, depending on how they define risks, risk appetite, personal risk assessment, and the sociopolitical environment where they work.

As a co-founder of Aegis Safety Alliance, an organization founded by six women and non-binary people with diverse backgrounds and expertise, we specialize in designing and running safety and security trainings that are trauma-informed, identity-aware, and culturally conscious. We met through the International Women's Media Foundation's Next Gen fellowship, which gathered a group of women and non-binary individuals to hone their skills and expertise on holistic safety.[28] The fellowship focused on how to make safety and security trainings like Hostile Environment Awareness Training (HEAT) and HEFAT more trauma-informed and identity-centric.[29]

Aegis worked with A Culture of Safety (ACOS) and the World Association of News Publishers (WAN-IFRA) to design interactive content for The Fundamentals of Safe Commissioning course, "a self-paced training course that equips editors with the skills they need to safely commission journalistic work, support the safety of freelancers they work with, and embed a culture of safety within their everyday practice."[30] Editors and managers learn how to work with journalists and freelancers on the different pillars of safety, discussing risk assessment and safety protocols and fulfilling their duty of care while supporting the psychological well-being of their teams.

Aegis helps journalists, newsrooms, and nonprofits with different versions of safety work, including modified and tailored HEAT and HEFAT trainings, such as identity-aware risk assessments, situational awareness, personal security, covering civil unrest and protests, digital security and online abuse, psychological and physical first aid, and with prepping for different assignments in the United States and internationally.

As the Senior Manager for Digital Safety and Free Expression at PEN America, I led the training program and resources on digital safety and online abuse. In addition to our work with journalists, writers, and human rights defenders, providing them with self-defense training and resources, we worked to address online abuse at a systemic level. As part of that systemic change, we worked with employers such as newsrooms, publishing houses, and nonprofits to help them fulfill their duty of care and support their staff and freelancers facing relentless online abuse. We also advocated with social media platforms to provide people with the tools and features necessary to mitigate online abuse and expedite efficient and timely support by social media platforms.

For too long, online abuse was not considered a real threat by newsrooms, often leaving journalists feeling isolated and abandoned. Now recognized as a severe threat to freedom of expression and the press, PEN America's digital safety team responded by creating several comprehensive resources for newsrooms, journalists, and their allies, such as the Online Harassment Field Manual, Digital Safety Snacks, and the Power of Peer Support.[31] As an advisory board member and newsroom lead with the Coalition Against Online Violence, we developed industry-wide best practices to equip newsrooms of all sizes to effectively prepare for and respond to online abuse and digital threats, and better support journalists facing online harassment.

The various forms of censorship—including the global rise in imprisonment and killings of journalists—paint a bleak future for press freedom. At the heart of press freedom, freedom of expression, and diversity and equity are pressing needs for holistic safety and security. With a trauma-informed and identity-aware approach to safety and security, we help ensure and protect the freedoms that democracy relies on.

JEJE MOHAMED is co-founder of Aegis Safety Alliance, a collective of women and non-binary media safety experts. She has more than a decade of experience in journalism, human rights, and safety and security. She offers holistic, trauma-informed, and identity-centered safety training for journalists, documentarians, media-makers, and human rights activists working in various contexts, focusing on newsrooms, media agencies, and NGOs. She developed safety and security resources, trainings, and courses for diverse organizations in different countries around the world, focusing on digital safety, physical safety, de-escalation, and psychological first aid. She serves on the advisory board for the Coalition Against Online Violence and was a fellow with the Online News Association's Women's Leadership Accelerator.

Notes

1. Hunter S. Thompson, *Fear and Loathing on the Campaign Trail '72* (San Francisco: Straight Arrow Books, 1973; New York: Simon & Schuster, 2022), 33.
2. Matthew Hahn, "Writing on the Wall: An Interview with Hunter S. Thompson," *The Atlantic*, August 26, 1997.
3. Hahn, "Writing on the Wall."
4. *Lancaster County District Attorney's Office v. Carter Walker and LNP/Lancaster Online*, 59 (2019) (statement of Craig Stedman, former Lancaster County District Attorney).
5. Dan Nephin, "Former Lancaster County Drug Task Force Head Sentenced to 8-22 Months in Prison for Theft [Update]," *Lancaster Online*, May 5, 2023.

6.   "Former Head of Lancaster County Drug Task Force Sentenced for Theft of Money Seized during Investigations," WGAL (Lancaster, PA), May 5, 2023.

7.   Louis D. Brandeis, "What Publicity Can Do," *Harper's Weekly*, December 20, 1913.

8.   "Hostilities in the Gaza Strip and Israel - Reported Impact | Day 213," United Nations Office for the Coordination of Humanitarian Affairs, May 6, 2024.

9.   Jason Lange and Matt Spetalnick, "US Public Support for Israel Drops: Majority Backs a Ceasefire, Reuters/Ipsos Shows," Reuters, November 15, 2023.

10. William Youmans, "Accounting for the Biases in U.S. Media Coverage of Gaza," DAWN, March 20, 2024.

11. Youmans, "Accounting for the Biases."

12. On *hasbara,* see Sam Hamad, "Understanding Hasbara: Israel's Propaganda Machine," *The New Arab*, November 18, 2023; on false allegation, see Robin Andersen, "Investigating the *New York Times* 'Investigation' of Hamas Mass Rape," *CounterPunch,* February 11, 2024, and Chapter 4 of this book.

13. Glenn Greenwald, "A Texas Elementary School Speech Pathologist Refused to Sign a Pro-Israel Oath, Now Mandatory in Many States — So She Lost Her Job," *The Intercept*, December 17, 2018.

14. Federica Marsi, "Will the US Adopt IHRA's Anti-Semitism Definition? What's the Controversy?" Al Jazeera, May 8, 2024.

15. Susan Svrluga and Danielle Douglas-Gabriel, "After Harvard and Penn Resignations, Who Wants to Be a College President?" *Washington Post*, January 12, 2024.

16. Rebecca Alter, "Melissa Barrera Fired from *Scream 7* over Pro-Palestine Posts," *Vulture*, January 24, 2024; Sergio Martínez-Beltrán, "Student Protestors Worry How School Disciplinary Actions Will Affect Their Futures," NPR, May 7, 2024.

17. Timothy Bella, "Online Posts about Israel-Gaza War Are Costing Some People Their Jobs," *Washington Post*, October 12, 2023; Benjamin Douglas, "US Workers Lack Free Speech Protections on Palestine or Anything Else," *Jacobin*, November 4, 2023.

18. Riham Alkousaa and Layli Foroudi, "Palestinian Keffiyeh Scarves - A Controversial Symbol of Solidarity," Reuters, December 15, 2023.

19. Lori Bindig Yousman, "Critical Media Literacy in the Age of the Neoliberal University: Challenges, Strategies, and Rewards," *The SoJo Journal: Educational Foundations and Social Justice Education* 3, no. 2 (2017): 35–48.

20. Ira Shor and Paulo Freire, *A Pedagogy for Liberation: Dialogues on Transforming Education* (South Hadley, MA: Bergin & Garvey, 1987), 106–8.

21. Monica Anderson, Michelle Faverio, and Jeffrey Gottfried, "Teens, Social Media and Technology 2023," Pew Research Center, December 11, 2023.

22. Cassandra Kunert, ed., "Weaving the Streets: Series Overview," *Weave News*, undated [accessed May 13, 2024].

23. "People's History Archive," undated [accessed May 13, 2024].

24. "What Does 'Born Digital' Mean?" Yale University, undated [accessed May 14, 2024]; "The Streets Are Talking: Public Forms of Creative Expression from around the World," JSTOR, undated [accessed May 16, 2024].

25. Kathy Jones, "Israel-Gaza War Brings 2023 Journalist Killings to Devastating High," Committee to Protect Journalists, undated [accessed May 15, 2024]; Arlene Getz, "2023 Prison Census: Jailed Journalist Numbers near Record High; Israel Imprisonments Spike," Committee to Protect Journalists, undated [accessed May 15, 2024].

26. "Threats That Silence: Trends in the Safety of Journalists," UNESCO, undated [accessed May 14, 2024]; Marigo Farr, "Threats against Journalists on the Rise," *Nieman Reports*, May 9, 2023.

27. "Less Press Freedom than Ever in Egypt, 10 Years after Revolution," Reporters Without Borders, January 22, 2021; Cathrin Schaer, "Press Freedom? Egyptian Journalists Set to Stand Trial," DW, March 3, 2023; and "Egypt: Events of 2023," Human Rights Watch, undated [accessed May 14, 2024].

28. "Next Gen Safety Trainers," International Women's Media Foundation, undated [accessed May 21, 2024].

29. "What Is Heat Training?" International Location Safety, undated [accessed May 14, 2024]; "Physical Safety and Hostile Environment Training," International Women's Media Foundation, undated [accessed May 14, 2024].

30. Andrew Heslop, "ACOS Alliance and WAN-IFRA Launch the Editor Safety Hub," World Association of News Publishers, April 4, 2024.

31. "Online Harassment Field Manual," PEN America, undated [accessed May 14, 2024]; "Digital Safety Snacks," PEN America, undated [accessed May 14, 2024]; and Susan E. McGregor, Viktorya Vilk, and Jeje Mohamed, "The Power of Peer Support," PEN America, April 2024.

CHAPTER 6

Eleven Theses on Disinformation (with Apologies to Karl Marx)

BILL YOUSMAN

But we can't simply reject our false gods.
We must figure out what they've done for us.
—LESLIE JAMISON[1]

Terms like "post-truth" and "fake news" became common in public discourse in 2016, as observers commented on a deluge of lies from the Republican presidential candidate. "Post-truth" was even anointed by the Oxford Dictionary as its Word of the Year for 2016.[2] Discussion of misinformation and disinformation is now prevalent in academic journals, the popular press, and social media. While misinformation can be thought of as mistaken ideas inadvertently held and shared, disinformation is deliberate, a means to exert influence by knowingly spreading false or unsubstantiated material. Disinformation can thus be thought of as a subset of propaganda.

Some, however, dispute that we are experiencing an acceleration of disinformation, arguing that this distracts from more productive and urgently needed attention to the root causes of social and political turmoil. Furthermore, ideas might be labeled disinformation simply because they challenge prevailing beliefs or are disseminated by alternative rather than establishment media.

Attempts to challenge disinformation can, therefore, slide into censorious limitations on public discourse.[3]

The journalist and activist Naomi Klein, writing about being confused with one of the most prolific purveyors of disinformation, Naomi Wolf, frames the dilemma this way: "Are the political movements Other Naomi helps lead ridiculous, unworthy of attention—or are they part of a serious shift in our world that needs our urgent reckoning?"[4] I argue for thinking about that question dialectically. Because the political theorist Karl Marx's *Theses on Feuerbach* touched on the nature of truth, I somewhat playfully borrow from its structure in offering eleven theses on disinformation, avoiding a binary approach of either simply dismissing disinformation concerns or focusing on these worries exclusively while marginalizing other political problems.[5] Marx was responding to limitations in Feuerbach's approach to materialist philosophy, specifically a lack of context grounded in real conditions. Similarly, I'm responding to nondialectical, noncontextual approaches by some disinformation researchers and skeptics alike while challenging what bell hooks called "the either/or dualistic thinking that is the central ideological component of all systems of domination in Western society."[6]

The first five theses acknowledge the concerns of disinformation skeptics. The next five argue for taking disinformation seriously. Following a dialectical approach, I offer both thesis and antithesis, working toward an incomplete and always in-process synthesis. The goal is to embrace complexities and contradictions as an antidote to overly simplistic thinking about a significant social phenomenon.

1. Disinformation is not new, cannot be extinguished, and will always be with us.

It's important to establish that disinformation was not born when Donald Trump descended an escalator, announcing his presidential campaign, making verifiably false claims about his wealth, and misleadingly identifying Mexican immigrants as dangerous criminals. In their book *The Paradox of Democracy*, Zac Gershberg and Sean Illing point out, "We can't be 'post-truth' because we were never pre-truth. And we certainly never lived in truth."[7] Folk singer Pete Seeger said, "The truth is a rabbit in a bramble patch. All you can do is circle around saying, 'It's somewhere in there,' as you point in different directions. But you can't put your hands on its pulsing, furry little body."[8]

We can go back to the Sophists of ancient Greece, who taught that in persuasion, the only thing that matters is not telling the truth but winning the argument. Or we can look to US history for endless precursors to the current era of disinformation: accusations of "witchcraft," the "pretendians" of the Boston Tea Party, deceptive showmen like P.T. Barnum, the emergence of the yellow press and tabloid journalism, the rise of the public relations industry and their army of "crisis managers," the propaganda radio broadcasts of Fascist sympathizers, deceit about Vietnam, decades of falsehoods in political advertising, the rise of Rush Limbaugh and his right-wing radio descendants, corporate deceptions about tobacco and climate change, Iran-Contra, military and intelligence lies about Iraq after 9/11, and much more. Which is to say, Eric Alterman's book *When Presidents Lie: A History of Official Deception and Its Consequences* lives up to its title.[9]

However, Gershberg and Illing argue that newer technologies have supercharged these historical patterns. Kevin Young agrees: "Untruths spread faster and faster ... spawning whole faux movements like birthers and truthers, billionaire populists and the alt-right, whose euphemistic names describe exactly what they do not believe." When Alterman revised his 2004 book in 2020, he called it *Lying in State: Why Presidents Lie—And Why Trump Is Worse*.[10]

2. Disinformation is not the source of *all* political problems.

Global communities are suffering from severe economic and social inequality; lack of adequate health care and housing; racial, ethnic, and religious conflicts; and environmental degradation. Disinformation didn't *cause* any of these enduring problems. This is a key point in the materialist critique of disinformation research. For example, a magazine editor, criticizing the historian Heather Cox Richardson, tweeted, "You have to be willfully ignorant of the dire, profound, and well-documented consequences of half a century of Reaganism on vast swaths of the Rust Belt and rural America to think 'the main story of the past decade has been Russian disinformation to undermine U.S. democracy.'"[11]

We can also point to the many antidemocratic flaws of the US political system: the Electoral College, the non-representative makeup of the Senate, gerrymandering, voter suppression, virtually no checks on campaign contributions, corruption and abuses of power at the Supreme Court, etc. that make a mockery of imagining the United States as a true democracy. For several years, the Economist Intelligence Unit's Democracy Index has classified America as a flawed democracy, ranked twenty-ninth in 2023.[12]

Joseph Bernstein, contesting the centrality of social media disinformation to political dysfunction, argues for more context, including:

> an idiosyncratic electoral process and a two-party system that has asymmetrically polarized toward a nativist, rhetorically anti-elite right wing ... a deeply irresponsible national broadcast media, disappearing local news, an entertainment industry that glorifies violence, a bloated military, massive income inequality, a history of brutal and intractable racism that has time and again shattered class consciousness, conspiratorial habits of mind, and themes of world-historical declension and redemption.... To take the whole environment into view, or as much of it as we can, is to see how preposterously insufficient it is to blame these platforms for the sad extremities of our national life, up to and including the riot on January 6.[13]

As explored below, while it is important to recognize how disinformation may *contribute* to political turmoil, too many have seized upon it as the only source of dysfunction, thus overlooking severe material inequities and deep structural flaws in societies around the globe.

3. Disinformation cannot simply be attributed to foreign provocateurs.

In the 1979 film *When a Stranger Calls*, police tell a babysitter terrorized by threatening phone calls that the calls are coming from inside the house. Disinformation skeptics reject the claim that the 2016 election results can be attributed to Russian disinformation campaigns. That contention is both facile and simplistic, and it serves to cast the blame elsewhere while whitewashing profound weaknesses in the American political, economic, and cultural systems.

In a comprehensive study of online and broadcast media leading up to 2016, Harvard scholars Yochai Benkler, Robert Faris, and Hal Roberts found that, while there were attempts by Russian sources to spread disinformation through social media, the actual impact was negligible: "These efforts sought to build on and widen already existing fissures in American society but . . . they appear to have mostly amounted to little more than jumping on a bandwagon already well underway."[14] Russia, for example, didn't have to invent the racist fears that motivated many American voters. The resentments and anxieties of White voters have long been exploited by dog-whistle politics.[15] Hatred and suspicion are homegrown, not imported.

In contrast, disinformation disseminated by domestic right-wing media sources, such as Fox News, Breitbart, talk radio, and *Infowars*, influences about a third of the American population. Henry Giroux refers to this as the "weaponization of culture," arguing that "right-wing media has . . . created a safe space for the 'big lie' [about the 2020 election], racism, [and] conspiracy theories."[16]

Benkler, Faris, and Roberts point out, "Right-wing sites that do claim to follow journalistic norms ... do not in fact do so, and therefore fail to act as a truth-telling brake ... repeatedly we found Fox News accrediting and amplifying the excesses." Furthermore, horse race, scandal-driven, blandly "neutral" political coverage in corporate media distracts from significant issues related to ideological and policy differences. This allows right-wing disinformation to proliferate in establishment outlets.[17]

4. Establishment media is not and has never been innocent of disseminating disinformation.

Benkler, Faris, and Roberts thus demonstrate that disinformation does not stem solely from social media or alternative media sources. Historically, alternative media have offered important correctives to the lies and omissions of establishment media. From lynching investigations by Ida B. Wells in the Black press, to I.F. Stone's muckraking *Weekly*, to alternative newspapers like *The Village Voice* and *The Advocate*, to contemporary outlets like *Democracy Now!*, *In These Times*, *CounterPunch*, and many others, alternative media play a crucial role in the public sphere. While some alternative outlets are guilty of leveraging disinformation for both mayhem and profit (this means you, *Infowars*), this does not suggest that corporate media are paragons of truth and virtue.

One need look no further than the so-called "paper of record," the *New York Times*, to find a history of misleading and deceitful reporting, including its coverage of the Russian Revolution; Israel's occupation of Palestine; US military invasions and political interference throughout

Asia, Africa, the Middle East, and South America; and "weapons of mass destruction" in Iraq; among other examples. In December 2023, the *Times* prominently featured an investigation into alleged systematic sexual violence by Hamas, the veracity of which has since been questioned by many journalism professors and scholars.[18] Similar patterns prevail at the major television networks, CBS, ABC, NBC, CNN, and Fox.[19] The giant digital media corporations, including Facebook (Meta), Google (Alphabet), and Amazon, are also implicated, as absurdly exemplified by Amazon's "smart speaker" Alexa proclaiming that massive voter fraud allowed Biden to steal the 2020 election.[20]

Media studies professor Jack Banks puts it this way, "The only information [usually] included in [corporate] media . . . is that which supports the narratives of government, military, and big business to support their policies. Unsupported, inaccurate information that supports those narratives is presented as fact while anything that challenges that narrative is omitted or discounted as biased and extreme."[21]

5. Government intervention and/or corporate censorship is not a solution to disinformation.

In a media environment saturated with disinformation, it's unsurprising that some have called for restrictions on both traditional and social media companies. But one doesn't need to appeal to the First Amendment to see that censorship is ineffective and dangerous. As free expression advocates point out, censorship only drives people to other platforms while shuttering open discourse, creating societies where only the viewpoints of the powerful are sanctioned.

Despite these widely shared concerns, there have been calls for the US government to police disinformation. (Ironic when considering that it is often actually the *source* of disinformation.) In April 2022, the Department of Homeland Security (DHS) announced the creation of "the Disinformation Governance Board" to advise agencies on combatting disinformation. After a surge of criticism from across the political spectrum, the DHS initially put the board on hold and then eliminated it completely.[22]

Corporate censorship is similarly repressive. While private media companies always decide what they will or won't platform, silencing dissent should always concern those committed to vibrant public discourse. As Giroux points out, censorship by tech giants like Facebook, Google, YouTube, and X, the site formerly known as Twitter, has often been wielded most heavily against challenging perspectives from the left.[23] Journalist Chris Hedges charted how sites like *AlterNet*, *Democracy Now!*, *Common Dreams*, *Truthout*, *The Intercept*, and *CounterPunch* all experienced dramatic dips in traffic after Google introduced new algorithms to reduce "fake news."[24] Meanwhile, since billionaire Elon Musk took over Twitter, rebranding it as X, disinformation and hate speech surged.[25] This clearly presents a quandary for those devoted to a democratic and healthy public sphere.

Naomi Klein admits there is an information problem but points out that we can't expect tech overlords to solve it: "The spread of lies and conspiracies online is now so rampant that it threatens public health and, quite possibly, the survival of representative democracy. The solution to this informational crisis, however, is not to look to tech oligarchs to disappear people we don't like; it's to get serious about demanding an information commons that can be counted upon as a basic civic right."[26] ACLU attorney David Cole agrees, noting:

> I'm no happier about social media than the next person. But giving every state, or the next president ... the power to control what we see or don't see online is not the answer. Under the First Amendment, the government can't decide what private entities can and cannot say (or publish). But that doesn't mean there's nothing that can be done. A major source of the problem is the sheer concentration of power in the hands of a few companies. Antitrust law is designed to address that and does not involve government regulation of speech. Breaking up the large platforms would make the decisions of any particular platform less consequential for public debate.[27]

In other words, censoring content is not the answer, but giving media corporations free rein to pursue whatever profit-seeking practices they please is also detrimental to the health of the public sphere.

Ultimately, this conundrum is the price of democracy. Gershberg and Illing make this point forcefully: "We must live with the chaos of an open society and the cynicism and demagoguery that accompany it. We must tolerate bullshit from politicians who pander to the fickle tastes of public opinion as well as from our neighbors who recirculate false information on Facebook. No democratic system is immune to imperfect communication."[28] This understanding is particularly crucial for those in education, journalism, research, the arts, or any intellectual endeavor. As Susan Sontag wrote, "To be an intellectual is to be attached to the inherent value of plurality, and to the right of critical space (space for critical opposition within society)."[29]

6. The social impact of disinformation is real.

Despite the caveats offered above, we must acknowledge the real role that disinformation plays in the political and social environment: "What people believe is true is more important than what is actually true because what people do in the world is a function of what they believe about the world."[30] When a crusader fires a gun in a DC pizza parlor because he is there to free the sex slaves that Hillary Clinton is hiding in the basement, what really matters to him, and is fateful for the people that could be harmed, is his unwavering *belief*—rather than the *reality* that there are no sex slaves or even any basement.[31] Many rioters at the Capitol on January 6 sincerely believed Trump had won the election and that they were patriots protecting democracy. Yet people died and were injured, both storming and defending the Capitol. Many who died from COVID truly believed there was no virus or that the vaccines were more deadly than the disease. Similarly, measles is again spreading, sometimes taking lives, primarily because of antivaccination myths.[32] It is estimated that 16 percent of Americans and 25 percent of Republicans believe QAnon-type fantasies like these.[33]

Journalist Jeff Sharlet traveled the United States, talking to people from the far right and exploring what motivated their beliefs and actions. He listened as they echoed disinformation he had previously heard on Fox News and talk radio or seen in QAnon-related postings. The people he conversed with sincerely held a range of false ideas about both Democrats and Republicans and even basic facts about science, history, current events, race, gender, and the structures of American government and law. Sharlet's interviews thus support Benkler, Faris, and Roberts's quantitative analysis of how disinformation shapes the perceptions of listeners, readers, and viewers.[34]

Commentators have long minimized the impact of media and propaganda. This is an old pattern in media theorizing and debates about powerful or minimal media effects.[35] But there are endless examples of the real influence of disinformation. The journalist Elizabeth Williamson, for example, investigated the role that Alex Jones played in convincing listeners that school shootings are just false flags used to empower the government to seize guns. These outrageous claims led to vile harassment of grieving families.[36]

Furthermore, propaganda has historically been intertwined with racism and antisemitism.[37] David Icke, for example, who claims that all pandemics are hoaxes, is also a Holocaust denier, a promoter of the fabricated *Protocols of the Elders of Zion*, who says reptilian aliens are controlling the Earth. Some suggest that he employs this as a dog-whistle, a metaphor for Jewish people.[38] If that is correct, this only makes his rhetoric more pernicious. None of this keeps his books from receiving glowing five-star reviews on Goodreads.

Perhaps the most pernicious effect of disinformation is the way it distracts from efforts to confront social problems such as poverty, climate, wars, racism, sexism, and more. As Klein notes, "The confusion [disinformation purveyors] sow and the oxygen they absorb increasingly stand in the way of pretty much anything helpful or healthful that humans might, at some point, decide to accomplish together."[39]

7. Analysis of propaganda is a crucial element in the critique of power.

Disinformation is best understood as a subset of propaganda. Analysis of the social impact of propaganda has long been recognized as essential to left media criticism, as exemplified by the work of scholars such as Ed Herman, Noam Chomsky, Nancy Snow, Jacques Ellul, Norman Solomon, Robin Andersen, and many others. While propaganda cannot be considered the only variable in political and social power, it is a critical one, and its dismissal only allows propagandists to have their way. As the late social psychologist Alex Carey noted, "It is arguable that the success of business propaganda in persuading us, for so long, that we are free from propaganda is one of the most significant propaganda achievements of the twentieth century."[40]

Mass media effects researcher James Shanahan points out that dismissing the impact of propaganda is nothing new in media studies. Still, this negligence was an impediment in the past, and it is not useful now:

> In the standard version of the field's history, there was a move away from worry about propaganda, which empirical research seemed to suggest was never as powerful as originally supposed; it was

somewhat naïve to be concerned with propaganda. And yet ... propaganda is still everywhere
to be found ... Trends are worrisome enough
that we should probably look at the possibility of
direct propaganda playing a resurgent role ... For
media effects theorists, the time could come when
there is again a perceived need to understand propaganda, rather than casting it aside as an overly
simplistic view of the media world that we no
longer need.[41]

Propagandists benefit from our lack of awareness and
complicity. Bernstein notes that Jacques Ellul "dismissed
a 'common view of propaganda ... that it is the work of
a few evil men, seducers of the people ...' the propagan-
dist and the propagandee make propaganda together."
Anti-anti-disinformation campaigns contribute to an
environment where disinformation flourishes, thus
enabling the work of propaganda.[42]

8. Disinformation is not solely attributable to the left, right, or center.

The left should not assume disinformation only stems
from the right. While research reveals asymmetry,
with conservatives demonstrating a greater propen-
sity to believe and spread misinformation, this does not
mean that centrists, liberals, progressives, or leftists are
immune.[43] Benkler, Faris, and Roberts cite data indi-
cating "the Republican and Democratic leadership had
remarkably similar proportions of statements rated by
PolitiFact as 'mostly false' or worse ... Similarly, Rachel

Maddow ... is not systematically different ... than Bill O'Reilly ... or Sean Hannity."[44]

Many social-media influencers who spread health disinformation are people thought of as liberals or progressives, including 2024 presidential candidate Robert F. Kennedy Jr.[45] I personally find the most distressing examples of the calls coming from inside my own house to be the left media critics promoting disinformation about school shootings, vaccines, climate change, and more.[46]

It would be comforting and easier to deal with if disinformation was just a problem of the "other side." But this claim itself would be disinformation. Disinformation is nonideological in that it has no natural home in any segment of the political spectrum, and this contributes to it being a pervasive and vexing problem.

9. Political economic analysis of disinformation is essential.

Benkler, Faris, and Roberts state, "We take a political economy view of technology, suggesting that the fundamental mistake of 'the internet polarizes' narrative is that it adopts too naïve a view of how technology works and understates the degree to which institutions, culture, and politics shape technological adoption and diffusion patterns."[47] Political economic analysis is necessary for drawing a complete picture of any social phenomenon because it traces connections among wealth, discourse, social influence, and power.

Disinformation is not just politically, socially, and culturally significant but profitable. If it weren't, it would be less of a problem. Comparing media mogul Rupert

Murdoch to Logan Roy, his fictional counterpart from the television series *Succession*, media scholar Robin Andersen writes, "To Mr. Murdoch and Logan, creating streams of alarming and misleading newslike propaganda about issues they care little about was a counterprogramming business opportunity."[48] Corporate media's primary goal is profiteering. Former CBS CEO Les Moonves stated it nakedly when talking about Donald Trump's candidacy: "It may not be good for America, but it's damn good for CBS...The money's rolling in, this is fun...It's a terrible thing to say, but bring it on, Donald, go ahead, keep going."[49]

Disinformation profiteers are varied, ranging from establishment media, corporate interests, politicians, social media grifters, and Big Tech. Nothing is too horrible to be overlooked as a source of profit.[50] Not environmental collapse, pandemics, terrorism, or wars. For example, Elon Musk monetized disinformation about Israel's destruction of Gaza: "As false information about the rapidly changing war...proliferated...Musk personally recommended that users follow accounts notorious for promoting lies...That post was viewed 11 million times in three hours...before Musk deleted it."[51] Furthermore, X:

> became flooded with lies, misinformation, and spun-up fakery of the sort that might endanger people. It is obvious that this is the new normal: Whenever any similar, horrible event happens, Musk's Twitter will be there, to exacerbate the damage...users willing to spend $8 a month for a blue check can boost—and, in some cases, monetize—the spread of misinformation...the

social network demonstrated a singular ability to take a complex, fast-moving situation and make it more difficult to comprehend.[52]

There are also multitudes of online grifters such as Naomi Wolf, Steve Bannon, and Alex Jones (and thousands who are lesser known but still amass large follower counts) who use their platforms to sell all manner of suspect devices, concoctions, products, services, memberships, and swag.[53] In 2022, Bannon referred to his podcast, *War Room*, as "a cash machine."[54] A lawsuit directed at Jones was aimed specifically at the millions he made using lies about Sandy Hook as bait.[55] As Klein sums up, "This is what happens when we allow so many of our previously private actions to be enclosed by corporate tech platforms whose founders said they were connecting us but were always about extracting from us."[56]

10. Attention to disinformation should be part of the overall analysis of how power works in both democratic and authoritarian societies.

Some skeptics believe that concerns about disinformation are not just overblown but downright hysterical. However, political scientist Jan-Werner Müller, responding to those dismissive of the global threat of far-right authoritarianism, offers this applicable reminder: "Not all raising of alarm bells is alarmism, not all talk of fascism or even totalitarianism should casually be dismissed as Cold War hysteria."[57]

Dismissal of the critique of disinformation aligns with the myth that media have little influence over individuals and society. Certainly, other issues must be highlighted beyond the social impact of media. But Robert McChesney reminds us of a statement by former FCC commissioner Nicholas Johnson: "When speaking to activists and progressives, whatever your first issue of concern, media had better be your second, because without change in the media, progress in your primary area is far less likely."[58] What people *believe* about any political, social, or economic problem is critical to how they think it should be addressed or whether they even agree it is a problem at all. And those beliefs are shaped in profound ways by the media we use.

Klein emphasizes why topsy-turvy disinformation is destructive to political, social, and economic progress: "[Left] critiques of oligarchic rule are being fully absorbed by the hard right and turned into dark doppelgangers of themselves. The structural critiques of capitalism are gone, and in their place are discombobulated conspiracies . . ." Disinformation purveyors "have spent years mangling the meaning of the fight against authoritarianism, fascism, and genocide . . . And they have done it at a time when we are in dire need of robust anti-fascist alliance, in large part thanks to their own relentless inflammation and misinformation and the resentments they have sown."[59]

11. The point is to change it.

We've come to that place in an essay like this where the writer often feels pressed to offer solutions. Confession time: I don't have that. In fact, I'm fairly pessimistic. I still believe in Marx's plea at the end of the *Theses on Feuerbach*: "The philosophers have only interpreted the world in various ways; the point, however, is to change it."[60]

Marx wanted to change the economic basis of society. Hope could only be found in dismantling the capitalist economies that wreak misery, then and now. Capitalism, however, is a resilient beast. Attributing the phrase to both Fredric Jameson and Slavoj Žižek, Mark Fisher wrote that "it is easier to imagine the end of the world than it is to imagine the end of capitalism."[61]

The ravages of capitalism create societies primed for disinformation. Susan Maret points out that coverups, hidden information, and lack of transparency on the part of powerful entities all contribute to public acceptance of conspiratorial thinking. Maret cites the historian Kathryn S. Olmsted's argument that governmental deceit sows the seeds of distrust, and we can extend this insight to corporate crimes, corruption, and lies as well.[62] As Marcus Gilroy-Ware notes, "Abuse of power *begets* conspiracy allegations, and the men and women of conspiratorial capital at least partly have themselves to blame for the extreme and fictitious allegations made against them."[63] Or, as Anand Giridharadas puts it, "Where cults thrived, something in the society wasn't working right."[64] Power and profit-seeking conspiracies do exist, just not in the ways imagined by disinformation fantasists.[65] It's not QAnon, it's Exxon. Disinformation may be as intractable a problem as others wrought by capitalism: the climate crisis, severe global inequality, and dangerous international hostilities. Some might scoff at this comparison, but the point is that mediated disinformation plays a part in all these material world crises. Rosa Luxemburg believed that we must ultimately choose between barbarism and socialism.[66] But as much as we might work toward democratic socialist societies, if the demise of capitalism is not imminent, what else can be done?

Obviously, one key is critical thinking, along with media literacy and civic education.[67] Yet, there are structural barriers to critical pedagogy. Who's doing the educating? What would the GOP Florida governor Ron DeSantis's version of media literacy or civics education be? Or Meta's Mark Zuckerberg's? Further, as noted above, disinformation emerges even from the ranks of left educators and scholars. Marx disavowed those who had misinterpreted his ideas, saying that if their program was Marxism, "what is certain is that I myself am not a Marxist."[68] Looking at some examples of what passes for media education, I think that if that's media literacy, then I'm not a media educator. And yet . . .

We can't dismiss critical pedagogy entirely. But I've grown concerned about its limitations and whether we've been doing what we thought we were doing. Have we been encouraging critical thinking or nihilistic cynicism? Have we effectively made the case that the issues are structural, not individual? We don't need hyper-individualistic self-help programs when it comes to these problems. We also can't expect the tech and media industries to solve this. What we really need is daunting: economic, political, social, and cultural transformation.

We must first recognize disinformation as an ancient and ongoing problem closely related to issues of power and propaganda that all societies face. Jacqueline Rose, reflecting on the cultural studies scholar Stuart Hall's legacy, says, "For Hall, this is a political task . . . 'I have never believed in snatching some simple good alternative out of the mess. I think we are always, always working on the mess,' [Hall] writes . . . Only if you confront the 'mess' of things, delve beneath the surface, and let in the silenced voices of history clamoring at the gate is there the slightest prospect of understanding, let alone transforming, the nightmares of our contemporary world."[69] Scholars Rachel Kuo and Alice Marwick thus call for a type of critical disinformation studies that takes into account historical patterns; hierarchical power imbalances; and economic, social, cultural, and political injustices.[70]

Confronting this mess requires research, analysis, critique, and education, but it also demands activism: fighting the neoliberal turn in government and education, challenging corporate control of media, reining in the power of corporate and governmental surveillance technologies, supporting initiatives for publicly funded arts and nonprofit investigative and local journalism, demanding antitrust enforcement to dismantle gargantuan media conglomerates, and more.[71]

Victor Pickard, author of *Democracy without Journalism*, notes, "Transforming the US media system into a democratic force requires a robust policy program of regulating or breaking up information monopolies, creating public alternatives to commercial news media, and empowering media workers, consumers, and communities to engage with and create their own media."[72] The response ultimately must be collective and political, not individual. Although they come at it from different directions, challenging hyper-concentrated media power is one area where people from disparate sides of the political spectrum often land on common ground.

After 276 pages exploring the fragility of democracy, Gershberg and Illing attempt to simultaneously soothe and motivate: "We'll never quite get the democracy we want, and that's okay. That's the paradox. We all have work to do, then, in making the most of the democracies we have."[73] As they argue, it's a task that is never finished. Perhaps, then, the best way to close, for now, is with Samuel Beckett: "You must go on. I can't go on. I'll go on." And: "Ever tried. Ever failed. No matter. Try again. Fail again. Fail better."[74]

BILL YOUSMAN, PHD, is a Professor in the Media and Performing Arts Department at Sacred Heart University. His research focuses on media and the construction of racial ideology, critical media literacy, and the relationship between media and democracy. His scholarship has been published in many academic journals and edited volumes. His monographs include *Prime Time Prisons on U.S. TV: Representation of Incarceration* and *The Spike Lee Enigma: Challenge and Incorporation in Media Culture*, and he is a co-editor of the award-winning anthology series *Gender, Race and Class in Media*. Yousman is the former Managing Director of the Media Education Foundation and is a regular panelist on WNPR's *The Colin McEnroe Show*.

Notes

1. Leslie Jamison, "Why Barbie Must Be Punished," *New Yorker*, July 29, 2023.
2. "Word of the Year 2016," Oxford Languages, undated [accessed April 3, 2024].
3. Sam Adler-Bell, "The Liberal Obsession with 'Disinformation' Is Not Helping," *New York Magazine*, May 20, 2022; Joseph Bernstein, "Bad News," *Harper's Magazine*, September 2021; Jamelle Bouie, "Disinformation Is Not the Real Problem with Democracy," *New York Times*, March 11, 2023; Jack Bratich, "Civil Society Must Be Defended," *Communication, Culture and Critique* 13, no. 3 (September 2020): 311–32; Conor Friedersdorf, "How 'Big Disinformation' Can Overcome Its Skeptics," *The Atlantic*, April 21, 2022. For an earlier assessment of the phenomenon, see Emil Marmol and Lee Mager, "'Fake News': The Trojan Horse for Silencing Alternative News and Reestablishing Corporate Media Dominance," in *Censored 2020: Through the Looking Glass*, eds. Andy Lee Roth and Mickey Huff with Project Censored (New York: Seven Stories Press, 2019), 221–53, also archived on the Project Censored website.

4. Naomi Klein, *Doppelganger* (New York: Farrar, Straus and Giroux, 2023), 10.
5. Karl Marx, *Theses on Feuerbach* (1845); available online at Marxists.org.
6. bell hooks, *Feminist Theory* (Boston: South End Press, 1984), 29.
7. Zac Gershberg and Sean Illing, *The Paradox of Democracy* (Chicago: University of Chicago Press, 2022), 249.
8. Pete Seeger, quoted in David Hajdu, "Pete Seeger: 'For Too Much of My Life, I Preached to the Converted'," *New Republic*, January 28, 2014.
9. Eric Alterman, *When Presidents Lie* (New York: Penguin, 2004); Kurt Andersen, *Fantasyland* (New York: Random House, 2017); Joel Bakan, *The Corporation* (New York: Simon and Schuster, 2004); Gershberg and Illing, *Paradox*; Nolan Higdon, *The Anatomy of Fake News* (Oakland: University of California Press, 2020); Rachel Kuo and Alice Marwick, "Critical Disinformation Studies: History, Power, and Politics," *Harvard Kennedy School Misinformation Review* 2, no. 4 (August 2021); Naomi Oreskes and Erik M. Conway, *Merchants of Doubt* (New York: Bloomsbury, 2010); John Stauber and Sheldon Rampton, *Toxic Sludge is Good for You* (Monroe, ME: Common Courage Press, 1995); Kevin Young, *Bunk* (Minneapolis: Graywolf Press, 2017).
10. Gershberg and Illing, *Paradox*; Young, *Bunk*, 433; Eric Alterman, *Lying in State* (New York: Hatchette, 2020).
11. Sam Haselby (@samhaselby), "You have to be willfully ignorant," X, February 27, 2024.
12. "Democracy Index: Conflict and Polarisation Drive a New Low for Global Democracy," Economist Intelligence Unit, February 15, 2024.
13. Bernstein, "Bad News."
14. Yochai Benkler, Robert Faris, and Hal Roberts, *Network Propaganda* (New York: Oxford University Press, 2018), 385.
15. Ian Haney López, *Dog Whistle Politics* (New York: Oxford University Press, 2014).
16. Henry A. Giroux, *Insurrections* (London: Bloomsbury, 2023), 63.
17. Benkler, Faris, and Roberts, *Network Propaganda*, 14.
18. Amy Goodman, interview with Deepa Kumar, "60+ Journalism Profs Demand Investigation into Controversial NYT Article Alleging Mass Rape on Oct. 7," *Democracy Now!*, May 8, 2024. See Chapter 4 of this volume, on News Abuse, for more on this topic.
19. Robin Andersen, "Investigating the *New York Times* 'Investigation' of Hamas Mass Rape: Narratives of Demonization," *CounterPunch*, February 11, 2024; Jeet Heer, "The Nixonian *New York Times* Stonewalls on a Discredited Article About Hamas and Rape," *The Nation*, March 1, 2024; Edward S. Herman and Noam Chomsky, *Manufacturing Consent* (New York: Pantheon, 1988); Higdon, *Fake News*; Douglas Kellner, *The Persian Gulf TV War* (Boulder, CO: Westview Press, 1992); Sheldon Rampton and John Stauber, *Weapons of Mass Deception* (New York: Penguin, 2003); Danny Schechter, *When News Lies* (New York: SelectBooks, 2006).
20. Cat Zakrzewski, "Amazon's Alexa Has Been Claiming the 2020 Election Was Stolen," *Washington Post*, October 7, 2023.
21. Jack Banks (Director, School of Communication, University of Hartford) in discussion with the author, March 4, 2024.

22. Adler-Bell, "Liberal Obsession." See also, Reagan Haynie and Mickey Huff, "Leaks Reveal Homeland Security Plans to Regulate Disinformation Online," story #17 in *State of the Free Press 2024*, eds. Andy Lee Roth and Mickey Huff (Fair Oaks: The Censored Press; New York: Seven Stories Press, 2024), 72–74, also archived on the Project Censored website.
23. Giroux, *Insurrections*.
24. Chris Hedges, "American Commissars," *Chris Hedges Report* (Substack), April 17, 2022.
25. Vittoria Elliot, "Twitter Really Is Worse than Ever," *Wired*, May 3, 2023.
26. Klein, *Doppelganger*, 91.
27. David Cole, "The Right to Speak Freely Online," interview by Daniel Drake, *New York Review*, February 24, 2024.
28. Gershberg and Illing, *Paradox of Democracy*, 16.
29. Susan Sontag, *As Consciousness is Harnessed to Flesh* (New York: Farrar, Straus, Giroux, 2012), 381.
30. Gershberg and Illing, *Paradox of Democracy*, 272.
31. Camila Domonoske, "Man Fires Rifle inside D.C. Pizzeria, Cites Fictitious Conspiracy Theories," NPR, December 5, 2016.
32. Leana S. Wen, "Florida's Measles Outbreak Is a Devastating—and Preventable—Tragedy," *Washington Post*, March 5, 2024.
33. Anand Giridharadas, *The Persuaders* (New York: Knopf, 2022); "New PRRI Report Reveals Nearly One in Five Americans and One in Four Republicans Still Believe in Qanon Conspiracy Theories," PRRI, February 24, 2022.
34. Jeff Sharlet, *The Undertow* (New York: Norton, 2023); Benkler, Faris, and Roberts, *Network Propaganda*. Also see Dannagal Goldthwaite Young, *Wrong* (Baltimore: Johns Hopkins, 2023) for a summary of numerous studies on disinformation effects.
35. James Shanahan, *Media Effects* (Cambridge, UK: Polity, 2021).
36. Elizabeth Williamson, *Sandy Hook* (New York: Dutton, 2022).
37. Kuo and Marwick, "Critical Disinformation Studies"; Young, *Bunk*.
38. James McMahon, "The UK's Anti-lockdown Movement Has Welcomed David Icke and QAnon Believers," *Vice News*, September 1, 2020.
39. Klein, *Doppelganger*, 5.
40. Alex Carey, *Taking the Risk Out of Democracy* (Chicago: University of Chicago Press, 1995), 21.
41. Shanahan, *Media Effects*, 160–64.
42. Bernstein, "Bad News"; Jim Rutenberg and Steven Lee Myers, "How Trump's Allies Are Winning the War over Disinformation," *New York Times*, March 17, 2024.
43. Benkler, Faris, and Roberts, *Network Propaganda*; Dimitar Nikolov, Alesandro Flammini, and Filippo Menczer, "Right and Left, Partisanship Predicts (Asymmetric) Vulnerability to Misinformation," *Harvard Kennedy School Misinformation Review* 1, no. 7 (February 2021); Young, *Wrong*.
44. Benkler, Faris, and Roberts, *Network Propaganda*, 83.
45. Andersen, *Fantasyland*; Klein, *Doppelganger*.
46. Michael Bérubé and Jennifer Ruth, *It's Not Free Speech* (Baltimore: Johns Hopkins University Press, 2022); Mark Dery, "The Professor of Paranoia," *Chronicle of Higher Education*, May 12, 2021; Williamson, *Sandy Hook*.
47. Benkler, Faris, and Roberts, *Network Propaganda*, 8.

48. Kurt Andersen, "'Succession' Nailed the Unreal Way We Live Now," *New York Times*, May 29, 2023.

49. Lee Fang, "CBS CEO: 'For Us, Economically, Donald's Place in This Election Is a Good Thing'," *The Intercept*, February 29, 2016.

50. Naomi Klein, *The Shock Doctrine* (New York: Picador, 2007).

51. Joseph Menn, "As False War Information Spreads on X, Musk Promotes Unvetted Accounts," *Washington Post*, October 8, 2023.

52. Alex Shephard, "The Week Twitter Went Evil," *New Republic*, October 11, 2023.

53. Klein, *Doppelganger*.

54. Jennifer Senior, "American Rasputin," *The Atlantic*, June 6, 2022.

55. Williamson, *Sandy Hook*.

56. Klein, *Doppelganger*, 40.

57. Jan-Werner Müller quoted in Daniel Steinmetz-Jenkins, "Cold War Liberalism Is Still with Us," *Chronicle of Higher Education*, October 2, 2023.

58. Robert McChesney, "Waging the Media Battle," *American Prospect*, June 17, 2004. Johnson expanded on this idea in his book, *Your Second Priority* (Morrisville, NC: Lulu, 2008).

59. Klein, *Doppelganger*, 124, 71.

60. Marx, *Theses on Feuerbach*.

61. Mark Fisher, *Capitalist Realism* (Winchester, UK: Zero Books, 2014), 2; see also Zara Zimbardo, "It Is Easier to Imagine the Zombie Apocalypse than to Imagine the End of Capitalism," in *Censored 2015: Inspiring We The People*, eds. Andy Lee Roth and Mickey Huff with Project Censored (New York: Seven Stories Press, 2014), 269–94, also archived on the Project Censored website.

62. Susan Maret, "Contested Visions, Imperfect Information, and the Persistence of Conspiracy Theories," in *Censored 2017*, eds. Mickey Huff and Andy Lee Roth with Project Censored (New York: Seven Stories Press, 2016), 221–49, also archived on the Project Censored website; Kathryn S. Olmsted, "Government Secrecy and Conspiracy Theories," in *Government Secrecy (Research in Social Problems and Public Policy)*, 19), ed. Susan Maret (Bingley, UK: Emerald Group Publishing, 2011), 91–100.

63. Marcus Gilroy-Ware, *After the Fact?* (London: Repeater Books, 2020), 169.

64. Giridharadas, *The Persuaders*, 262.

65. Klein, *Doppelganger*.

66. Rosa Luxemburg, *Socialism or Barbarism* (London: Pluto, 2010).

67. Higdon, *Fake News*; Nolan Higdon and Mickey Huff, *United States of Distraction* (San Francisco: City Lights, 2019).

68. Karl Marx and Jules Guesde, *The Programme of the Parti Ouvrier* (1880); available online at Marxists.org.

69. Jacqueline Rose, "The Analyst," *New York Review*, September 21, 2023.

70. Kuo and Marwick, "Critical Disinformation Studies."

71. Higdon and Huff, *United States of Distraction*; Shoshana Zuboff, *The Age of Surveillance Capitalism* (New York: Hachette, 2019).

72. Victor Pickard, *Democracy without Journalism?* (New York: Oxford, 2020), 167.

73. Gershberg and Illing, *Paradox of Democracy*, 277.

74. Samuel Beckett, *The Unnamable* (New York: Grove Press, 1958), 119; Beckett, *Worstward Ho* (New York: Grove Press, 1983), 7.

Acknowledgments

This book represents the commitment, coordination, and contributions of many people. We welcome the opportunity to thank many of them here.

Nora Barrows-Friedman, Mischa Geracoulis, Veronica Santiago Liu, T.M. Scruggs, and Dan Simon serve with us on the editorial board of the Censored Press. Now entering its fifth year of operation under this group's wise guidance, the Censored Press publishes books that promote political engagement informed by independent journalism and critical media literacy.

At Seven Stories Press, we thank Dan Simon, publisher and editorial director; Jon Gilbert, operations director; Ruth Weiner, publicity director and co-publisher of Triangle Square Books for Young Readers; Stewart Cauley, art director; Claire Kelley, marketing director; Tal Mancini, production editor; Bill Rusin, sales director; Allison Paller, web marketing manager; James Webster, social media; Anastasia Damaskou, publicist; Silvia Stramenga, foreign rights director; Eva Sotomayor, publicity; Catherine Taylor, SSP UK; Oona Holahan, and Noa Mendoza.

Anson Stevens-Bollen created original artwork for *State of the Free Press 2025*. His cover image provides an apt preview of the turbulent currents in this year's book. We're energized by our ongoing partnership with Anson, who also created the story icons that add visual vim to Chapter 1.

We are grateful for the extraordinary generosity of our donors, many of whom have supported us for years, including James Coleman, Alma DeBisschop, Jan DeDeka, Robert DeMint, M.C. Dornan, Dmitry Egorov, Larry Gassan, Michael Hansen, Leo Horrigan, Susan Krebser, Sheldon Levy, Tony Litwinko, James March, Harry Mersmann, Christopher Oscar, Aaron Placensia, Allison Reilly, John and Lyn Roth, T.M. Scruggs, David Stanek, Lana Touchstone, Michelle Westover, and Montgomery Zukowski.

We also thank the Fred R. Martin Foundation, The Free Press, the Silicon Valley Community Foundation, ISL Enterprises, and the estate of Janet Strothman for essential support.

The Media Freedom Foundation's (MFF) board of directors, identified below, provides key counsel and support for our ongoing operations. We are grateful to them and our emeritus director/president, Peter Phillips, for his many years of service to the Project and its mission.

Since 2006, Adam Armstrong has worked to ensure that Project Censored engages a global audience. Adam continues to serve as the Project's director of communications and outreach. Adam also works as the Media Freedom Foundation's CFO, keeping our budget in order and our financial books squeaky clean.

Lorna Garano of Lorna Garano Book Publicity amplifies the impact of Project Censored's work and expands our circle of allies. In a media ecosystem where everyone is clamoring for attention, Lorna assures that the Project's signal (including each of the titles published by the Censored Press) never gets lost in the noise.

We are grateful to Lyssa Schmidt and all at Presence & Company for grant writing support. Partnering with Lyssa and her team during the past year has challenged us to think in new ways about how to best represent the Project and its mission.

In 2023–24, student interns working with Project Censored played a vital role in our day-to-day operations, supporting the Project's work behind the scenes while also contributing to Project publications, social media, and radio programs. Warm thanks and best wishes to our Summer 2023 interns, Riley Cummins, Grace Harty, Libby Meagher, and Ashton Sidford, for their great work and good cheer.

The credibility of the Project hinges on the factual accuracy of its work. *State of the Free Press 2025* has benefited from careful fact-checking and proofreading by Mischa Geracoulis, Reagan Haynie, Gavin Kelley, Cam Lippincott, Steve Macek, and Olivia Rosenberg.

The Project Censored Show on Pacifica Radio, which originates from the historic studios of KPFA in Berkeley, California, continues to broadcast on more than fifty stations around the United States, from Maui to New York. Special thanks to co-host and producer Eleanor Goldfield; our senior producer and man behind the curtain, Anthony Fest; and everyone at KPFA.

We are fortunate to work with wonderful people and organizations that not only share our mission to promote press freedoms but also help to spread the word about the Project's work, including Clayton Weimers of Reporters Without Borders; Maya Schenwar and Alana Yu-lan Price with *Truthout*; Seth Stern at the Freedom of the Press Foundation; Norm Stockwell and the team at *The Progressive*; Mnar Adley and Alan MacLeod at *MintPress News*; Heidi Boghosian and Marjorie Cohn of *Law and Disorder Radio*; Nolan Higdon, Allison Butler, and the organizing committee of the Critical Media Literacy Conference of the Americas; our friends and colleagues at the Union for Democratic Communications; our allies at the Society of Professional Journalists, including Ankita Kumar, Loretta McGraw, and Adam Sennott; Emily Keup and Alexandra Peterson at the Media Education Foundation; filmmaker Roger Stahl; Sonali Kolhatkar of *Rising Up With Sonali*; Sandy Sohcot and Jazzmin Gota of *The World As It Could Be* Human Rights Education Program; Michael Welch of *Global Research News Hour*; Jill Cody at *Be Bold America!* (KSQD); Geoffrey Riley, Angela Decker, and Nash Bennett of the *Jefferson Exchange*; Lee Camp, host of *Moment of Clarity*; Mitch Ratcliffe, host of the *Earth911* podcast; Joe Richey of *Hemispheres* (KGNU); Nancy Price, Jim Tarbell, and colleagues at the Alliance for Democracy; Annie Esposito and Steve Scalmanini, cohosts of *Corporations and Democracy* (KZYX); Lynn Feinerman at *Women Rising Radio*; Jeff Share; Karen Hunter of the *Karen Hunter Show*; Greg Godels and Pat Cummings of the *Coming From Left Field* podcast; Andrew Keen of the *Keen On* podcast; Matt Crawford of *The Curious Man* podcast; Jen Perelman and the *Jenerational Change* podcast; Rachel Hu and Chris Garaffa of the *CovertAction Bulletin*; Francesca Rheannon of *Writer's Voice*; *Bookin'* with Jason Jeffries; Jeffrey St. Clair and the rest of the crew at *CounterPunch*; Mitch Jeserich, host of *Letters and Politics* on Pacifica Radio; Davey D at *Hard Knock Radio*; Abby Martin of the *Empire Files*; Tracy Rosenberg of Media Alliance; *The Zero Hour* with Richard (RJ) Eskow; *Parallax Views* with J.G. Michael; *Tell Me Everything* with John Fugelsang; Max Tegmark and the

Future of Life Institute; Angie Tibbs and the team at *Dissident Voice*; Craig Seasholes and the Friends of the Winthrop Library; Danbert Nobacon; Greg Wright of the Methow Valley Authors Library; Bino Prassa and everyone at the Avid Reader Bookstore in Sacramento; Katie Desiato, Heather Grieshaber, Linda Heisley and all of the volunteers and staff at the Tucson Festival of Books; everyone at the League of Women Voters Diablo Valley Community Conversations Team; James Preston Allen and the staff at *Random Lengths News*; the Association of Alternative News Media; Kevin Gosztola, host of *The Dissenter* newsletter; Maximillian Alvarez and all our allies at The Real News Network; Raza Ahmad Rumi and Todd Schack at Ithaca College's Park Center for Independent Media; John Collins, Jana Morgan, Cecilia Hyland, and the entire *Weave News* crew; Julian Vigo at *Savage Minds*; Robert Scheer and the *ScheerPost* team; the Independent Media Institute; Lee Rowland and all at the National Coalition Against Censorship; and Betsy Gomez and the Banned Books Week Coalition.

At Diablo Valley College, Mickey thanks Obed Vazquez, outgoing Dean of Social Science; Lisa Martin, Carmina Quirarte, Matthew Powell, Nolan Higdon, Michael Levitin, Adam Bessie, Jason Mayfield; in the Social Justice Studies program, Sangha Niyogi and Albert Ponce; John Freytag and Lisa Smiley-Ratchford on the Academic Senate; Beth Arman, Dean of Career and Community Partnership; Vice President Joe Gorga and President Susan Lamb, as well as all of the students.

Mickey especially thanks his wife Meg and their two children for their ongoing love, patience, and support, as without them this work would not be possible. Shealeigh is very thankful for her family, friends, trivia team, and dog, Elizabeth Francine, who all bring all kinds of joy to her life. Andy is grateful to Elizabeth Boyd: "In the storm you are my destination, in the port you are my storm."

And, finally, thanks to you, our readers, for the continuous support and encouragement, which inspire and enhance the Project's work to promote press freedom, media literacy, and informed civic engagement.

MEDIA FREEDOM FOUNDATION BOARD OF DIRECTORS

PROJECT CENSORED 2023–24 JUDGES

*Indicates having been a Project Censored judge since our founding in 1976.

ROBIN ANDERSEN. Writer, commentator, and award-winning author. Professor Emerita of Communication and Media Studies at Fordham University. She edits the Routledge Focus Book Series on Media and Humanitarian Action. Her books include *Death in Paradise: A Critical Study of the BBC Series* and *Censorship, Digital Media, and the Global Crackdown on Freedom of Expression*. She writes regularly for Fairness & Accuracy in Reporting (FAIR).

AVRAM ANDERSON. Collection Management Librarian, California State University, Northridge. Member and advocate of the LGBTQI+ community researching LGBTQ bias and censorship. Co-author of *The Media and Me: A Guide to Critical Media Literacy for Young People* (2022), and "Censorship by Proxy and Moral Panics in the Digital Era" in *Censorship, Digital Media, and the Global Crackdown on Freedom of Expression* (2024). They also contribute to the *Index on Censorship*, *In These Times*, and *Truthout*.

HEIDI BOGHOSIAN. Attorney and activist. Author of *Spying on Democracy* (2013) and *I Have Nothing to Hide: And 20 Other Myths About Surveillance and Privacy* (2021), as well as several articles on the policing of First Amendment-protected activities. Co-host of *Law & Disorder Radio*.

KENN BURROWS. Teacher of Holistic Health Studies at San Francisco State University since 1991. Founder and Director of SFSU's Holistic Health Learning Center, an award-winning interdisciplinary library and community center. Since 2001, under his direction, the Center has hosted a biennial conference, "The Future of Healthcare," and annual educational events, including Food Awareness Month and the Gandhi-King Season for Nonviolence, an eighty-day educational campaign demonstrating how nonviolence empowers our personal and collective lives.

BRIAN COVERT. Journalist, author, and educator based in Japan. Worked as a staff reporter and editor for English-language daily newspapers in Japan and as a contributing writer to Japanese and overseas newspapers and magazines. Contributing author to past editions of the *Censored* yearbook series. He is currently a lecturer in the Department of Media, Journalism, and Communications at Doshisha University in Kyoto.

GEOFF DAVIDIAN. Investigative reporter, publisher, editor, war correspondent, and educator. He has taught journalism in the US, UK, and India and reported on international terrorism,

Middle Eastern affairs, Congress, local government corruption, and breaches of legal and judicial ethics, for which he twice received the Gavel Award from the State Bar of Texas. Founding publisher and editor of the *Putnam Pit*.

MISCHA GERACOULIS. Curriculum Development Coordinator at Project Censored, contributor to Project Censored's *State of the Free Press* yearbook series, and member of the editorial board of the Censored Press. Her writing focuses on critical media and information literacy, democracy and ethics, and press and academic freedoms.

NOLAN HIGDON. Founding member of the Critical Media Literacy Conference of the Americas, author, and lecturer at Merrill College and the Education Department at the University of California, Santa Cruz. Author of *The Anatomy of Fake News* (2020); coauthor of *Let's Agree to Disagree* (2022), *The Media And Me* (2022), and *Surveillance Education: Navigating the Conspicuous Absence of Privacy in Schools* (2024).

KEVIN HOWLEY (PhD, Indiana University, 1998). Writer and educator. His work has appeared in *Journalism: Theory, Practice and Criticism*; *Social Movement Studies*; *Literature/Film Quarterly*; and *Interactions: Studies in Communication and Culture*. His most recent book is *Drones: Media Discourse and the Public Imagination*.

NICHOLAS JOHNSON.* Author, *How to Talk Back to Your Television Set* (1970) and nine more books, including *Columns of Democracy* (2018) and *What Do You Mean and How Do You Know?* (2009). Commissioner, Federal Communications Commission (1966–1973); Professor, University of Iowa College of Law (1981–2014, media law and cyber law). More at nicholasjohnson.org.

NANCY KRANICH. Teaching Professor, School of Communication and Information, Rutgers University. Past president of the American Library Association (ALA) and member of

ALA's Freedom to Read Foundation Roll of Honor. Author of hundreds of publications, including *Libraries and Democracy: The Cornerstones of Liberty* (2001), "Libraries: Reuniting the Divided States of America" (2017), "Civic Literacy: Reimagining a Role for Libraries" (2024), and "Free People Read Freely" (2024).

MARTIN LEE. Investigative journalist and author. Co-founder of Fairness & Accuracy In Reporting (FAIR) and former editor of FAIR's magazine, *Extra!* Director of Project CBD, a medical science information nonprofit. Author of *Smoke Signals: A Social History of Marijuana—Medical, Recreational, and Scientific* (2012), *The Beast Reawakens: Fascism's Resurgence from Hitler's Spymasters to Today's Neo-Nazi Groups and Right-Wing Extremists* (2000), and *Acid Dreams: The Complete Social History of LSD* (with B. Shlain, 1985).

PETER LUDES. Visiting Positions in Sociology at the Universities of Newfoundland and Amsterdam; Professor of Culture and Media Science at the University of Siegen (Germany); Professor of Mass Communication, Jacobs University, Bremen, 2002–2017. Founder of the German Initiative on News Enlightenment (1997) at the University of Siegen. Recent publications on brutalization and banalization (2018) and collective myths and decivilizing processes (with Stefan Kramer, 2020).

DANIEL MÜLLER. Head of the Postgraduate Academy at the University of Siegen, in Germany. Researcher and educator in journalism, mass communication studies, and history at public universities for many years. Has published extensively on media history, media-minority relations in Germany, and nationality policies and ethnic relations of the Soviet Union and the post-Soviet successor states, particularly in the Caucasus. Jury member of the German Initiative on News Enlightenment.

JACK L. NELSON. * Distinguished Professor Emeritus, Graduate School of Education, Rutgers University. Former member, Committee on Academic Freedom and Tenure,

American Association of University Professors. Recipient, Academic Freedom Award, National Council for Social Studies. Author of seventeen books, including *Critical Issues in Education: Dialogues and Dialectics*, 9th ed. (with S. Palonsky and M.R. McCarthy, 2021) and *Human Impact of Natural Disasters* (with V.O. Pang and W.R. Fernekes, 2010), and about two hundred articles.

PETER PHILLIPS. Professor Emeritus of Political Sociology, Sonoma State University. Director, Project Censored, 1996–2010. President, Media Freedom Foundation, 2010–2016. Editor or co-editor of fourteen editions of the *Censored* yearbook series. Author of *Giants: The Global Power Elite* (2018) and *Titans of Capital* (2024). Co-editor (with Dennis Loo) of *Impeach the President: The Case Against Bush and Cheney* (2006).

MICHAEL RAVNITZKY. Attorney, writer, editor, engineer, and Freedom of Information Act expert who has developed tools to broaden access to public records in the public interest.

T.M. SCRUGGS. Professor Emeritus (token ethnomusicologist), University of Iowa. Print, audio, and/or video format publications on media in Nicaragua and Venezuela, as well as on Central American, Cuban, Venezuelan, and US music and dance. Involvement with community radio in Nicaragua, Venezuela, and the United States, including the KPFA (Berkeley, CA) Local Station Board and Pacifica National Board. Executive producer, *The Nine Lives of Barbara Dane*, and other documentaries. Board member, The Real News Network and *Truthout*.

PAUL STREET. Researcher, award-winning journalist, historian, author, and speaker. Author of ten books to date, including *This Happened Here: Amerikaners, Neoliberals, and the Trumping of America* (2021); *Hollow Resistance: Obama, Trump and the Politics of Appeasement* (2020); *They Rule: The 1% vs. Democracy* (2014); he writes regularly for *CounterPunch*.

SHEILA RABB WEIDENFELD.* Emmy Award-winning television producer. Former press secretary to Betty Ford and special assistant to the President; author, *First Lady's Lady*. President of DC Productions Ltd. Director of community relations of Phyto Management LLC and Maryland Cultivation and Processing LLC.

ROB WILLIAMS. Teaches media, communications, global studies, and journalism at Champlain and Saint Michael's Colleges and Northern Vermont University. Author of numerous articles on critical media literacy education. Publisher of the *Vermont Independent* online news journal. Author of *The Post (Truth) World* (2019) and *Media Mojo!* (2020), and co-editor of *Media Education for a Digital Generation* (with J. Frechette, 2016), and *Most Likely to Secede* (with R. Miller, 2013) about the Vermont independence movement.

This year, two of the Project's long-standing and esteemed contributors, Deepa Kumar and William Lutz, completed their service as judges. Special thanks to Deepa Kumar, who has provided insight and inspiration since becoming one of the Project's judges in 2011. We also note our deep gratitude to William Lutz, who began serving as a judge way back in 1980. Bill's insights and institutional knowledge have been invaluable to the Project's work for decades. We wish both Deepa and Bill all the best as they each take on new challenges.

How to Support Project Censored

NOMINATE A STORY

To nominate a *Censored* story, forward the URL to andy@projectcensored.org or mickey@projectcensored.org. The deadline to nominate stories for the next yearbook is March 31, 2025.

Criteria for Story Nominations

1) A censored news story reports information that the public has a right and a need to know but to which the public has had limited access.
2) The news story is recent, having been first reported no later than one year ago. Stories submitted for the 2024–25 news cycle should be no older than April 2024.
3) The story is fact-based, with clearly defined concepts and verifiable documentation. The story's claims should be supported by evidence—the more controversial the claims, the stronger the evidence necessary.
4) The news story has been published, either electronically or in print, in a publicly circulated newspaper, journal, magazine, newsletter, or similar publication from a journalistic source.

MAKE A TAX-DEDUCTIBLE DONATION

We depend on tax-deductible donations to continue our work. Project Censored is supported by the Media Freedom Foundation, a 501(c)(3) nonprofit organization. To support our efforts on behalf of independent journalism and freedom of information, send checks to the address below or donate online at projectcensored.org. Your generous donations help us oppose news censorship and promote media literacy.

Media Freedom Foundation
PO Box 9
Ithaca, NY 14851

About the Editors

MICKEY HUFF is the director of Project Censored and president of the nonprofit Media Freedom Foundation. To date, he has coedited sixteen editions of the Project's yearbook. He is also the co-author, with Nolan Higdon, of *Let's Agree to Disagree* (Routledge, 2022), a practical handbook on critical thinking and civil discourse, and *United States of Distraction* (City Lights, 2019); and a co-author of *The Media and Me: A Guide to Critical Media Literacy for Young People*. A professor of social science, history, and journalism at Diablo Valley College since 2000, Huff joined Ithaca College in fall 2024, where he serves as the Distinguished Director of the Park Center for Independent Media and professor of journalism. He is co-host and executive producer of *The Project Censored Show*, the Project's syndicated public affairs radio program. A musician and composer, he lives with his family in Ithaca, New York.

SHEALEIGH VOITL is the digital and print editor at Project Censored. She first began her research with the Project at North Central College alongside Steve Macek, co-authoring the Déjá Vu News chapter in the *State of the Free Press 2022* and *2023*, and the Top 25 chapter in *SFP 2023*. In addition to her editorial contributions to the yearbook series and work with the Campus Affiliates Program, Shealeigh helped develop the *State of the Free Press 2024* teaching guide and the Project's "Critical Media Literacy in Action" social media series. Her writing has also been featured in *Truthout*, *The Pro-*

gressive, and *Ms. Magazine*. Shealeigh lives in Chicago, Illinois, where she is often making or listening to music or watching *ER* (1994).

ANDY LEE ROTH is the associate director of Project Censored and co-editor of fifteen editions of the Project's yearbook. He helps coordinate the Project's Campus Affiliates Program, a news media research network of several hundred students and faculty at two dozen colleges and universities across North America. In addition to co-authoring *The Media and Me*, Project Censored's guide to critical media literacy for young people, Roth has published research and articles in the *Index on Censorship*; *The Progressive; In These Times*; *YES! Magazine*; *Truthout*; *Media, Culture & Society*; the *International Journal of Press/Politics*; and other outlets. He earned a PhD in sociology at the University of California, Los Angeles, and a BA in sociology and anthropology at Haverford College. He lives in Winthrop, Washington, with his sweetheart.

For more information about the editors, to invite them to speak at your school or in your community, or to conduct interviews, please visit projectcensored.org/press-room.

Index

[CP] THE CENSORED PRESS

The Censored Press is the publishing imprint of Project Censored and its nonprofit sponsor, the Media Freedom Foundation. Building on the Project's yearbook series, website, weekly radio show, and other educational programs, the Censored Press advances the Project's mission to promote independent investigative journalism, media literacy, and critical thinking.

To date, the Censored Press has published a number of award-winning titles, in partnership with Seven Stories Press. These books include *The Media and Me: A Guide to Critical Media Literacy for Young People*, by Project Censored and the Media Revolution Collective (2022); Kevin Gosztola's *Guilty of Journalism: The Political Case Against Julian Assange* (2023); Adam Bessie and Peter Glanting's *Going Remote: A Teacher's Journey* (2023); Peter Phillips's *Titans of Capital: How Concentrated Wealth Threatens Humanity* (2024); the four most recent volumes of Project Censored's *State of the Free Press* yearbook series; and Omar Zahzah's forthcoming *Terms of Servitude: Zionism, Silicon Valley, and Digital/Settler-Colonialism in the Palestinian Liberation Struggle*. Future titles from The Censored Press include Allison Butler's *The Judgment of Gender: Pop Culture Conversations that Center and Silence Women* and Cynthia Sandler's *Savvy: A Critical Media Literacy Roadmap for Educators*.

The generosity of several founding donors ensures that the Censored Press will be a sustainable publishing imprint, but generous support from new donors expands our capacity to produce additional titles and provide new opportunities for reporting, teaching, and thinking critically.

HTTPS://CENSOREDPRESS.ORG/